In Reverence We Stand

MEMORIES OF Phillips University

BOB BURKE AND KENNY A. FRANKS

FOREWORD BY DAVID L. BOREN

SERIES EDITOR: GINI MOORE CAMPBELL
ASSOCIATE EDITOR: ERIC DABNEY

OKLAHOMA HERITAGE ASSOCIATION OKLAHOMA CITY, OKLAHOMA
OKLAHOMA HORIZONS SERIES

Copyright ©2003 by Oklahoma Heritage Association

All rights reserved. No part of this book may be reproduced or utilized in any form or by any means, electronic or mechanical, including photocopying and recording, by any information storage and retrieval system, without permission of the publisher.

Printed in China
ISBN 1-885596-33-2
LC Number 2003109388

DESIGN, EDITORIAL ASSISTANCE, PRODUCTION:
Carol Haralson

Unless otherwise noted, photographs are courtesy of Phillips University.

OKLAHOMA HERITAGE ASSOCIATION BOARD OF DIRECTORS 2003

Clayton I. Bennett, Oklahoma City, *Chairman of the Board*

Roxana Lorton, Tulsa *Chairman Elect*

Pat Henry, Lawton *Chairman Emeritus*

Lee Allan Smith *Chairman Emeritus*

Bill Armor, Laverne, *Vice Chairman*
Bob Burke, Oklahoma City, *Vice Chairman*
Carol Crawford, Frederick, *Vice Chairman*
Vaughndean Fuller, Tulsa, *Vice Chairman*
Glen D. Johnson, Durant, *Vice Chairman*
Paul Massad, Norman, *Vice Chairman*
W.R. "Dick" Stubbs, Henryetta, *Vice Chairman*
Ben T. Walkingstick, Jr., Chandler, *Vice Chairman*
Becky J. Frank, Tulsa, *Corporate Secretary*
Bond Payne, Oklahoma City, *Treasurer*

Directors
Wanda L. Bass, McAlester
Everett Berry, Stillwater
G.T. Blankenship, Oklahoma City
L.D. Brittain, Lawton
Chester Cadieux, Tulsa
Luke Corbett, Oklahoma City
Bridge Cox, Ardmore
Betty Crow, Altus
Frederick Drummond, Pawhuska
Ken Fergeson, Altus

Martin D. Garber, Jr., Bartlesville
Jean G. Gumerson, Oklahoma City
Rick Holder, Gould
Gary Huckabay, Yukon
William E. Humphrey, Pauls Valley
David Kyle, Tulsa
Larry E. Lee, Tulsa
Karen Luke, Oklahoma City
Tom J. McDaniel, Oklahoma City
Robert P. "Bob" McSpadden, Vinita
Herman Meinders, Oklahoma City
Melvin Moran, Seminole
Tom Muchmore, Ponca City
John W. Nichols, Oklahoma City
John Nickle, Park Hill
George Nigh, Oklahoma City
Mary Jane Noble, Ardmore
C.D. Northcutt, Ponca City
Louise Painter, Oklahoma City
Leslie Paris, Tulsa
Robert Poe, Tulsa
Richard Poole, Stillwater
Julian J. Rothbaum, Tulsa
Sharon Shoulders, Henryetta
Jo Smart, Wewoka
Harland Stonecipher, Centrahoma
Steve Taylor, McAlester
Myra B. Ward, Enid
Martha Griffin White, Muskogee
Mollie Williford, Tulsa
Ray Ackerman, Oklahoma City, *ex-officio*
George Seminoff, Oklahoma City, *ex-officio*

In reverence we stand and declare to the land

The Glory of our Phillips U.

Her banner unfurl and her challenge we hurl,

Calling the loyal and true.

Those who have conquered stand ready to do

Tribute to our Phillips U.

Alma Mater, Alma Mater

Hail to Thee for whose honor we'll be

Ever faithful;

Alma Mater, Alma Mater,

May we be worthy and hold ever high

The standards of our Phillips U.

LYRICS BY DR. "JOE" EUGENE RECTOR, 1934
MUSIC BY ELIZABETH CLEAVER BICKFORD, 1934

CONTENTS

FOREWORD BY DAVID BOREN 9

CHAPTER 1   The Vision   11

CHAPTER 2   Oklahoma Christian University   17

CHAPTER 3   New Name, Same Mission   25

CHAPTER 4   Early Campus Life   33

CHAPTER 5   The Roaring Twenties   41

CHAPTER 6   Hard Times: The Great Depression   49

CHAPTER 7   World War II   61

CHAPTER 8   Post-war Growth   71

CHAPTER 9   A New Generation: The Sixties and Seventies   93

CHAPTER 10   Economic Woes: The Eighties and Nineties   117

CHAPTER 11   A Christian Learning Experience   137

CHAPTER 12   Excellence in Sports   145

CHAPTER 13   The End of an Era   165

CHAPTER 14   The Legacy Continues   177

ACKNOWLEDGMENTS 181

PRESERVING OUR LEGACY 182

LEADERSHIP AND AWARD RECIPIENTS 183

ENROLLMENT STATISTICS 186

HONORARY DEGREES BESTOWED 187

DEGREES AWARDED 189

BIBLIOGRAPHY 190

INDEX 192

FOREWORD

ONE OF THE REASONS Oklahoma is the envy of the rest of the world is its diversity in higher education. Not only are we blessed with thriving public universities—we have a strong tradition of private colleges and universities. One of Oklahoma's national and international strengths stems from the significant contribution made by private higher education to the state.

Phillips University in Enid was the first fully accredited private college in Oklahoma. The university's story is closely intertwined with the history of the state—both were born in 1907. For more than 90 years, Phillips served students from around the world, but most of them were children of Oklahoma families.

The Phillips experience was unique. With a strong emphasis on academic excellence that was a model for other private and public schools, the university provided a quality liberal arts education with a Christian emphasis that allowed personal growth and development of students. The small campus atmosphere aided the development that, for many students, is more difficult to achieve in larger institutions.

The academic excellence of Phillips University did not go unnoticed. In 1995, *U.S. News and World Report* selected Phillips as the fifth best private liberal arts college or university in the nation.

However, even with a rich history, superbly qualified faculty, success in athletic competition, and ability to provide students with a comprehensive college education or seminary degree, Phillips became the victim of increasing financial pressure upon private institutions of higher learning in America. University leaders valiantly tried to save the school but escalating costs of operation and growing debts forced the board of trustees to officially close the institution in 1998.

The closing of Phillips University is a loss for Oklahoma and for higher education. However, this history published by the Oklahoma Heritage Association, chronicles an environment in which thousands of Phillips graduates were prepared to become leaders in their churches, businesses, and professions, bettering Oklahoma and the nation.

The exceptional tradition of Phillips University will never die as long as friends and alumni of the university continue their commitment to the value of a broad liberal arts education with a spiritual dimension. Never has it been more important to have leaders in our society who are the products of that kind of education.

DAVID L. BOREN
April, 2003

David L. Boren is president of the University of Oklahoma. A graduate of Yale University, Oxford University, and the University of Oklahoma School of Law, Boren is a former governor of Oklahoma and United States senator. Before becoming governor, he taught at Oklahoma Baptist University. He is well known as a strong supporter of both public and private higher education.

The Vision

THERE WERE at least two reasons why a Christian school was needed in Oklahoma in 1907. One was a large increase in population. In the 18 years prior to statehood, thousands of square miles of land had been opened for settlement by land runs and lotteries. When the Twin Territories were combined to create the State of Oklahoma on November 16, 1907, Oklahoma Territory's population had grown to 733,062, with another 681,115 people living in neighboring Indian Territory. Another reason was the need for seminary-trained preachers. Among the early pioneers in the Twin Territories were ministers and members of the Christian Church (Disciples of Christ), hereinafter referred to as "Disciples" or the "Christian Church." As settlements

> were established and churches founded, it became apparent that a Christian university was needed both to train ministers and to provide higher education opportunities for laymen and their families.

O. Eugene "Gene" Moore, a Phillips graduate from the College of the Bible in 1939, with M.A. and B.D. degrees from the Graduate School in 1942 and 1944, believed one reason for the shortage of seminary-trained ministers was the strong tradition of Christian Church congregations practicing local autonomy. "Every congregation was responsible for its own destiny," Moore explained, "the members exercised their own autonomy in the calling of their minister" who served "at the pleasure of the congregation at a salary determined by the congregation." Any congregation could ordain anyone they thought was called to and worthy of the ministry.

Being worthy, according to Moore, did not necessarily mean having gone to any college or university. In fact, many of the congregations were suspicious of seminary-trained ministers. It was a common feeling among lay leaders in Disciples churches that seminary training ruined more ministers than it helped. A seminary education was not considered to be essential to being a minister in the Christian church. Even by the 1930s, less than one in ten Christian Church congregations were being served by a seminary graduate.

The Christian Church in America was organized in the early decades of the 19th century. Among its more prominent founders were two Presbyterian ministers—Barton W. Stone and Thomas Campbell.

Stone was born in Port Tobacco, Maryland, on December 4, 1772, and educated as a teacher at the Davis Caldwell Academy in North Carolina before migrating to Bourbon County, Kentucky, in 1796 where he served as a circuit lay preacher for local Presbyterians. Ordained in 1799 by the Transylvania Presbytery, Stone became the minister for the Cane Ridge, Kentucky, Presbyterian Church, so named because of the numerous cane breaks in the area.

Stone attended the emotional revival meetings of Presbyterian minister James McGready in nearby Logan County, Kentucky. McGready's camp meeting swept the frontier with religious zeal and Stone was astounded at the immediacy of conversion for believers. Many of those present became feverish and collapsed on the floor, jerking and rolling in anguish for their sins. Returning to Cane Ridge, Barton organized a revival for Bourbon County and, between August 7 and 12, 1801, held a series of camp meetings. The large number of religious converts marked the beginning of the Christian Church, later to be known as the Christian Church (Disciples of Christ).

Charged with failing to abide by the Presbyterian doctrine, Stone resigned from the Transylvania Presbytery and formed the Springfield Presbytery that denounced all human creeds and appealed to the Bible as the only rule of faith and practice. However, within a short time the presbytery was dissolved. At that time Stone published the *Last Will and Testament of the Springfield Presbytery* and formed a new sect, called Christians, which entered into unity with "the body of Christ at large."

The second founder, The Reverend Thomas Campbell, was born in County Down, Ireland, on February 1, 1763. He began his ministry in his home country, but in 1807, at age 45, left his family and church and migrated to the United States.

In America, Thomas Campbell became active in the movement to return the Presbyterian Church to its historic roots and clashed with local church officials over their refusal to allow open communion, his sympathy for the lay ministry, his desire to fellowship with other churches, his idea that preachers do not need a divine call, and his view that believers can live in this world without sinning. Campbell and his supporters became known as "Reformers" and the "Restoration Movement."

When Campbell invited Presbyterians of all parties to participate in communion during a sermon at Cannamugh, Pennsylvania, he was charged by local Presbyterian officials with violating the communion process. Found guilty, he was suspended, reinstated upon appeal, and suspended again.

Stripped of his position in the local Presbyterian Synod, Campbell organized the Christian Association of Washington, Pennsylvania, in 1808. Its motto was "Where the Scriptures speak, we speak, where the Scriptures are silent, we are silent."

In 1811, Campbell organized the Brush Run Church and published his *Declaration and Address* that later became a part of the foundation of the Christian Church and Disciples of Christ brotherhood. The concept that "the church of Christ upon earth is essentially, intentionally, and constitutionally one," became the first and key proposition to the new brotherhood that was formed for the "sole purpose of promoting simple evangelical Christianity, free from all mixture of human opinions and inventions of man."

In 1815, the Brush Run Church became a part of a nearby Baptist Association. The union lasted until 1830, when the Reformers left the Baptist organization and began calling themselves the "Disciples." Two years later, in 1832, at an historic meeting near Lexington, Kentucky, the two reform movements, the Christians and the Disciples of Christ, agreed on basic beliefs and aims and united with a formal handshake to form the Christian Church and Disciples of Christ movement, although their association would not become a formal religious denomination until 1968.

From the beginning, the Disciples had a strong vision of education, believing that both leaders and laymen should understand their beliefs. Alexander Campbell, the son of Thomas Campbell, founded Bethany College in Bethany, West Virginia, in 1840. The school became the principal training ground for Disciples ministers and established the practice of creating Christian schools of higher learning as the Disciples movement spread westward.

Garfield University was established west of Wichita, Kansas, by the Christian churches of Kansas in 1887. When it opened for classes, it boasted more floor space under one roof than any other educational facility west of the Mississippi River. Five hundred students enrolled the first year and 1,070 the following year. Unfortunately, Garfield University graduated only one senior class before closing in 1890. An effort was made to reopen the school as Garfield Memorial University in March of 1892 but it failed and the university closed for good on November 18, 1893. Five years later, in 1898, it was acquired by the Kansas Society of Friends and transformed into Friends University.

On September 8, 1889, Miss Meta Chesnutt founded El Meta Christian College at Silver City, Indian Territory. In 1890, the school was moved to near present-day Minco, Oklahoma. A new four-story building costing $119,000 was completed in 1894 and was shared with the Minco Christian Church. However, El Meta Christian College was more interested in educating Native American children than in training preachers.

This left Texas Christian University (TCU) as the nearest Disciples supported school for students interested in Christian service. Addison and Randolph Clark, two brothers who were also Disciples ministers, organized TCU as a private Christian school in Fort Worth, Texas, in 1868. The school was chartered by the state of Texas as AddRan Male and Female Academy in 1874 and moved to Thorp Spring, Texas.

In 1889, the Brotherhood of the Christian Church and Disciples of Christ acquired control of the school and changed its name to AddRan Christian University. In 1895, the school was moved to Waco, Texas. Its name was changed to Texas Christian University in 1902, and after a disastrous fire in 1910, the university was moved to Fort Worth.

As the movement for a Christian university in Oklahoma solidified, Ely Vaughn Zollars, the president of TCU, became the driving force behind the effort. Zollars was born September 19, 1847, at Lower Salem, Ohio. Both of his parents had been early converts to the Disciples. In 1863, shortly before he was 16 years old, Zollars was baptized into the Disciples, a commitment he would honor for the remainder of his life.

In the fall of 1871, Zollars enrolled in Bethany College. After he received his master's degree in 1876, he was hired as a financial agent for the school. In 1877, he assumed the presidency of Kentucky Classical and Business College, a Disciples school in North Middleton, Kentucky. Seven years later he resigned to devote his life to preaching.

In January of 1888, Zollars was selected as president of Hiram College in Hiram, Ohio. It was during this time that he became a friend of Thomas W. Phillips, a prominent oilman, leader, and philanthropist of the Christian Church. In June of 1892, Zollars received a LL.D. degree from Hiram College and 10 years later, in 1902, was named president of Texas Christian University.

As the president of TCU, Zollars was aware of the failure of Garfield University and the growing need for an additional Christian university in the lower Midwest. In February of 1906, Zollars announced his resignation from TCU for the purpose of starting a new school to train Disciples ministers.

Zollars discussed his plan over dinner with a longtime friend, Professor Frank H. Marshall, a former instructor at TCU. Marshall later recalled that during their meeting about the possibility of a new school, Zollars, after a few moments of silence and serious meditation, stepped to a large map of the United States hanging on the wall, dramatically pointed with his finger to the location he had chosen, and exclaimed, "I am going to start an entirely new school for the Brotherhood, and *Oklahoma will be the place!*" On that day, in that hour, *in that moment,* according to Marshall, Phillips University was conceived.

Zollars immediately wrote J. M. Monroe, secretary of the Christian Missionary Society for Oklahoma Territory, and S. R. Hawkins, secretary of the Christian Missionary Society for Indian Territory, for help and advice. Both replied that a Christian university was vitally needed and encouraged Zollars to pursue his mission.

The Vision 13

The founder and first president of Phillips University was Dr. Ely Vaughn Zollars. He served from September of 1907 to 1915.

Zollars, who already had been invited to Blackwell, Oklahoma Territory, to speak to the Ministerial Institute of Oklahoma, quickly headed north. His speech, titled "Christian Education," was well received and a resolution was passed unanimously calling on the two missionary societies to name a committee to organize a Christian university with Zollars as its first president. Thomas W. Phillips financed a one-year study to determine the feasibility of opening the school.

During the summer of 1906, Zollars, at the invitation of the two missionary societies, toured Indian and Oklahoma territories promoting the concept and seeking bids for its location. At the time, the Christian Church had 416 congregations with approximately 39,000 members in Oklahoma Territory and 75 congregations and 32,000 members in Indian Territory. Most of the congregations were small. There was an obvious shortage of ministers in the territories with only 212 ministers to care for 416 congregations in Oklahoma Territory. This was exactly the situation that Zollars hoped to correct by establishing a Christian university in the region.

Twenty-nine cities were visited and 38 speeches were given to Christian church groups and community organizations. At first, Zollars asked only for a Bible college—however, most community leaders preferred a four-year liberal arts college. To garner the necessary support, Zollars agreed.

On August 28, 29, and 30, 1906, the Missionary Board of Indian Territory met at its annual convention in South McAlester. Among other issues, the delegates approved a resolution supporting the creation of a Christian university of the soon to be State of Oklahoma. The school was to offer Biblical instruction for ministerial students as well as liberal arts classes for other students. Two hundred thousand dollars, to be raised between 1906 and 1911, was pledged to support the school.

J. R. Mason of Ardmore, T. R. Dean of South McAlester, Randolph Cook of Tulsa, W. R. Blake of Weleetka, and J. B. Martin of Holdenville were chosen to attend the Missionary Board of Oklahoma Territory's convention in September at El Reno to enlist its support. After hearing the proposal, the Oklahoma Territory board eagerly agreed and appointed Dick T. Morgan of Woodward, W. A. Humphrey of Guthrie, J. M. Monroe of Oklahoma City, E. B. Johnson of Norman, O. L. Smith of El Reno, and C. M. Jackman of Wichita, Kansas, to an educational committee.

When the two committees met on September 6, 1906, they convened as the board of trustees for the new university. Humphrey was chosen chairman, Johnson vice chairman, Blake treasurer, and Cook secretary.

Humphrey, Johnson, Cook, and Monroe formed the executive committee. Zollars was appointed president of the university.

From the beginning, the school received no government subsidy. During the early years the national church organization had no denominational treasury that could be tapped for its support, so the university was completely dependent on contributions from local congregations and individuals. It fell on Zollars and members of the board of trustees to raise the necessary funds to build and sustain the school.

The trustees solicited bids from any community interested in becoming the school's home. El Reno, Oklahoma City, Guthrie, Norman, Enid, Shawnee, and Tulsa replied. However, because they offered such little financial support, all proposals were rejected and new bids were solicited.

Another meeting was held in Guthrie to review the resubmitted proposals. Chickasha joined the original seven cities. While the committee debated and listened to the various proposals, the Enid delegation—Edmund Frantz, H. G. McKeever, F.L. Hamilton, J. M. Pieratt, Everett Purcell, and Al Lowen—telephoned the Enid Chamber of Commerce and was told, "Promise anything, get the school!"

By the time the bidding reached $70,000, only Enid and Shawnee remained in competition. The final deadlocked bid was $80,000. Enid then upped its proposal by agreeing to provide a $3,500 home for the school's president. The educational committee accepted. Zollars cast the deciding vote.

Enid's final offer included 40 acres of land two miles east of the town square valued at $12,000; a cash bonus of $75,000; four scholarships valued at $20,000; 200 preparatory scholarships worth $8,000; $5,000 in tuition for music students; $5,000 worth of water and sewer mains; $600 worth of water for five years; and 100 lots in the Sawyer's Addition valued at $10,000. Enid officials also promised to pave East Broadway to within one mile of the campus, to extend the town's streetcar line to the campus, to guarantee that the streetcar fare would not exceed five cents, and to work for reduced electric rates.

Another reason Enid was chosen was its excellent water supply and the fact that the city was the center of a large Disciples population. As Stephen J. England, the longtime dean of Phillips' College of the Bible explained, "All around Enid were scores of little [Christian] churches without preachers." This, according to England, presented "an excellent opportunity to build a large Bible college, whose ministerial students could serve these churches and thus strengthen them." In return, support received by the churches would help finance the school.

Once Enid's offer was accepted, the trustees adopted a policy to "employ on the faculty only such persons as are believers in the divinity of Jesus Christ and are avowed followers of our Lord and Master." The next day, October 9, 1906, Humphrey, Cook, Smith, Monroe, and Morgan traveled to Oklahoma City and prepared articles of incorporation for Oklahoma Christian University (OCU).

At the time it was a university in name only. The soon to be campus was a treeless alfalfa field. East Broadway, the main thoroughfare between the campus and Enid, was not yet completed. That part of the road that had been built was dirt and the dust quickly turned to mud when it rained. East Broadway ended at the top of a hill west of the campus. Visitors walked down hill and across a board placed over Sawyer's Creek to reach the campus. A weed-lined slough was southwest of the campus. The sluggish stream, first dammed in 1904-1905 to provide a watering hole for horses, eventually became University Lake. One-half mile to the south was Boggy Creek. To the north and east was nothing but open prairie.

While the legal incorporation was being completed, a meeting was held in Enid at the Garfield County Courthouse to raise the promised money. The Bank of Enid and the Garfield Exchange Bank pledged $5,000 each and Frank Hamilton contributed $2,000. Even one of the community's saloon owners and best-known gamblers gave $350. The Enid Chamber of Commerce pledged a bond for the promised amount and agreed on the terms of a contract between the school's board of trustees and Edmund Frantz and J. S. Hart, president and secretary of the chamber, and J. M. Pieratt and H. G. McKeever, president and secretary of the Enid University Investment and Development Company.

When the school's board of trustees reconvened in Enid on October 15, O. L. Smith of El Reno replaced Blake as treasurer and Zollars and Ford were named to meet with architects to design the school's buildings. Work quickly began on the Main Building, later called Old Main, a fine arts building, and a dormitory for female students. Contracts totaling $72,702 were approved for construction of the first three buildings.

While work was ongoing, Zollars opened an office on the third floor of the Chamber of Commerce Building in downtown Enid. Randolph Cook served as financial secretary and Ed W. McKinney, William N. LeMay, William L. E. Shane, W. A. Martin, and Mart Gary Smith were named field agents. All the school needed was a faculty and students.

The Vision 15

A chapel service in the auditorium of Old Main.

Oklahoma Christian University

2

OKLAHOMA CHRISTIAN UNIVERSITY was different from other schools related to the Christian church. Without the support of the church, the university probably could not have been founded, and without the financial support of the church, it probably would not have survived. In addition, the organization of its board of trustees was unique. When first organized, trustees were named by either the Indian Territory or Oklahoma Territory Missionary Societies. This process continued when the two societies were joined at statehood. Consequently the board of trustees became self-perpetuating and adopted a rule that the trustees must be active members in the Christian Church. As the service area of the university grew to include Oklahoma, Kansas, Arkansas, Colorado, and Wyoming, trustees were chosen from each of these states.

It became the policy to present the lists of nominees for trustees from the individual states to that state's church convention for consideration and approval.

William LeMay was the first student to enroll at OCU when classes began on September 17, 1907. Sixteen states were represented among students who came from a myriad of backgrounds. Some wore overalls—others were brought to enrollment in a carriage driven by a coachman.

Tuition was $25 a semester or $6 a month. Dr. Zollars taught apologetics and doctrine, Samuel H. Horn was professor of history and economics, and Dr. Frank H. Marshall was named professor of Biblical Greek language and literature. Becky Proudfoot remembered Dr. Marshall speaking to the students at chapel. "He was pretty intimidating," she recalled, but "I enjoyed watching him in chapel when he spoke because he would use his bony right forefinger to flip through his well-worn Bible to find a passage to read." Marshall would finally snap the Bible shut over his forefinger and quote the passage from memory. Proudfoot thought the professor grew tired of looking for the passage, and just quoted it to save time.

Arthur F. Reiter was professor of mathematics and astronomy and Rein Dyksterhus was professor of music, violin, and piano. Dyksterhus was Claudia Zollars Page's music violin instructor. Claudia was President Zollars' granddaughter and Zollars wanted to bring Dyksterhus to Enid to teach private music lessons so his granddaughter could continue her music education. Maude Waite Marshall was instructor of the Special Entrance Department. All formerly taught at TCU.

Miss Grace Reynolds taught voice and Henrietta Siegal taught art. Other instructors for the first year were Burton Woodford, T. L. Noblitt, Ison Roberts, Aaron P. Aten, B. F. Brown, Katherine Roberts, Mary E. Wood, and Sarah A. Dodson.

Zollars assigned Professor Marshall

East Maine Street connected the main entrance on the south side of Oklahoma Christian University with the square in downtown Enid, two miles to the west. This is the Library Building, as seen from the East Maine entrance.

Old Main, right, and the Fine Arts Building, left, as they appeared in February of 1908. Note the boards laid across the ground in the right foreground. They were necessary to keep the students out of the mud when it rained. The brick and stone colonnade archway connecting the two buildings had yet to be built.

the task of preparing OCU's academic policy and catalog. Marshall stressed the education of the "whole man." An education at OCU would provide for the development of the entire person—religious, mental, and physical. However, the orientation toward the Christian Church was emphatic. The attendance of all students at chapel exercises four days a week was required, as were courses in the New and Old Testament.

OCU consisted of a Preparatory School, College of Liberal Arts, College of the Bible, School for Church Workers, College of Music, College of Business, Teacher's College, School of Oratory, School of Fine Arts, School of Domestic Science, Correspondence School, and Postgraduate School. When classes began, Oklahoma statehood, November 16, 1907, was two months away and carpenters were still at work in the buildings. Instructors and students moved from room to room to make way for construction workers.

Furniture, chalkboards, and laboratory equipment had not been installed. The only way to get from the first floor to the upper floors of Old Main was by ladders. Nail kegs were used as chairs and boards formed improvised desks and benches. The workers' tool shack was used as a refectory. Its sawdust floor became a quagmire when rain poured through the makeshift roof. There were no sidewalks, only muddy paths in the red clay between buildings. Water mains had not yet been connected and sanitation facilities were poor. Students were called to class by a bell in Old Main's tower.

Athenian Hall, the dormitory for female students, remained unfinished. During the first few weeks of classes, a makeshift dormitory was opened in the Fine Arts Building. Its windows were unscreened and the girls were plagued by swarms of mosquitoes from Sawyer's Creek, Boggy Creek, and a nearby slough. To keep insects away, girls sweltered beneath sheets during the hot Oklahoma summer nights. A temporary dining hall was housed under an awning. Once during a heavy rain, the tarpaper roof gave way and those at dinner were soaked. Several students contracted typhoid fever, probably from germs carried by flies attracted to the bowls of food on tables in the outdoor dining hall. One student, Rosecrans Everts of Dallas, Texas, died of the disease.

Eventually Athenian Hall was finished and the female students moved into a proper dormitory. Unfortunately, when the fall rains started, the building's drainage system

Athenian Hall was the first residence dormitory built on the Oklahoma Christian University campus.

Oklahoma Christian University 19

The president's home on the southwest corner of East Broadway and 22nd Street, now South University Avenue, was never used as such—instead it was converted into the College of the Bible. In 1947 the College of the Bible moved into the new Marshall Building and the old building was converted into the headquarters for the Business Division. In 1975 the Business Division moved into the new Student Center by the campus store and the old building was once again converted, this time into the Communications Building. For a while *The Haymaker,* the student newspaper, was published from its second floor offices. Eventually, the Communications Department also moved into the building with the Business Division and the old College of the Bible building was converted to storage space. Courtesy Jack N. Taylor.

Facing, above: a class of homiletics, the art of preaching, being taught by President Ely Vaughn Zollars ca. 1908 at Oklahoma Christian University. First row, left to right: Claude C. Taylor, Wm. L. E. Shane, John E. Gorton, and James Crain. Second row, left to right, Carl Hibbs, unidentified, Enid E. Barnes, Lloyd Shapp, and Charles Funk. Third row, left to right, Charles A. Burkhart, Walter S. Roberts, William S. Rehorn, Elbert A. Taylor, and Frank Hargrove. Fourth row, left to right, Mart Gary Smith, Elmer Underwood, Andrew G. Smith, and Orville Hodge. Fifth row, left to right, Frank Lash, Walter G. Scates, Arthur Aikins, unidentified, and unidentified.

Facing, below: The University Dames was composed of wives of Phillips' faculty. Among those who are identified are (1) Mrs. Frank Wellman; (2) Mrs. Reuben Welty; (3) Mrs. Manley; (4) Mrs. Frank Marshall; (5) Mrs. Ora Cleveland, the mother of Maude Butts Briggs; (6) Mrs. Boggess; (7) Mrs. Brawner; (8) Mrs. Fred Suley; (9) Mrs. W. I. Palmer; (10) Mrs. Theis; (11) Mrs. J. Lee Rilford; (12) Mrs. Buley; (13) Mrs. Lincoln; and (14) Mrs. Gibble.

proved inadequate and its basement flooded. The water forced the kitchen and dining hall to close.

The entrance requirements for OCU were the same as for state supported institutions—15 units of high school work—or the completion of four years study at a first class high school.

Many local schools failed to provide the basic requirements and most of the 256 students enrolled the first year were placed in the Preparatory School. Only 20 freshmen in the initial class had completed high school.

Minnie Coleman Edwards was typical of the high school students who attended Phillips High School. Born outside Helena in Alfalfa County, she was sent to Phillips High School because there was no high school close to the family farm, and at Phillips she could live in the girl's dormitory.

From its founding, OCU had the support of Enid's citizens and the city's institutions, such as University Hospital, founded in 1907 by Dr. S.N. Mayberry. The hospital was one of the most modern and up-to-date facilities in the state. As part of the hospital's educational program, Mayberry instituted a Training School for Nurses. Classes were taught by the faculty of OCU. The three-year nursing course consisted of practical bedside training and classes taught by physicians on caring for the sick and the science of medicine. Upon the successful completion

20 IN REVERENCE WE STAND

of the program, the graduates received diplomas in a joint graduation program with OCU and the hospital.

In October of 1907, America was struck by a panic in the financial world that was triggered by a seven-month decline in the stock market. Faced with a shortage of cash, many Enid banks restricted withdrawals to $5 per day per customer. At the same time W. A. Humphrey, president of OCU's board of trustees who had used his personal credit to underwrite OCU's finances, died. The University Investment and Development Company had backed its pledges to OCU with farmland that it hoped to sell as the town of Enid grew. With the economic downturn, the expected growth did not take place and as the contractor neared completion of the original building program, there was no money to pay. Creditors filed more than 100 lawsuits against the university.

Many of the trustees wanted to close the school, but Zollars refused, as did most of the faculty who offered to teach without pay. In January of 1908, the trustees voted to issue interest-bearing bonds to see the school through the financial crisis. Most local businessmen, such as physician Dr. S.N. Mayberry and grocery store owner F. W. Buttrey, honored the warrants.

President Zollar's health deteriorated. He had not been in good health when he came to Enid, and the hot summers made his condition worse. The stress of securing adequate financing for OCU took its toll. At the May 5, 1908, board of trustees meeting he offered to resign. Instead, the trustees approved a long vacation to the Pacific Northwest and a period of rest at the home of Zollars' son-in-law, Dr. Harlan M. Page, in Warren, Ohio. While Zollars remained president of OCU, T. W. Blackman was moved from chairman of the board to treasurer and ex-officio business manager of the school and O. L. Smith became the new chairman of the board.

On June 3, 1908, OCU's first class was graduated. F. K. Hargrove, Orville Hodge, E. W. Schenke, Wm. L. E. Shane, C. C. Taylor, Sara W. Garrison, and A. E. Underwood were awarded bachelor degrees. William LeMay received a master of arts diploma.

By the close of the first year's classes, between 1,200 and 1,500 books had been secured for the library. Chemistry, biological, and physical laboratories were in operation. Most of the classrooms and offices were fur-

Dean Arthur F. Reiter's science laboratory was modern and up-to-date when completed. Each student had his own water spigot and natural gas burner, plus an electric light directly above the work station. Dean Reiter is leaning against the column in the center of the photograph taken in 1910.

nished with desks and chairs and an electric clock and bell system installed. Grading the campus had been completed, greatly improving its drainage system, and the campus had been landscaped with trees planted by ministerial students.

As a result of the efforts to beautify the campus, the once open fields were covered with thick grass lawns bordered by broad sidewalks. Ruth Wolfinger, the daughter of Roy J. Wolfinger, recalled long walks across campus with her father. There were stone benches on the lawn where students and faculty often sat while children played.

Zollars also was hard at work implementing a practice-preaching program for OCU's ministerial students. One of the primary objectives of the school's Bible College was to provide training for Christian Church preachers. An important aspect of this training was a pastoral practicum or Field Placement Program designed to find preaching and pastoral work for students preparing for the ministry to allow them to get on-the-job training. This not only gave budding preachers first hand experience, it also provided smaller congregations with preachers at a relatively low cost.

Within a short time of the opening of the Bible College, Zollars had succeeded in placing ministerial students in Christian Churches in Medford, Pond Creek, Hunter, Morrison, Drummond, Hennessey, Orlando, Agra, Tecumseh, Yukon, Carney, Ames, Cleo Springs, and Hitchcock in Oklahoma and in Council Hill, Kansas. In the following years the area covered by the Field Placement Service expanded the area served by Phillips ministerial students to include northern Oklahoma, southern Kansas, and the Panhandle of Texas.

Zollars was well aware that many of the ministerial students, or "preacher boys" as they called themselves, did not have adequate finances for an education and he took a personal interest in helping them find jobs. When Walter A. Smith and a friend enrolled at OCU they were broke. They went to the president's office and told him of their plight. After hearing their story, Zollars put on his hat and walked with them the two miles to Enid where he got them jobs as newspaper carriers.

By the fall of 1908 Enid's streetcar line had been built to within two blocks of the west side of the campus. There it halted at the bank of the same small stream that thwarted local farmers. Anyone going to or coming from OCU had to wade through two blocks of muddy paths to reach the streetcar line.

The streetcar conductors and OCU students often feuded. Once when a conductor ejected a student from a streetcar, the students retaliated that night by soaping the streetcar tracks near the campus. The first streetcar to campus the following morning began slipping on the soaped tracks and derailed. The police were called and suspects were arrested, but the incident never came to trial.

Zollars returned to Enid in late 1908. While he had been away the University Investment and Development Company made good its obligations to finance OCU's initial building program, but still owed $24,000 for scholarships and other commitments. Zollars immediately planned an extensive fund raising program throughout the Southwest. Trustees approved the hiring of William LeMay as a financial agent. LeMay accompanied Zollars, who often made as many as three speeches a week, up and down the main line of the Chicago, Rock Island, and Pacific Railroad in Kansas and Oklahoma.

Zollars was zealous in his search for funding to keep the university open. While in Cherokee, Oklahoma, soliciting financial support from the local Christian Church, Zollars spent the night with its pastor G. J. Chapman. Chapman awoke about 2:00 in the morning to find Zollars "kneeling beside his bed in prayer" seeking guidance for his fund raising. By January of 1909, pledges totaling $30,000 had been secured.

The successful fund raising came just in time. When Oliver N. Roth was hired as chancellor on January 1, 1909, he was shocked to find only $5.96 in cash and a balance of less than $300 on deposit at Enid's First National Bank. The situation was so critical that the school ran out of coal to heat its buildings. Fortunately, Roth found a coal dealer who would supply 40 tons of coal on credit until the school could collect on the pledges secured by Zollars and LeMay.

University administrators recognized the need for communicating with students. The first issue of *The Slate* was printed in September of 1909 "for and by the students of O.C.U." The monthly publications cost 10 cents per issue or 75 cents per year. Although often only a mimeographed newssheet, it helped give the university an identity. Ethel McElroy was the first editor. Plans were made to include editors for the senior, junior, sophomore, and freshman classes as well as for the Art Department, Music Department, College of the Bible, Literary Club, athletics, and exchange students.

At first *The Slate* was more of an annual, presenting a history of the various classes and the college as well as photographs of the students. Later, *The Slate* evolved into a monthly booklet and by the opening of school in 1916, it was a bi-weekly campus newspaper.

With the help of the community and Christian Church officials, OCU continued its growth, despite financial setbacks.

New Name
Same Mission

EVEN THOUGH progress was being made toward economic stability for OCU, President Zollars continued to strengthen the school's financial basis. In 1911, R. A. Long of Kansas City, Missouri, took interest in the university. Long, who had made his fortune in the lumber industry, was asked by Zollars for support. Impressed by Zollars' presentation, Long immediately donated $5,500 and agreed to aid in the raising of a $100,000 endowment fund. In addition, C. M. Jackman, J. N. Haymaker, and S. M. Naftzger, of the Fourth National Bank of Wichita, Kansas, paid off the $15,000 mortgage against OCU's buildings.

Because many of the local high schools in Oklahoma were deficient in the preparation of students for a college education, Phillips operated its own high school until 1924. This is the Phillips High School Class of 1912. Front row, left to right, Ray Balch, Maude Cleveland, A. G. Smith, Claudia Page, and John Charlton. Second row, left to right, Edna Ewing, Everett Hages, unidentified, Claud Peavey, and Maida Young.

Benefactor Thomas W. Phillips. Following his death, the university's name was changed from Oklahoma Christian University to Phillips University in his honor.

On January 11, 1912, another $18,000 in money and real estate was received from the Enid University Investment and Development Company.

With OCU debt free, Zollars embarked on a leave of absence to tour Europe and the Holy Land. W. J. Wright served as acting president during his absence.

Upon his return, Zollars lost one of his long time supporters. On July 21, 1912, Thomas W. Phillips died. Phillips had been one of the largest financial contributors to OCU during the school's early years, and Zollars left immediately for New Castle, Pennsylvania, Phillips' hometown. In his will, Phillips left $25,000 to OCU's endowment fund and another $5,000 to its loan fund.

As his quest for money expanded, Zollars realized that the name Oklahoma Christian University limited the appeal of the school to many would be donors who lived outside the state. As early as the summer of 1908 Zollars had decided to drop the word "Oklahoma" from the school's name to broaden its appeal and increase its financial support.

26 IN REVERENCE WE STAND

In a visit with Thomas W. Phillips, Jr., Zollars suggested naming the university after Phillips' late father. The younger Phillips was receptive to the name change, agreed to continue to pay Zollars salary as president, and pledged that the family would make a substantial contribution to OCU's endowment fund. On August 9, 1912, Zollars called a special meeting of OCU's board of trustees and introduced a motion to change the name of the school to Phillips Christian University (PCU). The trustees agreed and two years later, on December 23, 1914, when the university's articles of incorporation were revised, the name was shortened to Phillips University.

Not everyone supported the name change. R. A. Long had previously promised $25,000 toward the endowment fund if another $75,000 could be raised. The Phillips family contributed the necessary $75,000, $50,000 for the endowment fund and $25,000 for a building fund. Long honored his commitment and contributed his $25,000, but told Zollars, "Men of wealth do not care to memorialize other rich men through institutions that bear their names." Long never again contributed to Phillips.

With the new name came an increase in academic awareness. Phillips was in the area served by the North Central Association, one of the

The Phillips Christian University Band during the 1912-1913 school year. For several terms after its formation the university's band had no uniforms. Eventually, when an Oklahoma National Guard Unit was formed at the school following World War I, the band became a regimental band for the guardsmen.

leading accrediting institutions in the country. To gain full accreditation by North Central would be a tremendous boost in prestige; however, it would involve considerable expense. Dean Marshall of the College of the Bible and Dean Reiter of the College of Liberal Arts were charged with preparing Phillips for accreditation.

A larger library was the university's primary requirement to gain accreditation. Also, to comply with North Central recommendations, the university was reorganized into eight departments—English, mathematics, history, social sciences, biological science, physical science, modern language, and ancient language. The requirement of a $200,000 endowment fund fell $50,000 short. Phillips High School was accredited but Phillips University had to wait until March 23, 1919, to receive full North Central accreditation.

It was important to Marshall that the university's Bible College be included in the North Central accreditation. At the time of the founding of Phillips many presidents of Christian Church schools were laymen who were often more interested in copying the work of the state universities than in training ministers to serve the churches. This, according to Dean England, resulted in their Colleges of Liberal Arts limiting the number of Bible subjects accredited toward a bachelor degree. Many prospective preachers were not attracted to such programs and the result was a shortage of Christian church preachers. In addition, many congregations were "suspicious" of an educated preacher.

Dean Marshall disagreed with both concepts. He insisted that Christian church preachers should hold bachelor degrees. Likewise, he rejected the idea of what was called "a trade school" approach to ministerial education.

He demanded that a bachelor's degree from the College of the Bible be "an honest one" and he instituted a curriculum with basic requirements of science, English, history, and Biblical Greek as well as elective classes in both the Liberal Arts and Biblical interpretation. This, Marshall believed, would provide the ministerial students the proficiency to preach and prepare them for advanced study at the graduate level.

There was to be no shirking of academic standards. A degree from the College of the Bible was as "rigorously demanding of the minister as the courses for teachers and scientists."

In 1914, Chancellor Oliver N. Roth took over the duties of the office of the president. He served in the position until 1916.

Because of Dean Marshall's insistence on such high standards, Phillips' College of the Bible was included in the North Central Association's accreditation.

Phillips was the first private university in Oklahoma to receive North Central accreditation and one of only three universities in the state accredited. Later, Phillips was granted membership in the American Association of Colleges. Eventually the university was also accredited by the National Association of Schools of Music Education, the Training Board of American Speech and Hearing Association, the Board of Higher Education of the Christian Church, and the Veterans Administration.

An example of rigorous training was a tactic used by Roy J. Wolfinger who had arrived at Phillips in 1912 to oversee the university's English Department. He did so for the next 22 years. He was perhaps best known for requiring his students to come up with 10 original ideas as a composition assignment. Should there be a mistake on an assignment handed in by a student, Professor Wolfinger would simply clip the corner of the page without marking the error and place it on the student's desk. It was the responsibility of the student to locate the mistake and correct it. Wolfinger also wrote and produced numerous plays presented by the university's comedy class. Whenever he lectured, he would pace the floor, using frequent gestures and a keen sense of humor to keep the attention of students.

In 1913, university officials organized a School of Education. Phillips had always provided teacher training, but it was in the form of review in preparation for certificate examination. A dean of education was appointed and professional educational courses were introduced. In 1920, the program was accredited by the American Association of Colleges for Teacher Education. A Future Teachers of America organization also was active on campus. Later it was replaced by the Student Education Association.

In 1913, the Enid Commercial Club announced it would underwrite the construction of a new ladies gym-

28 In Reverence We Stand

nasium. Completed during the 1914-1915 school year, the brick structure had a 25-foot ceiling and a 60- by 80-foot main room. It contained a running track that hung like a balcony over the basketball court. There were no bleachers—spectators stood around the outside of the basketball court. Prior to the completion of the new gymnasium, female students at Phillips, with the exception of those participating in basketball or tennis, had no athletic facilities. Now regular gymnasium classes were available for girls.

President Zollars was suffering from diabetes, and by September of 1914, was unable to maintain the hectic pace of teaching and running the school. On March 4, 1915, Zollars resigned as president and accepted the position as president emeritus. His final official act was to sign the diplomas for the Class of 1915. He spent the rest of his life with his daughter, Addie, and her husband in Warren, Ohio. He died on February 10, 1916.

To replace Zollars, the Phillips board of trustees named Oliver N. Roth acting president. Roth had worn many hats at Phillips for seven years, including being responsible for running the school's business affairs. He was married to long time Phillips music teacher Ethel Mae Harris.

Roth introduced summer school sessions and oversaw Phillips' application for accreditation by the Oklahoma State Board of Education. The accreditation was necessary because state law required teachers to take courses at approved educational institutions. On June 21, 1916, the State Board of Education met in Oklahoma City to hear the applications of all church related schools in Oklahoma. Dr. Wilbur H. Cramblet presented Phillips'

The Ladies Gymnasium was completed in 1915. Chapel services and commencement services were held in the building in addition to athletic events. The gym was also the location of the annual Halloween Masquerade. Black and orange crepe paper was draped around the balcony. A grand march was held and couples paraded around the gymnasium floor as judges chose the most original, prettiest, and funniest costumes.

New Name, Same Mission 29

Dr. Isaac Newton McCash became president of Phillips University in 1916 and served more than two decades until 1938.

Frank A. Wellman was professor of history and political science. He arrived on the Phillips campus in 1918.

case that morning and the application was approved. The board then adjourned without hearing the other accreditation requests until that afternoon—thus Phillips University was the first church college in Oklahoma to be accredited by the State Department of Education.

Phillips officials actively sought the admission of students from outside Oklahoma and surrounding states. The first international student was a young Armenian, Naseef Monsour, who was brought from the Holy Land by John W. Umphries, an evangelist and Phillips alumnus. Monsour was enrolled in Phillips High School in 1914. That winter he joined University Place Church and several of Phillips' ministerial students took him to University Lake to be baptized.

Unfortunately Monsour was not familiar with the practice, and as the party made its way through the fields surrounding the lake, he became convinced that he was about to be murdered. When one of the ministerial students picked up a branch to knock down some sunflowers, Monsour fled, screaming for help. It took some time to locate him in a rooming house where he was hiding.

On March 10, 1916, Dr. Isaac Newton McCash was chosen as Phillips' new president. He assumed the post on August 3 of that year. Born in Cumberland County, Illinois, on June 5, 1861, McCash attended Peabody Seminary in Georgia and received degrees from State Teachers College in Lebanon, Ohio, and Drake University in Des Moines, Iowa. Before coming to Phillips, McCash had served as principal of Ewington Academy in Gallia County, Ohio, and as superintendent of schools at Lyons, Kansas.

McCash pastored churches in Des Moines and Berkeley, California, from 1890 until 1909 when he was named the corresponding secretary of the American Christian Missionary Society. In 1913, he became the president of Spokane University in Washington. He was inaugurated president of Phillips University on November 16, 1916.

McCash's vision for Phillips was similar to that of the school's founder, Dr. Ely Zollars. Specifically, McCash wanted to make sure the university continued to adequately prepare ministerial students. To raise necessary funds required by the North Central Association's accreditation, he instituted a Tri-State Missionary Movement, headed by T. T. Roberts. Directed toward Christian churches in Oklahoma, Kansas, and Arkansas, it was designed to increase the university's endowment and recruit ministerial students.

When McCash became president, Phillips had no debt. Unfortunately, that luxury quickly changed during the post-World War I depression. As money became tight, donations dropped, and by 1921, the university was nearly $100,000 in debt.

McCash envisioned an extensive building program and active participation with the Men and Millions Movement to increase Phillips' endowment. But America's entry into World War I on April 2, 1917, postponed future expansion for several years. The war also imposed hardships on many Phillips students.

At the opening of the 1918 school year Phillips was designated a Government Military School and First Lieutenant H. E. Embach was assigned to oversee the school's Student Army Training Corps (SATC). On October

30 IN REVERENCE WE STAND

1, 1918, federal officials approved Phillips as a training location for military officers. Twelve thousand dollars was raised by Enid businessmen to fund the completion of a military barracks on the Phillips campus, as well as gas, water, and sewer lines. The barracks were built opposite the library on the south side of East Maine Street.

One hundred men took the oath of allegiance inducting them into the army in the school chapel. Drill was conducted on the campus grounds. As training, sergeants taught the would-be soldiers how to march. The trainees marched in unison to classrooms for instruction by both Phillips faculty and military instructors.

There were some confrontations between the SATC men and ministerial students in the College of the Bible. The ministerial students were exempt from the draft and were viewed as "slackers" by some of the military trainees. On several occasions individual ministerial students were seized and thrown into University Lake by the trainees. University officials had no control of the men in the army, but when the training officer heard about what had happened, the harassment stopped.

The Student Friendship (War) Fund was formed by the Young Men's Christian Association and the Young Women's Christian Association and raised $1,200 in the fall of 1917 to aid those in the armed services. A United War Work Campaign was organized on campus as well, and in October of 1918 raised $1,500 for the war effort.

With the Armistice of November 11, 1918, the SATC program was closed. The last official formation at Phillips was held on December 14, 1918. The military barracks were converted first to student housing and later to riding stables.

With the end of the war, university administrators concentrated on catering to returning veterans and developing new programs for the coming decade. By 1919, Phillips had 1,015 students on campus—triple the number of students just seven years earlier.

The staff of the student newspaper, *The Slate*, in 1915. O. Page Manley and Austin C. Cleveland were managing editors. The newspaper printed stories of students and clubs and messages from university administrators.

New Name, Same Mission 31

Professor Rein Dyksterhus, second from the left, and a violin quartet at Oklahoma Christian University, ca. 1912-1913. Dyksterhus taught music, violin, and piano at Oklahoma Christian University.

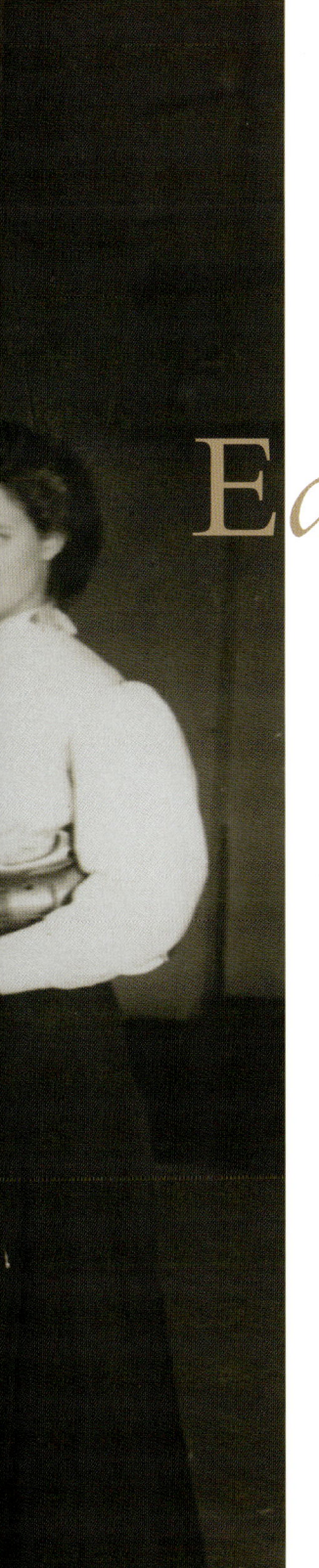

Early Campus Life

ONE of the most famous of the early students at OCU was Marquis James, the Pulitzer Prize winning author. Although James was born in Missouri in 1891, his parents moved to Oklahoma Territory to participate in the Run of 1893 when the Cherokee Outlet along the present Kansas-Oklahoma border was opened to homesteaders. When James was ten years old, the family relocated to Enid. James graduated from Enid High School in 1910 and enrolled in OCU that fall semester to continue his education. James later wrote about the three motion "picture shows" in Enid that OCU students could frequent as well as a roofless summer theater known as Delmar Garden. Silent movies sometimes were shown in the basement of the OG&E Building. However the movie theaters closed before 10:00 p.m. At 11:00 p.m.

the night policeman made his rounds of the town square, called the White Way because it was lined with iron posts, each with three street lights. The officer would turn off two of the three lights on each post. Also at 11:00 p.m., the drugstore soda fountains closed to allow the students to catch the "owl" streetcars, so named because they made their last run at midnight. The only establishments remaining open were the saloons, gambling houses, and the Midway Dance Hall, which, according to James, "closed only in the daytime."

While enrolled at OCU, James served as the college's reporter for the local newspaper, the *Enid Eagle*, and wrote stories for the newspaper detailing university life. He was paid $6.00 per week. Unfortunately, a few months after enrolling, his father died unexpectedly and James dropped out of the university to work full time as a newspaper reporter to help support his mother.

Most faculty members and students at OCU were active in the Christian Church but the closest congregation was Central Christian Church in downtown Enid. As early as 1909, a university Sunday school had been organized to better serve the university community. At first, classes were held in private homes. On February 1, 1910, Professor Marshall of the Bible College was selected to preach to the group that met in the university chapel, the beginning of University Place Christian Church.

On April 12, 1912, the group officially organized. That fall the congregation purchased the First Methodist Church building in Enid and moved it near the Phillips campus. T. H. Mathieson became the church's first full-time minister in 1920.

Campus life for OCU students, faculty, and administration was unique. Students approved of the official policy that social fraternities and sororities along the Greek system were prohibited. However, officials recognized the need for fellowship outside the classroom and encouraged the creation of social/service clubs and other student organizations.

The YWCA, Student Volunteers, and Student Ministerial Alliance were organized in the 1913-1914 school year and were open to everyone, especially students in the College of the Bible. Members of Phillips' Student Volunteers worked diligently with local missionary projects to prepare its members for foreign mission service. They offered Saturday Bible School classes at the Booker T. Washington School, the segregated school for black students. The area was one of the most depressed in Enid and the school was a welcome diversion for local children. The volunteers also offered Bible services at the County Poor Farm, a home for indigent elderly citizens.

During that same time the German Club was formed. The Philolathuian, Crown, Olympian, Cerropian, and Delphi literary societies flourished. The Crown Literary Society often presented three-act plays for the student body.

Students from states other than Oklahoma generally formed their state organization—for example the Kansas Klub, first organized in 1914, sponsored the Kansas Klub Taffy Pull. Its members proudly proclaimed:

Jayhawk Talk, Talk Jayhawk
Say Kansas
We're Phillips Jayhawks,
With a Phillips rah, and a Jayhawk Ray,
Rah, Rah, Rah

The Texas Club was made up of Phillips students from the Lone Star State. At its monthly meetings its members were obligated to "tell the truth, the whole truth and nothing but the truth" about their home state. On a more serious note they actively recruited prospective students in Texas. Likewise Oregon Club, Arkansas Club, Arizona Club, Colorado Club, and Missouri Club members came from those states.

The Timothy Club, organized by President Zollars, was open to younger ministerial students. The Ramblers, an unauthorized secret organization specialized in pranks around campus and sponsored an annual picnic in the red hills south of the school. When the Ramblers began to help themselves to milk that members of the Timothy Club left outside at night to cool, the ministerial students laced the milk with ipecac. Offending Ramblers became ill and President Zollars ordered them disbanded. However, the club existed at various times, even into the 1990s.

Incoming freshmen at Phillips were subjected to "Frosh Initiation" designed to build a sense of unity. Under rules adopted by the Student Council, which had been organized in 1914, freshmen at Phillips wore green beanies until after the Thanksgiving football game each year. Later, the color of the head adornment changed. In the 1950s, the beanies were maroon and white. Freshmen women were assigned a sophomore man who was her "Big Brother."

Whenever freshmen met a sophomore who said "Button, Freshie," the freshmen had to kneel, reach on top of their head, and touch the button on top of their cap while yelling, "Yea, Haymakers!"

The Sunken Garden was used by students as a Kangaroo Court for incoming freshmen who were tried for such crimes as not having their shirts or coats buttoned. Those found guilty were covered with paint or mud and then thrown into University Lake. Freshmen retaliated by roaming the campus looking for sophomores. Any caught were hauled to the lake and also thrown in.

The OCU campus provided one special bonus for Enid residents. The girls of Athenian Hall attracted the attention of local young men. Those with automobiles would make the two-mile drive from downtown Enid along East Broadway to OCU and then race around the campus throwing up clouds of dust to attract the girls' attention. At the sound of the approaching autos, the girls usually rushed to their windows to wave at the visitors. Most of this activity took place in the evenings after classes. At

Students on the steps of Athenian Hall holding an Oklahoma Christian University pennant. Many early students at OCU were poor and could hardly afford the $25 per semester tuition. Note the second student from the left in the second row. He obviously has borrowed a much too large suit to have this photograph made. The trouser legs are rolled up and the coat hangs down to his mid-thighs.

Early Campus Life 35

The interior of the Library at Oklahoma Christian University crowded with students from both the university and the university's high school.

the time President Zollars and his wife were living in Athenian Hall. When the noise became too great, Zollars would yell up the stairs to "be quiet."

Zollars enforced strict discipline. Card games, smoking, liquor, and dancing were prohibited. Most students observed the prohibition; however, some continued to smoke cigarettes. Zollars was horrified when he found some students openly smoking on campus. "I do not know that anyone is ever justified in concealing his evil habits," he thundered, "but if one ever is, it is the habit of tobacco." He continued, "Young men, if you must smoke . . .Go to your room, enter your closet, and shut the door, and there in secret offer up your burnt offerings to whatever god you think is suitable."

Not all students willingly accepted Zollars' discipline. During the 1910-1911 school year, the president was hung in effigy in the chapel. To deal with rowdy students, Zollars appointed a disciplinary committee. Offenders usually were suspended until they made an apology. Once, the human skeleton from OCU's Physiological Laboratory was hung between Old

36 IN REVERENCE WE STAND

Above: Miss Grace Reynolds, center forefront, and the Oklahoma Christian University Girls Glee Club, ca. 1910. Among its members were Etta Charlton, Noda Eby, Clyde Payne, Dixie Williams, Irma McMillan, Effie Payne, Ella Payne, Flo Williams, Opal Blakslee, Martha D. Mason, and Bonnie Goode. Miss Reynolds taught voice at the university.

C. C. Taylor, Elmer Schenke, and A. G. Smith of the Oklahoma Christian University Debate Team. Here the members pose with the Lion Store Cup won in a debate tournament with Epworth University, later Oklahoma City University, in November of 1908.

Early Campus Life 37

The modern science room at Oklahoma Christian University as it appeared in 1910. Geological specimens and various organs of the human body are displayed on the table in the foreground. On the wall in the background is a human skeleton.

Main and the Fine Arts Building with a placard bearing the name of the chairman of the discipline committee. On another occasion, pranksters led a cow to the top of the central tower of Old Main and left it there.

Some of the most popular organizations on campus were the debate teams first organized by Professor R. G. Sears. In the 1913-1914 school year, the Webster and Lincoln Debating Society was formed. In 1914, the Madison Debating Club was organized. Sears annually presented a gold medal to the school's best debater.

Most College of the Bible students were members of the Ministerial Association at Phillips. Its goal was to support the spiritual welfare of the campus and bring its members into contact with the areas of church service that could not be taught in regular classroom work.

Soon after McCash assumed his post, the question of Greek letter fraternities and sororities again became an issue on campus. Phillips had always had a ban on Greek letter fraternities and sororities. Nonetheless, some unofficial fraternities and sororities had been organized. Their members began to push the school's board of trustees to change their position and recognize them.

When word spread of the movement it triggered a backlash from other students. Those opposed to the Greek organizations maintained that the intent of the school was that "the rich and poor should meet together on a common level" and that "character and conduct, not clothes, or money, should determine the student's standing."

The issue dragged on for two years before, on February 5, 1918, Phillips' board of trustees voted to ban any Greek letter organizations. They maintained that they were discriminatory and contrary to the principles of Christian education for which Phillips University stood. For a few years thereafter, students were required to sign a statement that they would not join Greek letter societies.

In spite of the ban on Greek letter organizations, other student clubs flourished and an Inter-Club Council was formed to promote cooperation among the numerous social and service clubs and administer rules governing "rushing" incoming freshmen. Pledging of the social clubs took place during the second semester. Each club held a special formal social function. Pledging took the better part of a month during which the new members were required to carry out specific duties for the various clubs. The favorite activity of the men's clubs was serenading the residents of Athenian Hall.

English students formed the Zollars Literary Society during the fall semester of 1917. It was the oldest society at Phillips and its members claimed that Zollars stood for Zealous, Original, Lovable, Laughing, Amiable, Righteous, Students. Lawrence L. Lounsbury was the first president. It presented a multitude of original plays, songs, readings, jokes, and stories at Zollars Hall. When the roll was called for their monthly meetings, members were expected to answer with a memorized quotation.

In the university's first years, the men's honor society was Blue Key. The women's honor society was Cardinal Key. Who's Who in American Colleges and Universities also was active on campus. The Silver Scroll was the academic organization for freshmen and sophomores.

Music was important to both faculty and students. One hundred music scholarships were awarded in the first few years of classes. A band was organized although there was not sufficient money to buy uniforms. The campus was filled with talented men and women whose voices and instruments were used to entertain both students and members of the community in frequent concerts.

The people of Enid and the Christian Church were both happy with the progress of the fledgling Phillips University.

The "shoot the chute" on University Lake on the Phillips campus. The lake was a popular gathering place for students, with facilities for fishing, boating, picnicking, swimming, volleyball, dodge ball, pass ball, quoits, brevit, croquet, and tennis.

Early Campus Life 39

MUSIC HALL

The Roaring Twenties

IN THE 1920S, the American economy recovered from the recession caused by World War I. The recovery allowed Christian churches to provide more support for Phillips. The larger budget allowed the university to expand its programs and improve its already superior academic standing among colleges and universities in the region.

In January of 1919, Phillips became one of only two colleges in Oklahoma authorized to form a Reserve Officers' Training Corps (ROTC) unit. First Lieutenant George A. Neale was assigned as professor of military science and tactics. Phillips' trustees voted to create a permanent ROTC unit in March of that same year. All male students over 18 years of age were eligible to join. Those who enlisted were issued uniforms, ordinance, rifles, 60 rounds of ammunition, and haversacks.

The members of First Headquarters Battalion, Headquarters Battery and Combat Train, 189th Field Artillery Regiment posing in front of the Oklahoma National Guard Armory at Phillips University. The unit was stationed on the university's campus from 1921 until 1936 and for many years was commanded by Captain Stephen J. England, the dean of Phillips' College of the Bible. In 1940, the Phillips University Band became the 189th's regimental band.

Frank E. Knowles taught at Phillips University from 1920 to 1956. He was professor of physics and dean of men.

Unfortunately, by the opening of the fall term, the federal government had decided to close all ROTC units that had not existed prior to World War I. The ROTC unit was replaced on September 21, 1921, by a unit of the Oklahoma National Guard.

As a result, the First Battalion Headquarters Detachment and Combat Training, 189th Field Artillery Regiment, Oklahoma National Guard, was organized on September 21, 1921, under the command of Captain George E. Hutchinson. Federal recognition was received on November 17, 1921, and equipment was issued to the unit. Among the equipment received were large White trucks, which were a big hit on campus as the guardsmen drove them around the school.

The establishment of a National Guard unit on campus offered welcome financial aid for many students. Guardsmen were paid between $1.00

The 1927 yearbook featured Phillipian missionaries serving on foreign fields in Africa, China, and Tibet.

The Roaring Twenties 43

In the 1920s, the Zollars Club banquet was held each February. Balloons and confetti helped students celebrate the lives of great men born in February.

The Zonta Club banquet in 1929. The Zontas were distinctive, dressed in colorful jackets and white pleated skirts.

and $2.80 per weekly drill, a substantial sum of money for the time. In addition, they attended a two-week summer camp. Phillips also received federal money for renting a drill hall to the National Guard. With the large number of veterans on campus after the war, filling the ranks of the unit was no problem. The unit's primary duty was communications between the firing batteries and observers, and the men trained in telephone, blinker, wig-wag, semaphore, and runner. In the summer of 1925, a new armory was built on campus.

The University Post Office Station was opened in a brick building on the northwest corner of the campus following World War I. A frame building, called Phillips Lunch and later the Haymaker Inn, was also constructed to provide more rooms to rent to students and to serve as a dining hall for students.

The retreat at University Lake began hosting Young People's Conferences in 1919. In 1920, the name was changed to the Southwest Young People's Summer Conference. Youth from Oklahoma, Kansas, Colorado, Texas, and New Mexico participated.

In 1919, Phillips' School of Expression and Dramatic Art began annual performances of Charles Dickens' *A Christmas Carol* under the direction of Earl W. Oberg. Presented in the auditorium of Old Main, the program became so popular that it was broadcast by AM and short wave radio locally and coast-to-coast. The entire cast was portrayed by Oberg, who flawlessly recited every line of the book.

The Masquers, a dramatic society, was formed that same year. Its members came from the School of Expression and Dramatic Art who presented dramatic recitals and novelty programs both on campus and in Enid. The School of Expression and Dramatic Art also presented an annual Shakespearian play in the school's stadium.

44 In Reverence We Stand

In 1931, the Zelotai Club celebrated its tenth anniversary. Zelotai, a club for wives of students enrolled in the College of the Bible, was established by Marietta Tandy McCash, the wife of President Isaac Newton McCash.

The 1926 Masquers Club, a dramatic society composed of members of the School of Expression and Dramatic Art and others interested in dramatic arts. Esther Lillian Moss was president of the newly-formed club.

In 1920, Jefferson D. Hoy Lamb, of China, became the first Oriental to graduate from Phillips. After graduation he returned to his homeland. It was the beginning of an extensive effort by Phillips to expand its program of Christian education to Asia. In the following years numerous students from overseas were sent to Phillips by the United Christian Missionary Society. Likewise many Phillips' students traveled to Asia as missionaries.

Both student leaders and administrators at Phillips realized the importance of social/service clubs. In 1923, the Gridiron Club was organized by Stephen J. England, Emory Cameron, and Jones Graves. Members of the Gridiron Club were primarily from the College of the Bible and the organization was referred to as the "preachers' club." The Gridiron Club oversaw the annual Football Queen Contest at Phillips. When Phillips dropped football from its athletic program in 1933, the Gridiron Club shifted its purpose to the support of other athletic programs. Annual watermelon feeds and rind fights, freshmen parties, barbecues, and a spring sweetheart banquet were sponsored.

After graduation of the senior class of 1924, Phillips High School was closed. There simply was no longer the need for a preparatory school. Local educational facilities had improved to the point that public schools were adequate to prepare students for admission to Phillips.

During this time President McCash launched a program to raise $1 million in endowment. Called the Phillips University Endowment Crusade, the effort began in September of 1924 and by October of 1926 had cash and pledges of more than $1.2 million.

The Roaring Twenties 45

The Phillips story was easy to convey to congregations and potential donors. In the 1920s, reports from all Disciples-related colleges and universities showed that Phillips was spending only $174 per student for administration, operation and maintenance of the physical plant, and instruction. That figure was substantially lower than the other dozen Disciples schools in the nation.

In 1925, the School of Education became the College of Education and in 1931 a graduate department of education was formed and a masters degree in education offered. Local schools pro-

President Isaac Newton McCash built a private home on the southeast corner of South University and East Maine. After his presidency, he donated the home to Phillips. Subsequent presidents lived in the home until a new president's home was constructed in 1969. After 1969, it was used by the Music Department.

vided classrooms for education students to observe and practice and Phillips became the major source of substitute teachers for the Enid public schools.

The Zontas and The Tenth Muse, organized in 1926 and 1927 respectively, also were active in campus life. The Zonta Club members wore white wool skirts and white pigskin jackets and hosted an annual Sweetheart Formal, Abnormal Formal, Line Party, weenie roast, skating party, Kodak-Picnic, and Mothers' Day Breakfast. According to Sandra Anne Parish Remmert, Zonta was one of the most active service clubs on campus.

The Red Peppers, formed in 1925, was another popular girl's club. Its goal was the promotion of school spirit, loyalty, and pep as well as to emphasize attendance at all university activities—literary, musical, or athletic. Their cry of "We're the Red-pep-pep-Peppers" soon became well known on campus. An all-male pep club—the Triple R—was formed. RRR stood for Rip Roaring Rooters and its members wore bright red shirts and white bow ties.

A Girls' Drum Corps was formed in 1927-1928. Members' costumes were made by parents and the drums were provided by the university. Boasting 12 snare drums, a bass drum, a tenor drum, and cymbals, the drum corps performed at many athletic events. They dressed in maroon-colored capes and skirts, overseas caps, and white Russian blouses. The drum major dressed entirely in white.

An art club was organized with Rose Wright as its first president. Its goal was the development of an appreciation and responsibility for beauty and good taste on the campus and in the community through fine and applied arts.

In 1926, the Maroon Pencil Club was formed as an organization for students studying journalism. Its members formed the core staff for *The Slate*. The first president of the Maroon Pencil Club was Gladys Linden. New members were called "cubs," as in cub reporter, until they obtained full membership. In 1929, the name of *The Slate* was changed to *The Haymaker*. The name change took effect the following year in 1930.

In 1929, the Knights of Knowledge was organized for students and staff of the library. "The right book to the right person at the right time and in the right spirit" was the organization's motto.

Not all student activity was structured or approved by the administration. Some students were enamored with the leading comic strip characters of the day and took their nicknames from them. "Boob" McNutt, "Bud" Fisher, "Moon" Mullins, and friends went to great lengths to carry out a prank during chapel. Hearing that the university choral group would be singing "The Awakening Chorus" at chapel the next morning, the boys "borrowed" dozens of alarm clocks from dorms and rooming houses. The clocks clanged and rang loudly a few minutes after the chorus began to sing "Awake! Awake!" Kay Taylor remembered, "If those guys weren't well known on campus before this exercise, they certainly were from then on."

The 1920s had been a decade of unprecedented growth for the university. Unfortunately, the economic boom of the Roaring Twenties was about to end with the stock market crash of October of 1929. The onset of the Great Depression would have a devastating effect on Phillips University.

In 1938, Champlin Oil Company of Enid presented the Harvesters men's club four Corinthian columns from the Enid Bank and Trust Building built in 1913. The columns were used to landscape the Sunken Garden as representations of the four facets of education—physical, spiritual, social, and intellectual. When completed, the Sunken Garden was the site of concerts, Shakespeare plays, and Greek Theater. The columns were moved when the Mabee Center was built on the property where the Sunken Garden were located. This is a 2003 photograph of the columns. Courtesy Jack N. Taylor.

Hard Times

The Great Depression

AS PHILLIPS UNIVERSITY'S silver anniversary approached, the nation was gripped by the economic hardships of the Great Depression. In the states that formed Phillips' service area, residents were struck by the twin disasters of the dust bowl and depression. The effects of the nearly decade long drought soon were evident on Phillips' campus. Much work had gone into landscaping the university but the shortage of rain turned the once lush green campus a dirty brown. Many of the campus' 220 trees had died. When the rains returned, efforts were made to replace the trees lost to the dust bowl. E. W. Marland, Oklahoma oilman and governor, presented the university with $1,750 worth of shrubbery from the nursery at his Ponca City mansion. The Enid Garden Club provided the transportation to bring the shrubbery to the Phillips campus. The Enid American Business Club donated another 200 trees.

Phillips celebrated its 25th anniversary on September 17, 1932. Phillips students presented a three-part historical pageant held in the athletic stadium at University Lake for the event. Episode one portrayed the Native American heritage of the region with dancing by Ponca and Otoe Indians, prairie schooners, a living representation of the Pioneer Woman statue, and a re-enactment of the Run of September 16, 1893. The second episode focused on the uniting of the Twin Territories into the State of Oklahoma and the third act dramatized the founding of Phillips University and its history.

The silver anniversary celebration was overshadowed by the sobering effects of the depression. As income from agriculture plummeted, the price of wheat at Enid dropped to 52 cents per bushel in October of 1933. Money needed to keep Phillips University active slowed to a trickle. Income from church contributions decreased as congregations could no longer honor their pledges. Tuition payments plummeted as students no longer had the financial resources to attend college and enrollment decreased. Special gifts also dropped off as the economic depression worsened. Many student loans went unpaid.

School officials found it difficult to pay salaries. At the end of the 1931-1932 school term, faculty members were issued promissory notes for the unpaid balance of their salary. In 1932-1933, even with salary cuts of between 10 and 20 percent, promissory notes were again issued in lieu of money. In 1933-1934, the faculty was told that only three months of their salary could be paid and that the money would be allocated on a pro rata basis. Fortunately, the faculty members agreed to continue teaching.

Because the faculty members were no longer salaried employees, but more or less partners of the university, the board of trustees organized a three-member Faculty Participation Committee to help oversee expenditures. John C. Lappin, Stephen J. England, and J. Clifford Shirley were appointed to the committee. By the spring of 1934, the crisis passed and regular salary payments were resumed.

It was the willingness of the faculty to sacrifice, according to Thurman J. White, that allowed Phillips to survive the depths of the depression. This dedication to Christian education was what made the Phillips alumni of the depression era dearly treasure their alma mater. The value and vision of this "Phillips Tradition," according to Druie L. "Pete" Warren and Patricia Cravens Warren, was what made an education at the university so valuable.

One of the major suggestions of the Faculty Participation Committee was to support the effort of Bayne Driskill to formulate a plan to liquidate the depression debt. Driskill was named director of the Bureau of Public Relations in February of 1936 and Stephen J. England was moved from teaching to serve as controller of finance. This reorganization was part of a "Million Dollar Drive" to raise $1,000,000 by 1939, enroll 350 ministerial students, build a new Bible College building, Science Hall, dormitories, and an auditorium.

The Bureau of Public Relations was charged with finding employment for Phillips students needing financial help. The office kept files on local employers that hired students and regularly checked with them to see if any positions were available. The bureau also was in charge of student recruitment. In an effort to boost enrollment, Phillips, for the first time, actively recruited prospective students. C. V. Covey was in charge of the recruitment program.

Although not in the dust bowl proper, many of the dust storms that formed in the Texas Panhandle, western Kansas, and eastern Colorado blew across Enid. They were described as "sinister, eerie, deathly quiet, gray days." The years 1934 and 1935 were especially bad for dust storms. As William "Bill" Briggs, son of the university president, recalled, "We'd close up the house as best we could and stay inside unless we absolutely had to go out." People held damp cloths over their mouths when they ventured outside. Much of the blowing soil came from the red hills around Enid and local residents called the dust storms "red blizzards."

To keep out the blowing soil, students and faculty at Phillips sealed doors with tape and hung wet sheets over windows. Still the choking, powder-fine dust found its way inside. It seeped into every house and building, covering everything with a reddish gray coat.

Many students survived the depression and completed their education because of Miss Nona Wright, a 1925 graduate of the College

Members of the 1932 faculty of the College of Fine Arts. Front row, left to right, L.L. Lacy, Louise Allen, Aline Wilson, Marie Crosby. Second row, C.D. Hahn, Russell Wiley, Earl Oberg.

of the Bible. At the onset of the Depression she managed the Haymaker Inn, which served as a rooming house and dining room for students. When money became tight, Miss Wright continued to allow students to eat at the Haymaker Inn on credit. The facility became a favorite gathering place and religious center for those who met there informally. Wednesday night was "cocoa night" at the Haymaker. The fare consisted of cocoa and dried toast from the school cafeteria. Roland K. Huff recalled Wright always referred to the students that lived at the Haymaker Inn as "her boys." She even cared for them when they were ill. Huff remembers her cooking potato soup for him after a tonsillectomy.

Miss Wright also helped establish a Mexican mission in Enid to help Hispanic students studying for the ministry. She later became the manager of the cafeteria in the Phillips Student Union when it opened in 1942.

The plight of Phillips' employees during the depression was made somewhat easier by the attitude of local merchants such as A. H. Ray, owner of Ray's Grocery near the Phillips campus. Ray extended interest-free credit to both faculty members and students. Customers telephoned Ray with a list of what they needed. Ray or one of his employees would fill the order for pickup or Ray would have it delivered at no additional charge.

A local Enid dentist wanted to send his daughter to Phillips, but lacked the funds for her tuition. He worked out a barter arrangement between the university and a faculty member who needed dental work. The dentist performed the dental work for the faculty member, his daughter was enrolled at Phillips, and the cost of the dental work was deducted from the money owed the faculty member.

The head of the university's English Department, Roy J. Wolfinger, visited local farmers and asked permission to capture pigeons in their barns. Once they agreed, he would go in at night, close all the openings, and capture as many of the birds as he could. He then took them home where he kept them in a pen. As his son Birge Wolfinger, who often helped on these expeditions, later recalled, "We ate a lot of pigeons in those years."

The children of Phillips' ministerial students, as well as children of all ministers, were called PKs, the abbreviation of "preacher's kids." Most children of Phillips' employees or students attended Adams Elementary School or Longfellow Junior High School before moving on to Enid High School. A. H. Ray usually included a small bag of candy for the PKs when their parents ordered food from his grocery store.

During the depression, prices were low, if one had the money to pay. Frank Hawkins Grocery offered beef roast at 10 cents a pound, beef ribs at 6 cents a pound, and pork neck bones at 5 pounds for 15 cents. A 2-pound can of Folgers Coffee at Tapps Grocery was 29½ cents. H. Mogab's grocery store sold frying hens for 7 cents each. Pig livers at Nick H. Nicholas' grocery were 2 pounds for 9 cents. The Waken Grocery sold 20 pounds of sugar for 48 cents. Tomatoes, hominy, peas, corn, peaches, kraut, or tomato juice brought 5 cents per can. Peanut butter was 2 pounds for 23 cents and 21 cents would purchase 2 cans of salmon.

Tiny Murdock Grimes recalled that she lived with her sister Zeta Murdock, Wilma More Tye, and Margaret Smith in an upstairs apartment just off campus. They each put $25 a month into their grocery money which was sufficient, if they were "frugal," to keep them in food.

With the onset of President Franklin D. Roosevelt's New Deal, the financial stress of some Phillips' students was eased. In June of 1935, Congress passed legislation creating the National Youth Administration (NYA), a work-relief and employment program for high school and college youth designed to allow them to continue their education. An important aspect was a part-time employment program

Hard Times: The Great Depression 51

This group of distinguished professors trained Phillips students for service in churches throughout America. Left to right: Front row, Dr. Wilfred Evans Powell, professor of religious education; Dr. Robert G. Martin, Sr., professor of Old Testament and later dean of the Bible College; dean emeritus Frank Hamilton Marshall, who came to Phillips in 1907; Dr. C. C. Taylor. Back row, Dr. S. M. Smith; Dr. Stephen J. England, Bible College dean; Dr. G. Edwin Osborn, Phillips chaplain and professor of practical theology; professor of philosophy Dr. Ralph W. Nelson; and professor of speech J. A. Morris.

for college students and graduate students. Professor Frank A. Wellman was the NYA administrator for Phillips and through his efforts several hundred students were provided jobs so they could remain in school. In 1938 alone the NYA provided $5,130 to aid 38 students.

Most Phillips students worked to help support themselves during the depression. Bill Briggs turned a four-by six-foot coal bin in the basement of his parent's house into a darkroom. He then took candid photographs of events around the Phillips campus such as Stunt Night or Freshmen Girls. He made an 8 x 10 inch montage and sold copies for 50 cents each.

Stunt Night was a diversion from the ravages of the depression for students and faculty. It was an annual fun event where members of six to ten organizations performed. The stunts were humorous, satirical, romantic, dramatic, energetic, and every other possibility that creative students could imagine. The professors' stunt was always one of the best—they had no inhibitions about how they appeared or what they were called on to say and do.

Not all stories from the Depression were sad. One of the biology students at Phillips in the early 1930s was Cecil R. Williams. In 1932 and 1933, Williams was a laboratory assistant in the Biology Department for Dr. J. Clifford Shirley. Along with Eugene Highland, Williams compiled a collection of every snake native to Oklahoma. The snakes were kept in cages in the basement of Old Main. The poisonous ones were under lock and key, but the others were kept in unlocked cages.

One morning Williams and Highland reported to work to find that all the unlocked cages had been opened and the snakes had escaped. Williams recalled, "All day long whenever we heard a scream from some room, one or both of us would dash and recover the lost reptile." One very large bull snake was found on the porch of Athenian Hall, the girl's dorm. Needless to say all cages were locked from then on.

Some students were fortunate to have support from hometown churches. Patricia Vandersall Crowl managed to work her way through Phillips after arriving on campus with $89 in her pocket. She was employed by the President's Office as a part-time secretary. In addition, the local Christian Church congregation in Muskogee, Oklahoma, sent her sufficient money for her room while members of a church social group from several churches sent her a "love offering" every month, which Patricia credited more than once in "keeping me from starving." Patricia eventually graduated in 1946 with a degree in Christian education.

Many of the students at Phillips during the depression years came from nearby farms. Rose Miller Shaklee was one of eight members of her family to attend Phillips. She helped pay her expenses by working in a downtown ladies store, babysitting, and sorting books at the Phillips Library. Because extra money was non-existent, she often took fellow classmates home with her for entertainment. Her parents welcomed them with parties, hayrides, and wiener roasts.

Other students came from great distances. Ernest E. Durham hitchhiked from Tacoma, Washington, to Enid in August of 1935. He left with a leather brief case, a Bible, some clothes, a road map, and $20. He arrived in

Enid on September 1 with six dollars and took the bus to Phillips' campus. One of the first people he met was Dr. Madison Love Perkins who offered him a room on the second floor in exchange for working around the house. He found work at the university for 25 cents an hour, which was credited toward his tuition, and at the Snack Shack where he worked as a fry cook and waiter in exchange for food.

During the 1930s, Phillips students were allowed to have automobiles "for transportation only." Bill Briggs had a tandem bicycle that he and his date could both ride. Students in Athenian Hall could have radios in their rooms only if the housemother approved and, if they paid an additional 75 cents per month for the privilege. Dancing, card playing, and smoking were prohibited on campus or in any Phillips-owned building. Simmons Grocery, which also contained a small delicatessen, was one of the few places where students could eat and smoke at the same time.

Many young men took their dates to one of five movie theaters in Enid, of which the Aztec was the best. It carried first run movies and generally showed three different features each week. Sunday, Monday, and Tuesday evenings were the days the top-rated movies were shown. A movie preview was shown on Sunday, but the girls had to sneak out of Athenian Hall to attend because it did not begin until midnight. On Saturday mornings, children were admitted for a nickel. Two B-Western movies were shown and the child received an ice cream cone. Other movie houses were the Mecca, Criterion, Royal, and Rialto.

The Enid Police Department owned only two patrol cars and most traffic control was performed by a single motorcycle officer. Bill Gould patrolled the area around Phillips on a Harley-Davidson motorcycle. However, the motorcycle was only effective on paved streets and Phillips students quickly learned to head for the nearest dirt road if Gould chased them.

At the beginning of the depression, Russell L. Wiley established the University Band that quickly grew from 10 to 34 members. Dressed in maroon jackets and white pants, the band was a big hit with students and Enid residents. The university also maintained an orchestra which annually presented two formal programs, the Messiah each spring and a Christmas season program. Many Phillips students also played in the Enid Symphony Orchestra.

Once Wiley had established the Phillips University Band, he envisioned inviting high school bands to Enid for a contest so that he could recruit band students. The university's administration and Enid officials encouraged Wiley to hold a festival to celebrate Band Day in 1932. What became the Tri-State Band Festival, and later the Tri-State Music Festival, featured Dr. Edwin Franko Goldman, one of

Professor Milburn Ernest Carey directed the Phillips band and enlarged the Tri-State Band Festival on the Phillips campus after he began his service at Phillips in 1934.

The Phillips University Band appeared at all Phillips sporting events and held annual concerts for citizens of Enid.

Hard Times: The Great Depression 53

America's most renowned band leaders from New York City, and Carl Busch, a composer and director of the Kansas City Symphony. Seven bands attended the first Tri-State Band Festival.

The festival was so successful that Wiley expanded the event the following year "to promote a greater interest for, and a warmer feeling between the high school and university bands in this section of the country." He also wanted to aid in the development of school bands, symphonic bands, and greater skill in wind instruments. At the same time he wanted the festival to expose participants to leading musicians and conductors.

Wiley convinced the Enid Chamber of Commerce and the Retail Merchants Association to support a massive festival, featuring bands from Oklahoma and surrounding states. In 1934, 50 bands from Kansas, Oklahoma, Arkansas, and Texas attended the three-day event. Solo performances were held in Enid's Central Christian Church. Highlighting the festival was a performance of 500 specially selected musicians directed by bandleader Goldman.

In 1934, orchestra competition was added to the festival, and in 1936 massed choruses participated. When Wiley left Phillips in 1934 to eventually become the director of the University of Kansas bands, Frederick Green headed the festival. The following year, Milburn Carey assumed responsibility for the event. In 1953, the event was renamed the Tri-State Music Festival and grew into an international event, attracting participants from around the world.

The festival was used as a recruiting tool by the Music Department at Phillips. Jeanette O'Connor Ice enrolled at Phillips in the late 1930s on a Tri-State Piano Scholarship and worked with many of the music department's professors. Among the professors who contributed to the success of the music program were Mauritz Kesnear, who helped secure Ice's scholarship; Henry Hobart, who taught voice; Aline Wilson, who was a piano instructor; and Marie Crosby, who specialized in organ, music harmony, and counterpoint.

Students spent a lot of time involved in campus activities. A men's and a women's glee club, opera club, and orchestra were favorites among fine arts students. The women's glee club usually toured churches in Oklahoma and Kansas during the summer. Sarah Kathryn Alloway Couch was an active member of the women's glee club. She remembered traveling by bus throughout the region, eating evening meals at a local church, and then spending the night and eating breakfast in a parishioner's home. Couch was the glee club's treasurer and whenever the bus would stop at noon, she would hand each girl a quarter for lunch.

The men's glee club tour of Oklahoma and surrounding states was used as a recruiting tool for Phillips. In 1935, the group stopped at Larned, Kansas, to present a program. Among its members were Charles Livingston, Henry Harmon, Bill Smith, W. L. Wicky Kingen, DeWitt Adams, and Paul Cook. Gene Moore attended and was impressed. Moore had been considering becoming a minister and attending Phillips and when he saw the "preacher boys" in the glee club, he thought to himself, "If they can be ministers, I can too." Later that year, Moore enrolled in the College of the Bible.

Moore was one of a family of five. His father was a day laborer, earning $15 a week. Until he was called to be a minister, Moore had no thought of going to college. Then, he remembered, "I felt I could not be a minister unless I went to college. And that meant Phillips." He knew his family could provide little financial support but he had heard stories from students he knew who had gone to Phillips and worked their way through school. After working for a year and saving $150, Moore was "determined to give it a try."

When he arrived on campus, he discovered that Bible College scholarships paid only $75.00 per year in tuition, half of the total tuition cost. To supplement his income he found a job at the J. C. Penney Store, working mostly on Saturdays. His salary was $2.50 per week. He paid $1.00 per week for a room and had $1.50 left over for food and spending money. "The pickings were thin," Moore recalled, "and there were more than a few Wednesdays that came when I didn't have two nickels to rub together. But I got by."

Paul Sharp, who later was president of the University of Oklahoma from 1971 to 1978, enrolled at Phillips in 1936 as a history major. His favorite professor was Dr. Frank Wellman, who personalized his classes and encouraged Sharp to continue his education, which he did, receiving his Ph.D. from the University of Minnesota after graduating from Phillips in 1938. As a junior, Sharp was editor of the *Phillipian*. Sharp met his future wife, Rose Anderson, while at Phillips and she echoed his praise of the faculty. It was not uncommon, according to Sharp, for the faculty to entertain students in their homes. Paul and Rose chose Dr. Wellman to perform their wedding ceremony.

One of the innovative concepts of the McCash era was the United States Department of State's approval of Phillips to educate foreign students. Many Japanese and Chinese students were recruited to attend Phillips and most returned to their homeland after graduation. To provide financial aid for the foreign students, the Enid YWCA and Phillips sponsored an annual Japanese Christian Bazaar.

INSPIRATION POINT

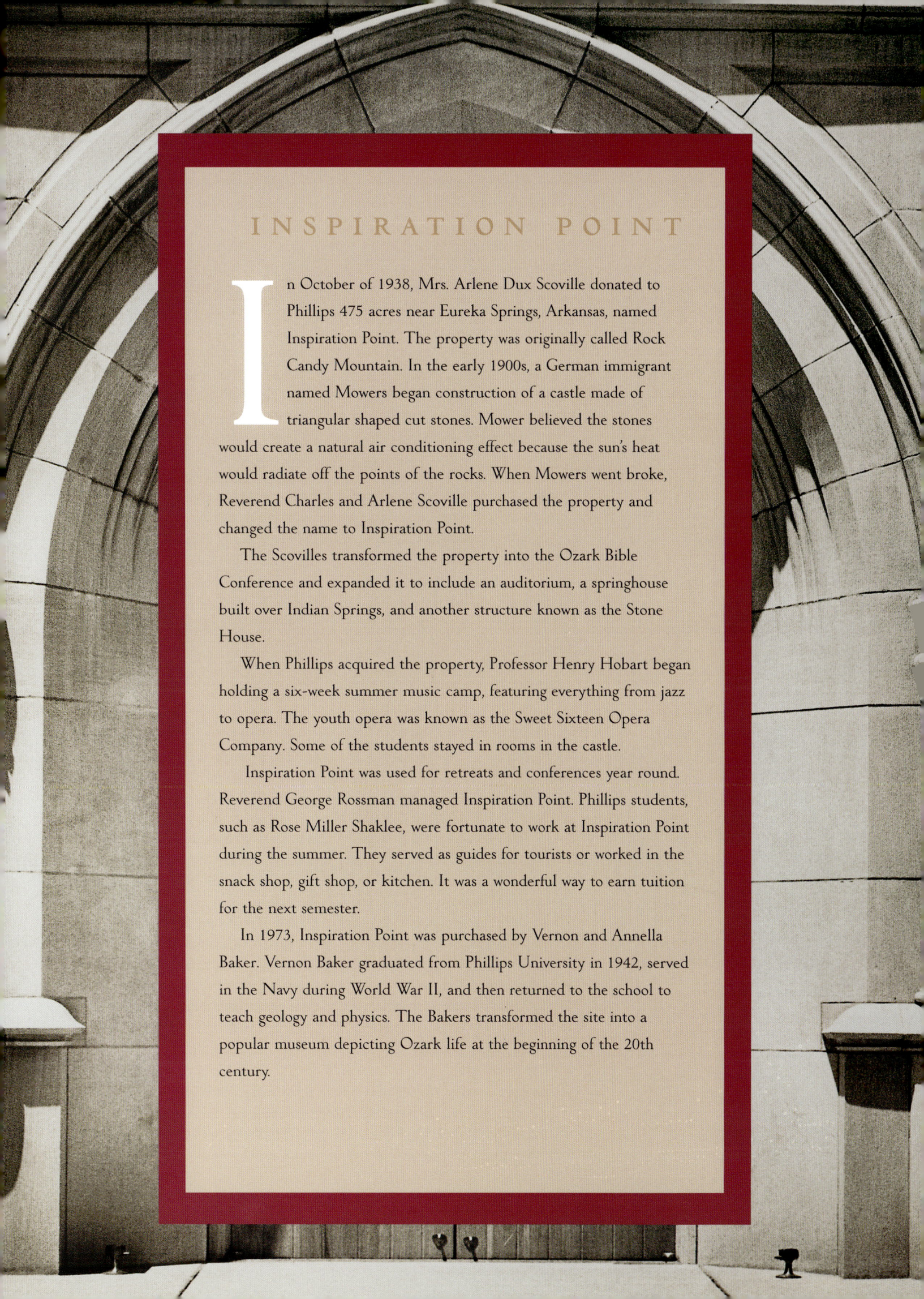

In October of 1938, Mrs. Arlene Dux Scoville donated to Phillips 475 acres near Eureka Springs, Arkansas, named Inspiration Point. The property was originally called Rock Candy Mountain. In the early 1900s, a German immigrant named Mowers began construction of a castle made of triangular shaped cut stones. Mower believed the stones would create a natural air conditioning effect because the sun's heat would radiate off the points of the rocks. When Mowers went broke, Reverend Charles and Arlene Scoville purchased the property and changed the name to Inspiration Point.

The Scovilles transformed the property into the Ozark Bible Conference and expanded it to include an auditorium, a springhouse built over Indian Springs, and another structure known as the Stone House.

When Phillips acquired the property, Professor Henry Hobart began holding a six-week summer music camp, featuring everything from jazz to opera. The youth opera was known as the Sweet Sixteen Opera Company. Some of the students stayed in rooms in the castle.

Inspiration Point was used for retreats and conferences year round. Reverend George Rossman managed Inspiration Point. Phillips students, such as Rose Miller Shaklee, were fortunate to work at Inspiration Point during the summer. They served as guides for tourists or worked in the snack shop, gift shop, or kitchen. It was a wonderful way to earn tuition for the next semester.

In 1973, Inspiration Point was purchased by Vernon and Annella Baker. Vernon Baker graduated from Phillips University in 1942, served in the Navy during World War II, and then returned to the school to teach geology and physics. The Bakers transformed the site into a popular museum depicting Ozark life at the beginning of the 20th century.

Unfortunately, the expanding conflict between Japan and China during the 1930s caused the suspension of recruitment of Asian students. After World War II, the enrollment of foreign students grew and a Students' Foreign Aid Fund was established to provide financial support.

A change in leadership at Phillips occurred in the late 1930s. On May 24, 1937, President McCash submitted his retirement request to the board of trustees. Errett Newby, A. M. Ehly, and Lawrence Lounsbury were appointed to a committee charged with searching for a new president. They recommended Dr. Eugene Stephen Briggs, who was unanimously approved by the board of trustees on December 16, 1937.

Before coming to Phillips, Briggs, who had received his Ph.D. from Columbia University in New York City, had been superintendent of schools in Okmulgee, Oklahoma; president of Southeastern Teachers College at Durant, Oklahoma, for five years;

Phillips' longest serving president was Dr. Eugene Stephen Briggs who headed the university from 1938 to 1961. His children, Bill and Sue, were graduates of Phillips. His wife was a popular first lady and served as a surrogate mother for international students.

and president of Christian College at Columbia, Missouri, for three years. Briggs assumed the Phillips post on February 1, 1938, and was inaugurated on October 12, 1939.

Robert E. Lee, a longtime supporter of Phillips and Enid newspaperman, called Dr. Briggs "truly a gentleman of the old school, a symbol to me of all Phillips University stood for."

Mary Gentry Briggs, Dr. Briggs' first wife, acted as the first lady for Phillips and was very active in helping new students. She was instrumental in forming the Cosmopolitan Club to aid foreign students in making the adjustment from their homeland to Oklahoma. Her front door was always open to students.

C. William "Bill" Nichols recalled arriving on the Phillips campus from Baxter Springs, Kansas. Charlie Briggs, a Phillips recruiter, had visited his hometown. When Nichols told him he could not afford to go to college, Briggs told him to come anyway and he would get him a job. Nichols took a bus to Enid and then got into a taxi. He asked the driver if he knew a "Mr. Briggs." The taxi driver took him to the president's home, instead of Charlie Briggs' residence.

Nichols walked up to the door and rang the bell. When Mary Briggs answered, he said, "Mrs. Briggs, I'm here." The president's wife invited the new student inside, fed him breakfast, and then directed him to the president's office. When Nichols walked inside the office, he knew he had made a mistake—the wrong Mr. Briggs. Nonetheless, the promise was kept. Nichols landed a job, graduated from Phillips, and was elected general minister and president of the Christian Church (Disciples of Christ) in 1991 for a two-year term.

President Briggs faced the difficult task of leading the university out of the economic doldrums of the Great Depression. Many of the buildings had deteriorated because of the lack of maintenance and no new major buildings had been completed in nearly two decades. It looked "like a poor man's college," Dean Marshall recalled.

Scholarship continued to improve at Phillips University. By 1938, the library collection had grown to 28,000 volumes, thanks to the Dillinger, Alice, and John See Library Endowment Fund that had been established a dozen years before. Students Joseph Ogle and Tom McLaughlin were named Rhodes Scholars.

Briggs' 23-year tenure as president was described as "the period of greatest advance" for the university. He was an experienced academic administrator and the paradigm of a visionary leader. He strongly believed that Christian education is the hope of the world. He pressed that message throughout the Phillips University territory and student ministers and other students returning to their home churches on holidays and vacations spread the conviction. Many churches and individuals joined with the school to accomplish Briggs' vision.

During his administration, nine new buildings were built on campus, the value of the school's facilities increased twenty fold, seminary salaries increased 239 percent, scholarships grew by 227 percent, and relationships were established with 370 Phillips Lifeline Churches.

In May of 1938, the university's board of trustees voted to implement a night school program that opened an entirely new student market for Phillips among working adults who were unable to attend day classes. At the same time, Phillips' service territory was expanded to include Colorado and Wyoming.

For years the golf course by University Lake was the scene of an annual tug-of-war between freshmen and sophomore classes. A heavy rope was stretched across waist-deep water and the two classes took opposite ends of the rope and pulled with all their might. A huge crowd always gathered to see which class would be dragged into the water.

The annual tug-of-war between Phillips' freshmen and sophomore classes reached a new high in October of 1938, when members of the freshman class climbed the campus flagpole and hoisted their flag. Outraged, a group of sophomores climbed a nearby tree, attached a burning torch to a fishing pole, and burned the freshman flag. The next day freshmen hoisted a piece of tin, which would not burn, with their flag painted on it. They also greased the flagpole to make it difficult to climb.

The sophomores retaliated by climbing the pole and taking the flag down. They also kidnapped the president of the freshman class and any other freshmen they could find. Some were taken to University Lake and thrown into the water. Others were hauled outside of town in automobiles and left to make their way home as best they could.

Biding their time, the freshmen gathered a supply of "big, ripe, red, juicy" tomatoes and began to pelt sophomores as they crossed campus. While the upper classmen were held at bay, other freshmen climbed to the top of the flagpole to reattach their flag. The freshmen won the "battle of the flagpole" in 1938, but university officials made them clean off the grease and replace the rope. Turning the punishment into an advantage, the freshmen class sold lengths of the rope as souvenirs for 10 cents per foot.

In 1939, an Acappella Choir was organized by the Music Department to present concerts, chamber recitals, and other promotional activities for the university. The choir later became the Phillipian Choristers which performed a myriad of hymns, spirituals, anthems, light operas, cantatas, and oratorios. In 1941, the Phillips University School of Music was selected by the American Musical Art

The Tenth Muse was the youngest club on the Phillips campus in 1938. The club's stated purpose was to promote democracy, give organized service, and sponsor a wholesome social atmosphere. Left to right, front row, Ruth Hoffines, Alma Bird, Mildred Rather, Kathleen Shannon, Helen Parker, Laura Frances Bixler. Second row, Wilma More, Lorraine More, Mrs. Robert Martin, sponsor, Mary Gwinn, Wilma Peter, Louise Grimes. Third row, Barbara Baldwin, Joan Adams, Dorothy Campbell, Doris Dellenback, Sally Elliott, Wilma Jean Darst, Evelyn Ashcraft. Fourth row, Lorraine Plank, Loretta West, Helen Burkhart, Betty Wallingsford.

Hard Times: The Great Depression

To foster a spirit of unity among the women of Phillips, the Women's Self-Governing Association (WSGA) was formed with representatives from major student organizations and clubs. In 1938, WSGA members were, left to right, Viola Clark, Verna Conley, Jean Claire Gettel, Vernal Harrison, Dr. Ethel Manahan—sponsor, Wanda Kreie, Bobbie Mae Holt, Prudence Osborn, Ruth Latchaw.

Members of the Ministerial Association form a cross in front of the Sunken Garden. All students of the Bible College were members of the Ministerial Association.

Facing: Brush and Pencil Club members in 1939 helped create posters for the publicity department, campus clubs, and for professors' use in the classroom.

58 In Reverence We Stand

Foundation of New York as one of 23 college music departments in the United States that were "especially outstanding."

The Gridiron Minstrels Club was formed to provide campus-wide entertainment in the 1930s. Its main competition came from the Harvesters Club, which drew its membership mainly from the College of Arts and Sciences. The Harvesters called any Gridiron member "Gus." Organized in the spring of 1937, the Harvesters Club did much of the planning and work on the university's Sunken Garden. Members of the Harvesters Club could be readily identified by their bright red jackets. In September of 1939, a new men's club, Varsity, was founded. It was primarily a social organization sponsoring parties, picnics, and formal dances.

In spite of the effects of the depression, Phillips University continued to have a vital economic impact on Enid and Garfield County. By the close of the "Dirty Thirties," as the era was called, the school and its students annually spent an estimated $795,000 in Enid. The payroll accounted for $108,000 and another $72,000 came from school maintenance. University students spent an average of $520,000 annually. These totals, when combined with money generated by speech, band, debate, art, and other tournaments, amounted to 19 percent of the retail business in Enid.

Top: Members of the Cardinal Key Club in 1944 were, front row, left to right, Ruth Silvee, Helen Stephenson, Betty Goodness, Lois Simpson, Betty Frances Lovejoy, Lorraine Hood. Second row, Dorothy Bank, Muriel Watkins, Mildred King, Kathrine Hopper.

Above: *The Haymaker* was a well-written and professionally-produced student newspaper. The 1942 editorial staff, left to right, seated, Betty Hilsabeck, Ken Teegarden. Standing, Loren Horton, Dorothy Ann Thurman, Jean Quillin, Sam Smith, Casey Cohlmia, Kathryn Hopper. Teegarden later was elected general minister and president of the Christian Church (Disciples of Christ).

World War II

AS THE WORST of the Great Depression passed, the Enid Chamber of Commerce undertook the financing of a new gymnasium and swimming pool on the Phillips campus. Everett Purcell, editor of *Enid Events,* was the chairman of the fund raising effort. Ground was broken for the new building on October 11, 1940. A wartime emergency unfortunately interfered with the completion of the new gymnasium as building materials were rationed. However, Phillips' administrators improvised whenever possible. When iron pipes could not be found for the building's natural gas lines, pipes beneath the old gymnasium were dug up and reused. Old lockers were refurbished and repainted for the new gymnasium which was opened for its first official basketball game against Oklahoma A&M on December 1, 1944. The gymnasium was named the Enid Building.

The Enid Building was a gift of the citizens of Enid in 1944. A heated swimming pool was added in 1951. Years later, the building was incorporated into the Mabee Center.

Funding for a Student Union, located on Maine Street, was requested from members of the First Christian Church in Oklahoma City. Forty thousand dollars was forthcoming from the Oklahoma City congregation and the new facility was dedicated on May 28, 1940. It contained a cafeteria that could serve between 250 and 300 meals per hour. The Mothers Association of Phillips furnished the union's lounge, which boasted a parquet floor, semi-round ceiling dome, fireplace, and mantel.

A popular girls club, the Comets, was formed in 1940. "Personal development" was the motto of the club in early years. Club members sponsored a number of annual events such as style shows, Christmas parties for underprivileged children, painting campus buildings, and babysitting for sponsors and Zelotai members. Each spring, the Comets hosted an alumni tea and spring formal.

Work on a new girl's dormitory began before America's entry into World War II. After wartime delays, the four-story dorm was built overlooking University Lake and originally contained facilities for 120 female students. It was later enlarged.

The girls' dorm was named in honor of Robert Henry Clay of Medicine Lodge, Kansas. Clay was a third cousin of the statesman Henry Clay. Robert Clay's wife, Sadie, donated $25,000 toward the construction costs of the building. Additional funds were raised by the American University Women's "Buy a Brick" campaign, which sold bricks for five cents each. The cornerstone for Clay Hall was laid on October 9, 1941, but the effects of World War II halted construction. As part of the war effort federal officials froze all non-essential construction, and Clay Hall was not deemed essential.

The 1940 Bisophians. Left to right, front row, Mrs. Shirley, Minnie Henson, Eldon Farley, Glenn Seibel, Hettie Ruth Carnell, Dean Shirley. Standing, Donna Hammer, T.J. Howard, Vernon Scott, Verle Rennick, Anna Regier, Jack Enos, Norman Dunnington, Mary Scrivner, Monnette Yewell, Patty Vance, Frances Hayes, Elaine Shelton, Ray Carlson, Virginia Sheeks, Armon Meis.

Central Christian Church, at Broadway and Adams in Enid, was church home to hundreds of Phillips students. Many university professors attended the church and occasionally taught Sunday school classes.

Facing: The Student Union formally opened on December 2, 1940. Later, the Student Union became the Music Building.

World War II

Clay Hall across University Lake. Courtesy Jack N. Taylor.

64 In Reverence We Stand

Below: In 1941, the Red Peppers were easy to spot on the Phillips campus in their bright red jackets. The Peppers was a versatile group—its members came from all disciplines of study.

Below: Breakfast and lunch were served cafeteria style in Clay Hall. The dinner meal was served family style, with the person sitting at the head of the table responsible for passing the various dishes.

Below: Zonta was a popular club on campus in 1941. Legend had it that the word "zonta" meant trustworthy. The club's main event each year was a sweetheart formal in February.

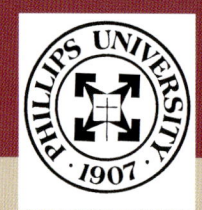

THE PHILLIPS SEAL

In the 1940s, considerable thought was given to designing a new seal or symbol for the university. Ever since its founding, Phillips' seal had been a burning lamp—the general symbol of education. However, many faculty and students wanted a new symbol, one more representative of the role of Christian education. A committee of Errett Newby, Harvey Everest, and First Lady Mary Briggs was appointed to design a new seal for the university, one that would be more distinctive. A seal with four columns—representing the physical, spiritual, social, and intellectual aspect of education—was adopted. Between the columns was a large open book stamped with the word "Truth." Above the columns were the words "Phillips University." Below them was the motto "Christian Education, the Hope of the World." Mrs. Briggs, the first lady of the university, wrote the official description of the new Phillips' symbol:

In this symbol, Phillips University speaks of the ideals that lie at the heart of her being. She would be a true UNI-versity thru which Youth shall pass and go equipped to cooperate with those who would create a new world in answer to the prayer, 'Thy will be done on earth.'

The outer frame of the symbol with its four sides and its four columns, in maroon and white, represents the school with its four-fold emphases on the Intellectual, the Physical, the Social, and the Spiritual.

The radiant globe is the New Earth to be brought into being. The dynamics to be used are Truth and Love.

The open book symbolizes the accumulated knowledge of mankind. It is Truth only we would glean from its pages, true formulae to bring desired results in Science; exact rules for the solution of the problems of Mathematics; correct use of language to convey true Meanings; true principles applied to the Art of Living to insure peaceful and happy relations with God and our Fellowmen.

Our second dynamic is Love. We would extend the supreme Love, consummated on the Cross, thru the heart of the world.

At the center of it all, at the point on which the pivot rested which guided the compass in a true circumference of our planet is the letter U. Y-O-U are Phillips University, wherever YOU are, whatever YOU do, however YOU serve. On YOU, as students and alumni, faculty, and administration, rests the responsibility for the fulfillment of the ideals represented here.

Top: Four seals of the University. From left to right, the first, second (designed in the 1940s), third (adopted in the late 1950s), and fourth and final seal.

University officials had intended for Clay Hall to replace the aging Athenian Hall. When they were left to make do with Athenian Hall, several renovations were hurriedly completed to make it habitable. Clay Hall finally was opened in 1946.

As war spread across Europe and Asia, America began to build up its fighting forces. As a part of the rearmament program, federal officials began an expanded pilot training program officially designated as the Civilian Pilot Training Program (CPTP). Its purpose was to create a pool of training pilots that could be summoned for service in the Army Air Corps.

Phillips was one of 166 educational institutions approved by the federal government to train civilian pilots under the Civil Aeronautics Authority. The program began in 1940, with student pilots receiving 72 hours of ground training and 35 to 50 hours of flight training at nearby Woodring Air Field.

Among the Phillips students selected for the CPTP program was Tommy Campbell. After he completed the program, he became a civilian flight instructor for the Royal Air Force (RAF) and trained British pilots at Ponca City, Oklahoma. Other graduates from the Phillips training program signed up with the British Royal Air Force and fought in the Battle of Britain in 1940.

Everett Mayberry and Phil Long were in the CPTP program. Mayberry flew both bombing and supply missions from China and India, including 97 round trips over the Hump. Long flew similar missions in the battles for the islands of the West Pacific.

When John E. Bloss arrived on campus in June of 1943 at the height of wartime restrictions, he had been given the name of Dean Stephen J. England from whom to seek guidance. England helped Bloss find a place to live even though housing was in short supply because of World War II. Bloss credited England's encouragement and patience with keeping him in seminary, when the pressures of wartime and society would have shoved him aside into something else.

Dean England always took a personal interest in what he considered "his" students and helped them whenever he could. Eldon E. Jandebeur had to drop out of Phillips for a semester because of his father's illness. Before he left, he visited with England and explained his plight. Returning to school the next fall, Jandebeur found that England had applied his previous tuition payment to his new registration fees. It was, as Jandebeur recalled, a "pleasant surprise."

On September 1, 1940, the Oklahoma National Guard, including the 189th Regimental Band, was called to federal service. Many other Phillips students also were members of the National Guard. On September 16, 1940, Congress approved the first peacetime draft in American history, and on October 29, the first men were called to service.

Many Phillips students opposed America's entry into a war. In a poll taken in 1940, 98 percent of the students polled were "not in favor" of American involvement. However, after the Japanese attack on Pearl Harbor on December 7, 1941, that attitude changed.

As Bill Briggs recalled, there was an emergency chapel service held on the day after the attack on Pearl Harbor. Both G. Edwin Osborn, a professor of religion, and President Briggs spoke about the role of America in the war. According to John Ireland, whose education at Phillips was interrupted by World War II service with the United States Marines, almost every male student at the university wanted to enlist in the armed forces immediately. Dr. J. Clifford Shirley convinced most of

Since medieval times, presidents of universities have carried two ensigns of authority to official functions—the seal of the university and a mace. Phillips did not have a mace until Professor Paul Denny designed and built one of ceramic during the administration of President Hallie Gantz. This photograph shows a later mace made by Professor Jim Stroup. The cross, the world, and a flame were symbols contained in the mace. Inscribed on bands around the head of the mace is the motto, Vincit Omnia Veritas (Truth Prevails Over All Things), the year of the university's founding, and the name of the university. The flame was carved from soapstone by President Robert Peck who designed the mace.

World War II 67

Even during World War II, the Tri-State Band Festival drew huge crowds of high school band students to Enid. In 1942, Bill Briggs prepared this montage of photographs showing some of the 4,000 students who helped celebrate the 10th anniversary of the festival. The highlight of the festival was the world premiere of the "Phillipian Festival March," composed by Karl King. King conducted the combined bands in the piece which was dedicated to Professor Milburn Carey.

them to join the reserves instead and wait to be called. After the war, Ireland returned to Phillips to graduate in 1947. He returned again to become director of teacher education from 1969 to 1991.

Many Phillips students suddenly found their education on hold as they were called into the military. Eric W. Berg had traveled from Forest Lake, Minnesota, to enroll in Phillips in 1939, and had found a job at the Chenoweth and Green Music Company in Enid. Following Pearl Harbor, Berg, like many others, withdrew from school and entered the military. Fortunately, he survived the war and returned in 1946 to complete his education and graduate in 1947. Bill Briggs received his diploma in absentia in May of 1945 while on active duty with the Navy at Okinawa.

Not all veterans were men. Elizabeth D. Votaw graduated from Phillips in May of 1943 with a degree in religious education and joined the WAVES.

Travel during the war years was discouraged. Because it was difficult for out-of-town students to make travel plans for the holiday, Phillips held classes the day after Thanksgiving. However, as Nancy L. Webster recalled, on Thanksgiving Day every out-of-town student was invited to the home of a faculty member or local resident for dinner.

Private automobiles were rare on campus. As Becky Proudfoot remembered, "The very few students who had cars didn't have enough rationing coupons to go much of anywhere, and no one had the cash to buy the gas anyway." When it was necessary to go to town, Nancy Webster and the other students caught the local bus at the bookstore-post office. There was a table in the corner where students could safely leave their books to be picked up when they returned.

Movies were still the major source of entertainment for students. Many hours each week were spent listening to the radio for news of the war. However, according to Proudfoot, who was a freshman in the fall of 1942, there were fewer men than usual on campus as many students joined the military. The shortage of college men was offset by the number of trainees pouring into Enid's Army Air Corps base. "We did not live monastic lives," she recalled.

Phillips became a training station for Navy and Army Air Corps aviation cadets as well as Air Corps, Marine, and Navy reserves. Seventy-five graduates of Phillips' College of the Bible served as chaplains in the military in spite of the fact that they could have been granted deferrals from the draft. Phillips also became a training center for the Women's Auxiliary Corps. Because of these and other programs, Phillips' enrollment actually increased five percent in 1942.

One unusual source of new students was the Japanese-Americans relocated from the West Coast to the interior of the country in early 1942. Some of these Americans of Japanese ancestry were interned in Arkansas. As wartime restrictions were eased some of the young Japanese-Americans were released from the internment camps to attend college if they could find an American family to sponsor them. At the time Becky Proudfoot was attending Phillips and living off campus. Because she had a spare bed in her room, she was asked to share her room with one of the Japanese-American internees. The fall semester had not yet started and the young Japanese-American girl, named Susan, needed a place to stay until the dormitory opened.

Proudfoot became well acquainted with the student who was still at Phillips when World War II drew to a close. Proudfoot vividly remembered the news of the dropping of the atomic bomb on Nagasaki, Japan, on August 9, 1945, because Susan told her that her grandparents lived in Nagasaki.

The Mavon Club, organized on January 14, 1945, was an all-girls club distinguished by their Kelly green jackets. Its purpose was to promote loyalty to the university, the nation, and its members. The name came from the initial letters of Shakespeare's "Two Gentlemen from Verona."

A Phillips University Civilian Defense Committee, headed by College of the Bible Dean England, was formed. Most clubs and organizations on campus invested in Defense Bonds. Under the "Let Every Student Buy a Bond" plan, substantial funds were raised for the war effort. The Phillips Service League was organized by female employees and faculty wives. Among its goals was to provide recreational programs for military personnel stationed in Enid.

As a tribute to the men and women who served in the military, the University Service League of Women raised funds to build a new bridge across the stream at the upper end of University Lake near Clay Hall. Two bronze tablets on the bridge contained the names of almost 600 Phillips University veterans. The bridge became a major thoroughfare for students going to and from class.

As World War II drew to a close, President Briggs launched a Seven-Year Plan to provide for the anticipated post-war growth in education. Briggs realized that after the fighting ceased, there would be throngs of young Americans returning home to resume their education. It was expected that Phillips' enrollment would grow by nearly 700. The goal of Briggs' plan was to raise $2,000,000 to fund an expansion program to provide for the anticipated increase in enrollment.

In 1951, a new wing (sanctuary) was completed at University Place Christian Church, 2107 East Broadway. It served the spiritual needs of many Phillips students.

Post-war Growth

BY THE END of World War II, Phillips had achieved a reputation of providing a solid Christian education and of showing extraordinary interest in the individual student. The success of its graduates proved its academic excellence. In 1947, the university's alumni included six college presidents, eight college deans, 31 college professors, 40 missionaries, 100 chaplains, 1,200 ministers, 100 graduates of the school's Graduate College, and countless writers, military officers, doctors, scientists, business administrators, engineers, and educators. As returning veterans flocked to Phillips and America began to demobilize, a housing shortage quickly developed. John Ireland returned, and when he walked past Athenian Hall and headed for Old Main, thought, "I'm home." Many married students found housing with local residents. Dr. England had a small three-room house behind his home that he often rented to ministerial students. Glenn Cowperthwaite, along with his wife and four-year-old son, felt fortunate to live there while he attended the College of the Bible after World War II.

Other students, such as Nancy Webster, found rooms at the Broadway Dorm, located at 1706 East Broadway. The dorm originally had been built as a private residence and every bedroom had a fireplace. In the back yard was a fish pond, barbecue oven, and rose garden. Elizabeth D. Votaw roomed at the Perisho House, a block west of the campus.

Nearly 100 students enrolled under the provisions of the GI Bill for the fall semester of 1946, and by 1948, the number had increased to 300. Many students were married and some had children, making sufficient housing difficult to find. Dr. Henry Hobart was the director of veteran's affairs on campus and worked as the liaison between the university and the Veterans Administration.

A Veteran's Village mushroomed on the east side of the campus where university officials placed 25 trailer homes acquired from the army. The trailers were painted maroon. Lois Moore Wimpey remembered that residents of the trailers had a central bathhouse. She never forgot seeing students in robes carrying their towels and soap, walking from their trailers to the bathhouse.

Eugene and Bonnie Frazier lived in one of the trailers when they returned to Phillips following their honeymoon in 1949. The trailer was 20 feet long, with a table and two chairs in one end and a bed in the other. Between the two rooms was a kitchen area containing an electric hotplate, a small icebox, and a sink, which only produced cold water. That winter was very cold and the Fraziers were afraid to leave the natural gas heater on when they were away from home, especially on Sundays when Eugene preached at a small church in Kansas. When they returned to Phillips, they would stop in North Enid, use the bathroom, hurry home, thaw out the trailer padlock, light the heater, and go to bed with their coats on.

Two other married student additions were added. Varsity Courts was located north of the University Post Office. Campus Courts was built just to the east of the Enid Building. The homes were prefabricated, built by General Housing in Dallas, Texas, and were called the Texas Houses. They had kitchens, a bathroom, and other basic amenities, and according to Lois Moore Wimpy, were the most luxurious married student housing units available.

Campus Courts was Nancy McKeeman Moats' first home on the Phillips campus. Her mother tells of the walls of the housing units being so thin that babies like Nancy who chose to "vocalize" at night were not very popular with their neighbors who were studying. Nancy returned to the campus in the 1960s as a student.

There also were some small square cottages, covered with brick patterned tarpaper, located on Randolph Street near Adams School and A. H. Ray's Grocery. Many students living in the cottages did not have refrigerators and were allowed to keep a few things in Ray's cooler. Every Sunday, Ray would open early so the people could get their milk and meat out of the cooler in time for Sunday dinner. Then, he would close the store and go to church.

East Hall, a temporary frame structure, was built to house single men returning to school after World War II. Hot water for its occupants was often non-existent, causing students to shave with cold water. As Eldon Jandebeur recalled, the water pipes in East Hall

Phillips officials purchased several houses near the campus and converted them into student residence halls. Verna Dean Smith Roberts lived in such a house outfitted with bunk beds for 10 students.

University administrative offices were housed in a building known as "The White House," until the Everest Building was constructed in 1963.

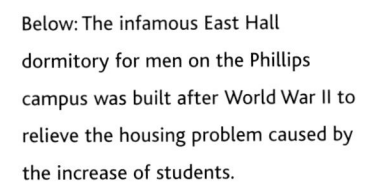

Below: The infamous East Hall dormitory for men on the Phillips campus was built after World War II to relieve the housing problem caused by the increase of students.

Top: Dr. Henry Hobart was director of Veterans Affairs. His job was to make smooth the transition of returning veterans to the Phillips campus. Hobart and his wife later founded the Inspiration Point Fine Arts Colony in Arkansas. Above: Dr. Roger Carstensen was a champion ping-pong player and piano virtuoso when not teaching Old Testament classes. He began teaching in 1949 and specialized in Bible story dramatizations. M. Rick Hendricks said, "He had a commanding presence and a voice that could shake the pillars of the Marshall Building." After his service at Phillips, Carstensen was founder and president of the Institute for Biblical Literacy.

ran along the ceilings of the rooms. Once he jumped up and grabbed a pipe that pulled loose and flooded his room with water. It was said that, "You will never be a true Phillipian until you prove that 'you can take it,' at East Hall."

In the spring of 1947, the Camelot Club for men was organized. Patterned after the legendary King Arthur, the Camelot Club members were pledged to "live spiritually, serve quietly, and to follow humbly with God and man." As Robert A. Bish recalled, pledges in the Camelot Club worked hard performing such chores as polishing shoes for members until they obtained "knighthood." After being initiated, the former pledges stood arms entwined outside the Marshall Building singing "On the Campus of Phillips U.," "Camelot Like the Knights of Old" and "My Camelot" to the tune of "Danny Boy." Knights of the Camelot Club participated in annual jousts that were held on a pole spanning the creek between Clay Hall and the golf course. The object was to force an opponent off the pole and into the water.

It was not until 1947 that a Greek letter fraternity, the Gamma Upsilon chapter of Phi Mu Alpha Sinfonia, was formed. A scholarly rather than social national honorary music fraternity, its goal was to advance the cause of music, to foster the mutual welfare and brotherhood of students of music, to develop the truest fraternal spirit among its members, and to encourage loyalty to the alma mater." It was followed in 1948 by the Eta chapter of Tau Beta Sigma, an honorary music sorority for girls. Another all-women professional music sorority was Mu Phi Epsilon. Alpha Beta Kappa was formed in 1954 for business administration majors and minors.

In 1950, the Oklahoma Kappa Chapter of Pi Kappa Delta, an honorary speech society, was organized at Phillips and opened to students studying speech, debate, or oratory. That same year the Knowles Physics Club was formed for students of physics. The members of Knowles purchased a 12.5-inch reflecting telescope and constructed an observatory on the campus.

One post-war student was James Pippin, who had served in the army and used the GI Bill to enroll at Phillips for the fall semester of 1946. Pippin made the trip from his home in Georgia by train. When he arrived at the depot at Enid he was fortunate to meet A. C. Cuppy, who offered him a ride to the campus. Because he was not married, Pippin could not live in the Veteran's Village. Instead he shared a room with Roscoe Babcock.

Pippin and Babcock's room was in the attic of the Babcock house. There were two beds in the room separated by about six feet. The only place you could stand up in the room was in the center of the attic, and when Pippin lay down, the ceiling of the attic was about two feet from his face. The house had one bathroom, and Pippin, Babcock, Babcock's sister and mother each were given specific times they could use it. Pippin usually ate at the school's snack shop. Pippin, like other veterans at Phillips, continued his military career by joining a local National Guard unit.

In the spring of 1947 Pippin enrolled in a psychology class. On the first day of class, Pippin struck up a conversation with the student sitting next to him. When Pippin asked his neighbor's name, the man replied "Oral." Pippin replied, "Oral? Is that your first name or your last name?" His new friend answered, "My last name is Roberts. My mama named me Oral because it was prophesied that I was to be an oracle for God and called to preach the gospel of Jesus Christ." At the time Roberts was the pastor of the Enid Pentecostal Holiness Church. Over the next 40 years, Oral Roberts

74 IN REVERENCE WE STAND

THE FRIENDSHIP FIRE

A campus tradition until the close of Phillips University, the Friendship Fire was a time when the entire campus came together to celebrate the start of a new school year. Each year, students threw items symbolizing the past and future intentions into the fire.

Old friends gathered to celebrate the strength of their friendship and new friendships were formed as incoming and returning students joined together to sing the alma mater.

The Friendship Fire truly represented the power of the friendships formed at Phillips. The editors of the 1992 *Phillipian* wrote, "The fire of friendship gives warmth when times are cold, and light when confusion darkens the horizon. The fire also represents the relationship that the students have to the university. The education which we gain here is not always contained in the books, but, like the fire, it is something that is part of us. It will light the path of our future."

Linda Danforth, editor of *The Phillipian*, tosses a copy of the previous year's yearbook into the 1958 Friendship Fire.

A mural, "The Hope of the World," by Noel Wyatt, hung in Old Main before it burned.

became the first preacher to successfully use television in his ministry. He founded Oral Roberts University in Tulsa, Oklahoma.

The university's progressive building program received a setback when Old Main burned on May 24, 1947. The fire, which investigators determined was the result of arson, was discovered about 2:00 a.m., and before it was extinguished, had destroyed nearly all of the classrooms; the administration and business offices; the science laboratories; and rooms housing the home economics, speech, radio, and business departments. The university's auditorium also was destroyed along with the pipe organ, the grand piano, and the stage scenery. The school museum lost its collections. Fortunately, student transcripts were stored in a fireproof vault and survived. Although the fire was doused, portions of the building continued to collapse throughout the next day. The only item that remained unscorched in the building's cornerstone was a Bible.

Many Phillips students were awakened by the fire. Dale E. Williams and other band members rushed to the second story of the Fine Arts Building, adjacent to Old Main, and removed the band's music instruments. Fortunately, the fire did not spread to the Fine Arts Building.

When Old Main burned, almost four decades of Phillips alumni records were destroyed. Following the fire, the Alumni Association hired a part-time paid secretary to help reconstruct the files, a humble beginning to the university's modern Alumni Association.

Don Mitchell had the job of replacing science equipment in the labs that had burned in Old Main. He searched surplus stores that had sprung up after the war so he could teach physics classes that fall. Mitchell was chairman of the construction committee that had the responsibility of building a new science facility. Mitchell stayed at Phillips long enough to graduate his first class of physics majors four years later.

Many of the returning veterans were smokers. According to Carl Books, many smokers gathered at what became known as "smokers corner," at the intersection of Broadway Avenue and the street in front of Old Main, just outside the Phillips campus. There was not enough room in the old Ladies Gym for the entire student body to attend required chapel, so it was held on two days, Tuesday and Thursday. There was always a large crowd of smokers on "smokers corner" on the day they were not in chapel.

The favorite meeting place for students around campus was the Varsity Shop on the northwest corner of Phillips. In addition to a post office substation, it had a soda fountain and four round marble-top tables. The Varsity Shop had the textbook concession from the university and also sold candy and sundry items. It was the only place on campus that sold refreshments. However, in keeping with university policy, smoking was forbidden. Likewise, it did not have a jukebox for music.

76 In Reverence We Stand

Flames leap from the burning hulk of Old Main early on the morning of May 24, 1947.

The cornerstone of the Marshall Building was laid October 10, 1947, during the fortieth anniversary of the founding of Phillips University. Students such as O. Edmund "Ed" Pendleton helped pay tuition costs by helping dig the basement for the new building. He later served 14 churches during 60 years of ministry.

Later, the Varsity Shop moved and the building became known as the Campus Store or "C-store," and even later was called the Coach House.

Across the street from the first Varsity Shop was the Snack Shack, with low-cost food and drinks. Because it was off campus, students could smoke and listen to music there. Froggie's, on Randolph Street near the old post office, was another favorite place for students to eat. Many couples had dinner at the White Castle, home of great hamburgers. Others went to the Silver Moon Cafe, which was open after the midnight preview and specialized in pancakes. Taking a date to the Boston Fruit Store for a coke and peanuts was popular. Dan and Bake's offered hamburgers for a nickel and chili for a dime. Bozo Lyles Barbecue Pit was another popular eatery. Weibels offered all the buttermilk that one could drink for five cents.

On October 11, 1946, ground was broken for a new Bible College facility, the Marshall Building. Completed during the 1950-1951 school year, the building's auditorium, Selman Hall, could seat 200 people. There were five large classrooms on the first floor, twelve on the second, and two on the third floor. A 126-feet tall tower topped the building. According to Gene Frazier, a student at the time and later a member of the university's board of trustees, students were recruited to help move library books and furniture from the old Bible College to the new facility. On the morning of the move, students picked up their desks and chairs and marched into their classrooms in the new building.

By 1947, the World Student Service Fund of the Intercollegiate Christian Council was helping place international students at Phillips. Five foreign students, Peter Solomon from India, and Betty, Esther, Sarah, and Ruth Managbanag from the Philippines, were enrolled at the university. The four Filipino sisters were recruited by Chaplain Edwin Kirtley who was stationed in the Philippines during World War II. The sisters were sponsored by the university's Cardinal Key Club. Peter proved so popular that the Mittrata Club was formed. The word "mittrata" means "friendship" in Hindi.

While plans were made to replace Old Main, the new Science Building was started just east of the Marshall Building. The cornerstone was laid on October 11, 1948, and it was dedicated on October 9, 1949. The $450,000 three-story building was built of concrete, stone, buff brick, and glass. Its 40 rooms contained the most up-to-date scientific equipment available.

By October 29, 1948, there were so many foreign students enrolled at Phillips that a Cosmopolitan Club was formed. Among its members were students from Korea, Cuba, Japan, China, India, the Philippines, Finland, Holland, and Hungary.

In 1948, Briggs was elected president of Lions International. Briggs had long been active in the Lions organization and a member of the Enid Lions Club. When Briggs was inaugurated president of Lions International, the Phillips University Band made the trip to New York City for the event. According to the Reverend Lloyd Lambert, who was a drummer in the band at the time, a special train was chartered to take the band to President Briggs' inauguration. Stops were made at Washington, D. C., and Niagara Falls, New York, along the way. To help cut costs, band members were housed in the Park Avenue Christian Church in New York City. The female members bathed in the nearby YWCA, while the male members utilized the church's huge kitchen sinks and the baptistry.

Phillips was blessed with innovative professors. Professor Earl W. Oberg had a unique way of making an impression upon new students. Oberg's class began sharply at 7:30 a.m. After he walked in, he locked the door. "If you were not in the room when class started," John Ireland remembered, "you never got in."

Geology, mathematics, and physics classrooms and laboratories, and a museum, were housed on the first floor of the Science Building. Chemistry and biology classes were held on the second floor. At one time, the Phillips University Press was located in the basement which also housed both live and preserved animals used in science experiments.

Post-war Growth 79

THE TEACHING WINDOWS

In the east wing of the second floor of the Marshall Building was the Mary E. Bivins Chapel, whose most famous features were stained glass windows by Henry Lee Willet of the Willet Stained Glass Company of Philadelphia, Pennsylvania. Five double-lancet windows on the east wall focused on aspects of the Christian mission—preaching, teaching, healing, helping, and transforming. The upper division of the Preaching Window blended Jesus in the synagogue at Nazareth and Jesus preaching from the boat off the shores of Galilee into a single unit. The middle level depicted a pioneer preacher and a modern pastor. The lower panel depicted the spirit of true vocations—work and music education.

The upper lancets of the Teaching Window represented the Sermon on the Mount and the Samaritan woman at the well from the Bible. The middle panels represented the Young People's Conference and the themes of home, church, and college as they were concerned with aspects of the teaching work of the church. The lower portion symbolized human art stimulated and inspired by the artistry of God.

The Healing Window represented the role of the church in medicine. The upper panels illustrated instances in which Jesus healed the blind and the lepers. The middle section depicted occupational therapy, counseling, and medical services. The lower panels emphasized the contributions made to health by recreation as well as by medical research.

The Helping Window was a vigorous assault on isolationism and complacency. Its panels were filled with striking reminders of the varied aspects of the ministry of helpfulness. The upper right symbolized "The Least of My Brethren" and the upper left "Feeding the Multitudes." The center focused on the theme of the underprivileged and feeding the hungry of the world.

The Transforming Window represented the inner transformation, a result of faith in God's love. The upper panels, titled "Come Unto Me" and "In Me...Peace," symbolized individual and social redemption, both as a present reality and as enduring hope in Jesus Christ. The two center panels, "Transforming the Community" and "Permeating the Nations," depicted the outreaching church, which sought to bring the Word to persons everywhere. The bottom panels, "Liberty and Justice for All" and "Toward a Better Future," were a call to personal commitment. At the base of each window were small instructive segments. Intertwined with art forms were streamers bearing legends from the Bible, hymns, and other literature.

Ewel Vaughan, who attended the Graduate Seminary from 1954 to 1959, recalled that the stained glass windows overlooked the chapel and while attending the weekly inspirational services, many students found themselves being "preached to" by the windows and found inspiration for their sermons.

The Preaching Window in the Mary E. Bivins Chapel in the Marshall Building. The high point in the long career of Graduate Seminary faculty member, Dr. Wilfred E. Powell, was his participation in the planning, design, and development of the Bivins Chapel windows. Powell's last publication was *The Mystic Harmony* in which he told the full story of the windows.

Other windows in the chapel include the Chancel Window on the north wall, which was more formal than the others. It had its own pattern and message—Jesus the Lord. Surrounding the central figure of Christ were suggestions of the Divine Drama from the Garden of Eden to the Eternal City of God. The upper portion portrayed responsibilities and future hope.

At the opposite end of the chapel, on the south wall, was the Rose Window. Its 12 diagonal sections surrounding a circle depicted symbols of prayer and praise, from praying hands to musical instruments.

Representative Phillipians in 1947 were John Ireland, of Florence, Kansas, and May Sweet of Hartshorne, Oklahoma. Later Ireland returned to the campus as a faculty member.

Facing: In 1950, Professor Earl W. Oberg was hospitalized for weeks but the work of the School of Drama continued under the watchful eye of his wife. Mrs. Oberg supervised, and student Robert Fleming directed *Blythe Spirit*.

One of America's best known television meteorologists graduated from Phillips University in 1945 with a degree in physics and mathematics. Harold Taft obtained his degree from Phillips in two and a half years, carrying as many as 28 credit hours per semester. After college and a tour as a meteorologist in the Air Force, he landed a job at WBAP-TV in Fort Worth, Texas, where he forecast the north Texas weather for 40 years. Taft was one of the first meteorologists in the country to use radar on television. His weather forecasts were also heard from coast to coast on clear channel WBAP-Radio. Taft died in 1991.

The four aims of the Comets were physical, spiritual, social, and intellectual growth. Aletha Page was president of the 1950 Comets. Front row, left to right, Ruthella Farris, Patty Gibson. Second row, Mrs. Arrel Gibson, Aletha Page, Donna Jean Scheen, Marilyn Crum, Jo Ann Crose, Midge Kidd. Third row, Barbara McHugh, Elinor Anderson, Mary Anna Barr, Barbara Semones, Deanie McMahan, Anna Louise Watts, Betty Strecker. Fourth row, Lois Young, Lois Hobart, Dorothy Jackson, Joy Lou Keen, Jerry Davis, Bessie Alyce Bishop, Jeanette Parsons.

Oberg directed many of the plays presented by Phillips' students and he insisted that at dress rehearsal the evening before a performance everyone had to know all their lines, with no mistakes. Once when the dress rehearsal was horrible, with many missed lines, Oberg called another rehearsal the next morning at 9:00 a.m. and told the students, "All will know their lines or the play will be canceled." As Ireland remembered, everyone studied all night so that the rehearsal would go well. Oberg frequently told his female students like Annella L. Baker, "I'll get you a degree or a husband."

Bob Seals and his wife were struggling financially when they first arrived at Phillips in the 1950s. He had no job, no tuition, and only 50 cents. His wife was walking out the front door to buy milk for their two daughters when she met Professor Roger Carstensen, who was working as a salesman during the summer. When the Sealses told Carstensen they could not afford to purchase any of his goods because they were about to spend the last of their money, Carstensen pointed to a nearby house and said, "I live in that house and I want you to know that you have a standing invitation to come directly to my house whenever you run out of food and bring your wife and daughters with you." Because of the "family" atmosphere, no one at Phillips went hungry.

On December 7, 1952, the College of the Bible received accreditation from the American Association of Theological Schools, the single standardizing agency for seminaries in the nation. Afterward, all students attending the Graduate Seminary could transfer credits to any other seminary in the United States. Likewise, those preparing to be chaplains in the military qualified for acceptance by the armed services.

Not only did the College of the Bible prepare ministers, but also, according to Mary Vaughan, it offered a practicum for minister's wives through the Zelotai Club. Originally organized by Mrs. I. N. McCash, the wife of the school's president, and Mrs. Frank H. Marshall, the wife of the dean of the Bible College, "Zelotai" meant "Glad Helpers" and was open to all wives of regularly enrolled ministerial students. Through both formal and informal gatherings the wives of potential Christian Church preachers were

Barbara Danforth, 1953 Junior Queen, and her escort, Don Angle. After their marriage, Barbara became affectionately known as the "cute angle," and Don was the "right angle."

given advice on how to successfully support their husband's ministry.

Another social organization open to ministerial students and their families was the Johnson Club, associated with the Johnson Bible College, located in Knoxville, Tennessee, in the foothills of the Great Smoky Mountains. Many students from Johnson Bible College continued their studies at Phillips and the club was to promote fellowship among former Johnson Bible College students.

The Pulpiteers was formed for men who were regularly and actively participating in the College of the Bible's student preaching program. The Bible College Fellowship was formed to serve Phillips' students and a Gospel Team was organized to conduct church services and youth programs throughout Oklahoma and Kansas. The King's Messengers Club was composed of students interested in becoming world missionaries. Its members, such as Jeannette Tonaki Okamura, organized outreach children's programs such as Saturday religious classes for black students in outlying areas.

During the 1952-1953 school year, three of Phillips' oldest social organizations disbanded—the Boosters Club, the Harvesters Club, and the Red Peppers. Replacing them was the Crusaders Club, which unfortunately only lasted a few years longer.

When Ewel and Mary Vaughan arrived in 1954, for Ewel to enroll in the Graduate Seminary, they were met by Dean England who astounded them by greeting them by their first names. They had previously met England only briefly. As Ewel discovered, "This was typical of the seminary faculty and students. We were family!" Indeed, students at Phillips often felt a special bond. Bob Williams, Gilbert Brawner, George Horne, and Victor Wellman all began the first grade together and graduated from Phillips together.

A custom among students in the College of the Bible was "throwing in the lake." Ministerial students were notoriously needy and most instructors encouraged them to refrain from marriage until graduation. Nonetheless, many fell in love and were married while still in college. The rule was simple—"If a senior gets married, throw him in once; if a junior, twice; if a sophomore, three times; if a freshman, first tie an anvil around his neck."

Don and Barbara Angle both were

graduates of Phillips who were among the many missionaries sent out to the world from the university. After attending Phillips in the early 1950s, they served together as missionaries in the Belgian Congo. The Angles returned to Phillips and in 1966 graduated from the seminary and then returned to Africa as missionaries until 1973. As Barbara explained, their education at Phillips prepared them for a missionary career, gave them lifelong friends, and made Enid their hometown for the rest of their lives. Both returned to Enid after their mission work and Don later became a professor in the university's art department. Since the closing of Phillips, the Angles have been at the forefront to preserve records and memorabilia relating to the history of Phillips University.

Music also continued to be an important part of the curriculum at Phillips during its second half century. The university became well known for its music programs through a series of traveling musical groups. For several years in the 1940s and 1950s Phillips commissioned a male quartet known as the Phillips Ambassadors to tour the region and promote music education at Phillips. The quartet would spend the summer touring neighboring states performing evening concerts at

The Phillips Science Camp was established for students to spend summers studying science in a remote corner of Colorado. There is a time capsule in one of the posts at the entrance to the camp.
Above left: A cross made of sticks tops a hill at the Phillips Science Camp.

Disciples churches. To help recoup expenses, special "love offerings" were taken after the performances. Special noon concerts were scheduled for local civic clubs. During the school term the Ambassadors performed closer to home and were accompanied by faculty members or a church relations counselor, usually Charlie Briggs, Gerard Taylor, Dr. Arthur Elliott, Dr. Arrel Gibson, or Dr. Fred Keller.

Other groups of Ambassadors and Presidential Singers were used to entertain audiences and spread the good news about Phillips until the university closed.

Roy McNaught, from Kingfisher, Oklahoma; Randy Rassmussen, from North Platte, Nebraska; Howard Clegg, from Hutchinson, Kansas; and Bill Williams, from Butler, Missouri, first met in 1952 when they were freshmen living in East Hall. All four sang in the university's chorus, conducted by Morris Poaster, and hoping to become the next Phillips Ambassadors, they informally formed a quartet and began practicing.

They were successful, and in 1953, they were chosen as the new Phillips Ambassadors. Keith Mielke, a sophomore music major from Enid and a member of the previous year's quartet, was named the group's coach and arranger. In exchange for their performances on behalf of Phillips, the group received free tuition and free uniforms.

After their first tour in 1953, the group changed its name to the Four Statesmen because all the members came from different states.

Some of the group's tours provided unexpected excitement. In the summer of 1955, the quartet was taking the "scenic route," through the Ozarks, which at the time meant driving along unpaved roads, on their way to Mountain Home, Arkansas. It was a hot summer day. Traveling in Bill Williams' 1950 Chevrolet, with most of their equipment and clothes packed on top in a luggage rack, the group came upon "a sparkling clear, cool and

Vernon R. Baker, below, joined the Phillips faculty in 1946 and taught geology. He spent his summers at the Phillips Science Camp in Colorado.

Dr. Lysle Mason (left, at chalkboard) returned to Phillips after World War II to teach a variety of mathematics courses, always striving to develop the best undergraduate mathematics program in Oklahoma.

Top left: Dr. Cecil Williams was a co-founder of the Phillips Science Camp. He and his wife, Lucile, spent a quarter century hosting students in the summer session in the Colorado mountains.

Harold Stewart was president of the 1950 Harvesters club. Left to right, front row, Tom Kenney, Cecil Williams, Aris Prewitt, Joel Wiens, Don Mitchell, Bob Killian. Second row, Ronnie Shafer, Dave Quintana, Ray Quintana, Harold Stewart, Wayne Stuart, Keith Stone, Paul Walker. Third row, Leroy Thomas, David Mitchell.

inviting river." It was too refreshing to pass and, believing they had plenty of time, they stopped and jumped in. When they resumed the trip they were startled to hear a radio announcer on a Mountain Home radio station say, "and in just 30 minutes the 'Four Statesmen Quartet' from Phillips University will be here in our studio to sing."

McNaught, Rasmussen, Clegg, Williams, and Mielke were dumbfounded. They thought they had plenty of time to get to Mountain Home. As Mielke recalled, "We raced off in a cloud of dust on the curvy road," but within a short distance the luggage rack came loose. "Suddenly arms came out of each of the four car windows," according to Mielke "hanging on for dear life to the swaying luggage rack." Twenty-five minutes later they stopped at a Mountain Home gasoline station, obtained directions to the radio station, and made it "with seconds to spare before air time." After performing in the Ozarks, the Statesmen closed out the summer tour of 1955 at the International Convention of the Disciples of Christ

86 In Reverence We Stand

in Toronto, Canada. It was the highlight of their musical career at Phillips. In 1986, the Four Statesmen were reunited for the annual alumni reunion at Phillips University where they sang the "Star Spangled Banner" prior to an alumni basketball game.

As a part of the expanding scientific curriculum, the Phillips University Science Camp was established in the Rocky Mountains of southern Colorado to give students a firsthand exposure to zoology and geology. The 160-acre camp was located along the Alamosa River in the San Juan Mountains in the Rio Grande National Forest about 25 miles southwest of Monte Vista, Colorado.

The idea for the summer science camp came from geology professor Vernon Baker and zoology professor Cecil Williams who liked the cooler weather in Colorado for a summer camp venue. They presented their idea to Dean Shirley who found the Colorado property while making a Phillips presentation at the Christian Church in Monte Vista. The son of a man who owned much of the town and the land that ultimately became the Phillips Science Camp was so interested in the project, he promised to donate the land. After two years of legal maneuvering, the land along the Alamosa River became the home of the Science Camp.

Dr. Williams took 15 students for the first summer science camp in 1950. Students traveled from all over the country study in the mountains. The camp immediately became a student favorite. A large building served as a mess hall and smaller cabins provided housing. Professors Williams and Baker taught zoology and geology courses. Professor John Randolph taught art classes. The professors and students built most of the camp's facilities. One group would attend class, while the other cleared land and constructed cabins and other buildings.

Over the years, many Phillips professors spent the summer at the camp. In the 1960s and 1970s, Hiram College sent professors and students to the camp.

It was possible for students to carry a maximum of nine hours credit in art, science, geology, humanities, or special problems classes at the eight-week camp. The area surrounding the camp provided unlimited subject matter for all classes. Field trips were often taken for further study and specimen collection. The Science Camp served two major purposes—a valuable learning experience and unique fellowship among students and professors and their families. At 10:00 p.m. each night, students could often be found in a professor's cabin enjoying popcorn, hot cocoa, and lots of fellowship.

The Boosters club began its 1951 spring semester with a drive to clean up the campus grounds. They were helped by their traditional Booster goat.

Post-war Growth 87

Officers of the Phillips University Chorus in 1952. Front row, left to right, secretary Wanda Davenport, treasurer Betty Hall, and vice president Marilyn Ellis. Second row, president Jim Spiller, robrarian Zane Knoy, librarian R.J. Murray, and robrarian Russell Money.

The 1952 staff of the Phillips Campus Book Store. Left to right, Lloyd Cleveland, manager Ethel Giffen, and Gene Curtis, who later became Phillips' librarian.

The mess hall at the Science Camp was large enough to hold the entire contingent of students, professors and their families, and any wayfaring guests that stopped in for lunch or overnight.

In his book, *Memories of the Science Camp*, Dr. Williams wrote, "To many students, the camp was a maturing experience and a time to learn values that are hard to come by in the hustle and bustle of the city campus." At least a dozen romances that began at the Science Camp led to marriage. For years after their learning experience, many students would stop by the camp on vacations in Colorado just to say hello.

In October of 1954, work began on the Earl Butts Dormitory for men. It was constructed east of the Enid Building and was made possible by a gift of $100,000 by Mrs. Earl Butts whose husband had served as United States secretary of agriculture.

Phillips played a leadership role in the desegregation of American society following World War II. As early as 1894 there had been several black Disciples congregations formed in Oklahoma Territory. By 1915, there were 220 Christian Churches in Oklahoma, 11 of which were black. Most of these were located in small rural communities. However, Tulsa, Muskogee, Okmulgee, Sapulpa, Oklahoma City, and Chickasha supported black Christian Churches. Interestingly, the Christian Church at Clearview was organized by A. C. Chi Chou, a Chinese evangelist.

Oklahoma, like most states in the Deep South, was a racially segregated state. In 1941, the state legislature passed a state law making it a misdemeanor for school administrators to admit black students to white schools, for teachers to teach mixed-race classes, and for white students to attend them.

However, after World War II, segregation began to crumble. As a part of the postwar civil rights movement, the National Association for the Advancement of Colored People (NAACP) launched a drive for equality. Originally formed in 1910, the NAACP launched a membership campaign open to all races in 1947 in an effort to bring down the barriers of segregation. Students at Phillips quickly organized a local NAACP chapter and

88 In Reverence We Stand

on October 7-9, 1947, 48 Phillips students pledged their moral support plus a dollar in financial support to join the university's chapter. Phillips and the University of Texas were the only two southern universities with NAACP chapters. On November 5-9, Phillips sent representatives to the ninth annual NAACP Youth Conference in Houston, Texas, and on February 12-13, 1948, the Phillips chapter hosted a two-day inter-racial institute featuring Bayard Rustin and Rosa Page Welch.

Desegregation came to Phillips University in 1954 on the heels of several court decisions that opened the doors of secondary and higher education to black students. Under prevailing state laws, blacks could only enroll in classes that were not offered at the state's all-black college, Langston University. As a result, the single black undergraduate student who had applied to Phillips had been denied admission. However, six black students already were attending graduate school at Phillips. On October 9, 1954, the Phillips board of trustees went on record and called for desegregation just as soon as the laws of Oklahoma allowed it.

After Phillips integrated, its students continued to work for the improvement of civil rights for minorities. In 1955, Art Scott and others received approval from President Briggs to help desegregate eating establishments in Enid. They staged a non-violent boycott of the Red Feather Café in Enid.

Construction of the Earl Butts Dormitory began in 1954. The campus cafeteria was later located in the building. The cafeteria was the scene of what seemed like continuous card games. Courtesy Jack N. Taylor.

Post-war Growth 89

In 1957, members of the Libra Club began assisting the Enid City Library to promote closer relations between the city of Enid and Phillips University. Libra was chartered in 1946.

Members of the Cosmopolitan Club in 1958 included, left to right, Henry Terre-Blanche, Despina Lyberopoulou, Joe Kim, Timothy Lee, and Alex Bilinski. Students from 17 nations belonged to the international club.

90 In Reverence We Stand

Because of a concern for the speech and hearing handicapped, the Phillips Speech and Hearing Center was built in 1956. The center was a combined project of Enid, Northern Oklahoma College, and Phillips. The campus building housed speech and hearing laboratories. Dr. Thayne Hedges taught speech and hearing therapy classes. Hedges was well-qualified to head the Speech and Hearing Center. He held two degrees from the University of Wichita and a Ph.D. from Ohio State University.

In the 1950s, student ministers continued to serve churches in an ever-widening radius of the Phillips campus. Most students traveled by automobile, train, or bus. According to Gene Moore, "A few had student pastorates that paid enough that they could ride the train, when aided and abetted by a clergy permit that enabled us to ride for a penny a mile." However, most student-preachers hitchhiked. Moore hitchhiked 200 miles each way from Enid to Snyder, Oklahoma, where he was assigned. He was paid $50 a month.

Ernest E. Durham hitchhiked 175 miles to and from Gage, Oklahoma, every weekend as a student preacher during the Great Depression, often receiving only $20 a month. A few students, who were pilots, flew private aircraft. Edward E. Bridwell, received his B.D. degree from Phillips in 1959 and his D. Min. in 1974. Bridwell flew 195 miles each week between Enid and Miami, Texas, where he preached in the local Disciples church. Although Bridwell admitted that he flew several times when "it would have been better to have been on the ground" he never missed a service in three years.

Ministerial students often had to maintain a harsh schedule, leaving Enid on Saturday to reach their congregations to preach on Sunday. No classes were held on Monday to allow the preachers ample time to return to Enid after Sunday night services. Classes resumed Tuesday morning.

Richard Allen Waldron, who attended the College of the Bible during the mid-1950s, drove 65 miles from his church at South Haven, Kansas, to Phillips every Tuesday morning. On Wednesday, he reversed the route to be at his church for Wednesday night services. Then he returned to Enid on Thursday morning and drove home to tend his church on Friday afternoon. He had Monday off from church and classes.

In 1957, Phillips University celebrated its golden anniversary. That spring, Charlene Brannen Imhoff became the 5,000th graduate of the university. On October 9, as a part of the semi-centennial celebration, the cornerstone was laid for Briggs Auditorium, which was dedicated on Founder's Day, October 9, 1958.

The auditorium, named for President Eugene S. Briggs, was the first structure on campus able to accommodate the entire student body since the burning of Old Main in 1947. The new facility had a seating capacity of 1,500 people.

The auditorium was the gift of the citizens of Enid, the university board of trustees, and the T. W. Phillips Foundation. Chairs and other furnishings were made possible by gifts from alumni and friends of the university. The air-conditioned auditorium had modern staging and single panel control lighting equipment.

As the 1950s came to a close, Phillips was flourishing. Students, administrators, and faculty members were all proud of their association with the university.

Briggs Auditorium was completed in 1958 and was used for a variety of student and community events for the remainder of the life of Phillips University. Many famous performers graced the Briggs stage, including Doc Severinsen, Ferrante and Teicher, Lillie Tomlin, Linda Ronstadt, and Dallas Holm. Courtesy Jack N. Taylor.

Post-war Growth 91

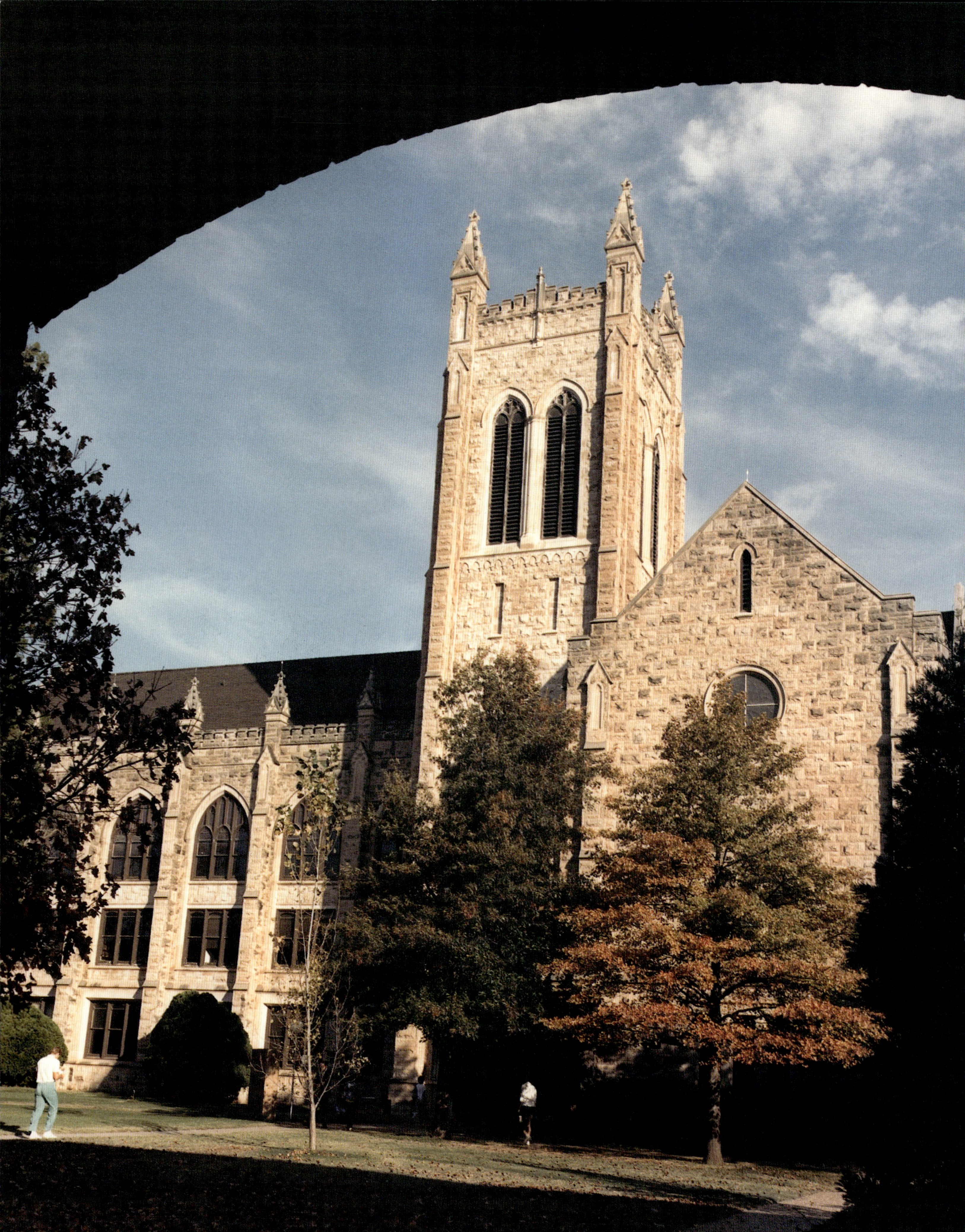

A New Generation

The Sixties and Seventies

The 1960s was one of the most unique decades in American history. It began with innocence and was filled with assassinations, race riots, anti-war demonstrations, and American astronauts landing on the moon. To some, it was called the "decade of discontent," as college students' voices could be heard across the land protesting the unpopular Vietnam War and expressing concern about the plight of minorities after race riots in Detroit, Michigan, and Los Angeles, California. Others called the 1960s the "decade of peace, love, and harmony" because of the peace movement and the emergence of "flower children."

At Phillips, the beginning of the 1960s was also innocent. The 1960 *Phillipian* was dedicated to the cherished Phillips University motto—Christian Education, the Hope of the World. Even though students were concerned about Sputnik and the Russians' entry into the space race, an aura of peace and tranquility still hovered over the Enid campus.

The influx of veterans after World War II had waned and the campus was full of bright-eyed students who wanted to further their education to make better citizens of themselves and improve their chances of succeeding in the business world and in Christian service.

"Phillips was a community of like-minded students, staff, and faculty who came together in a somewhat conservative but *not* stuffy or pious environment," said Barry Robinson, chair of the Phillips University, Inc. board. Even in a changing generation, students who often had been influenced by family, pastors, or teachers to seek a Christian environment were predisposed to take college seriously.

Robinson remembered, "There were a few unconventional characters among the students who adopted the 'beatnik' dress and aura, but most Phillips students were there to develop skills and accomplishments and later, leadership qualities."

However, Phillips was not immune to the change and discontent that hit every college and university campus in the land. Phillips students were likewise troubled by the uncertainty of the times. Students hovered around black and white television sets watching reports of the Cuban missile crisis, trying to determine the relevance of the events.

There was one campus protest in 1960. Barry Robinson and others were upset with the Sunday evening sack dinner given to residents of the Earl Butts Dormitory. Robinson described the "dinner" as a "tasteless bologna sandwich and cookie, maybe an apple." One Sunday, after the unappealing sack dinner was distributed, several male students took their sacks and threw them on the porch of the administration building. The years have dimmed Robinson's memory of President Briggs' response to the mild protest and the consequences of the action.

Television instantly conveyed radical changes in hairstyles and clothing that were sweeping the nation. In the 1960s, the look of the typical Phillips student changed—longer hair and long sideburns appeared, along with an occasional mustache and beard. However, Phillips students did not make the drastic change in appearance and attitude that impacted many major college campuses across the land. Barry Robinson reflected, "There was very little 'partying' on campus, and not much off-campus."

Students' language changed in the 1960s—new words not yet in Webster's dictionary dominated their conversation. "Boy," became an adjective in sentences like "Boy, that was a hard test!" "Beat it" was a verb that meant leave quickly. "Blast" was a noun describing a good time. "Bread" was no longer a food group, but was another word for money. "Bummer" was a noun describing a sudden bad turn of events.

Despite the changing attitudes and interests of students, the Phillips administration went about its business with an increased fervor for academic excellence. Phillips' presidents surrounded themselves with excellent staff people. In 1961, Homer Fortson was executive director of the university, running the business operations of the campus. Dr. Herbert Chase was vice president and Professor Henry Hobart was director of the community college for evening classes. George King headed up an active public relations department that was charged with spreading the word about the university. Dr. Arthur Elliott was director of special gifts, responsible for keeping donations coming into the school.

The quality of the Phillips staff was a hidden asset of the university. Sheldon Elliott explained, "After all, students have to be recruited, housed, fed on time, and cared for. The buildings have to be financed, built, modified, and maintained. The faculty have to be paid, records kept, bills paid, letters written, and appointments made. These things don't happen by magic."

Elliott believed that the cooperative, understanding, and encouraging staff that was developed at Phillips through the years was part of the successful execution of the plan to create an atmosphere of academic excellence. He said, "After all, a lot of the ambience of a place comes from the staff's attitude, particularly at a university."

Support for Phillips from the citizens of Enid continued to be strong. A great example of the combining of resources was the Enid-Phillips University Concert Orchestra. Under

94 In Reverence We Stand

Dr. James Clifford Shirley was professor of botany and bacteriology and later served as dean of the College of Arts and Sciences. He was named the Tenth Muse Club Sweetheart in the mid-1960s. He and Mrs. Shirley provided their beautiful garden for many club teas and gatherings. Dean Shirley often said he was the scientific botanist but that his wife grew the flowers. She planted many of the flowers on the Phillips campus.

Dr. J. Daniel Joyce became dean of the Graduate Seminary in 1962. He received his Ph.D. from Yale University and was one of the most respected theological school deans in America. Dr. Joyce recognized that Phillips' first obligation was to its own theological family but welcomed students from other church denominations.

the direction of Walter Wehner, 55 orchestra members, both students and private citizens who underwent rigorous auditions, practiced three times a week and performed many times a year at student gatherings and community events. A fall concert in 1961 featured Dr. Jon Nelson, professor of piano and music history, as a piano soloist. Just before Christmas each year, the orchestra and the university chorus presented *The Messiah,* which became a holiday tradition at Phillips.

Dr. Nelson influenced many of the university's music students. As Joyce Bridgman, who received her bachelor of music degree from Phillips in 1965, recalled, "He challenged many of us to accomplish more than we had even thought possible." "His productive critiques of our student performances," she continued, "were matched by his musical sensitivity, honesty, humility, human kindness, personal integrity, and spiritual insight." Many of Dr. Nelson's students continued their

Located on the west end of the campus, this building was a beehive of activity for decades. At various times, it was called the "C-store," or campus store, Student Center, and the Coach House, and consisted of a lounge, game room, student senate offices, a refreshment and snack bar, and a university bookstore. Later, the building housed business administration and communications classes.

In 1962, East Hall was torn down and replaced with Elliott-Goulter Apartments, named for Dr. and Mrs. Arthur Elliott, Phillips alumni who were missionaries to Paraguay, and Dr. and Mrs. Oswald Goulter, Phillips staff and faculty members who had served as missionaries to China. Courtesy Jack N. Taylor.

Barry Robinson was editor of the campus newspaper, *The Haymaker*, for two years. He was actually elected to the post, which paid $400 a year. In his senior year, the journalism experience allowed him to be hired in the Phillips public relations office for $1 an hour, when other campus jobs paid 65 to 75 cents an hour. Robinson later rose to the position of vice president of the Federal Reserve Bank in Kansas City and joined the Phillips University Board of Trustees in the early 1990s. He became chairman of the Phillips Board in 1997.

In 1959, the Graduate Seminary and the College of the Bible at Phillips University were administratively separated. These students made up the Seminary Council in 1960. Dr. Stephen J. England became the Graduate Seminary's first dean. The Graduate Seminary was a fully-accredited seminary with a stated goal of "helping men and women to become good ministers of Christ."

music education careers at other institutions of higher education. Bridgman became coordinator of keyboard studies at Oral Roberts University and Dr. Robert Bonham, bachelor of music, 1963, became a professor of music at Maryville College in Maryville, Tennessee.

Another music group that was formed at Phillips was the Surf Riders, which performed folk music in the early 1960s. Mike Crum, Vic Ehly, and C. E. Lear made up the trio. Crum later sang and played for the New Christy Minstrels.

With the new Briggs Auditorium providing an excellent venue for stage productions, the Phillips drama program excelled in the 1960s. Drama professor Duane A. Cline produced quality performances several times each year. The Phillips Players traveled to churches in the region to help promote the university. In

96 In Reverence We Stand

summer, the Traveling Players presented a repertoire of religious dramas in a five-state area.

Many Disciples churches across the state sent students to Phillips. John P. Moore, Jr., of Henryetta, Oklahoma, was planning to enroll at the University of Oklahoma in 1960 until Jack Nicholson, pastor of the Henryetta First Christian Church, convinced him to visit the Phillips campus. Nicholson even drove Moore to Enid to visit the school and introduce him to the faculty. Once there, Moore remembered feeling so comfortable and at home that he dropped plans to attend OU and enrolled at Phillips.

In 1961, President Briggs retired. His replacement was Dr. Hallie G. Gantz, the first president of the university to have graduated from Phillips. Gantz completed the requirements for three degrees at Phillips—a B.A. in 1931, an M.A. in 1932, and a B.D. in

Phillips President Dr. Hallie Gantz, right, shows an art exhibit to members of Oklahoma's first family in 1963. Left to right, Ann Bellmon, First Lady Shirley Bellmon, and newly-elected Governor Henry Bellmon. Dr. Hallie George Gantz served as president of Phillips University from 1961 to 1972.

The Lankard Apartments were built by the university in 1960 as an air-conditioned apartment building for married students.

A New Generation: The Sixties and Seventies

Downtown Enid in 1964, at night. Businesses in Enid provided a close and convenient shopping venue for Phillips University students who had cars. However, the lack of services within a reasonable walking distance was an ongoing concern for students.

1937. Afterward, he completed graduate work at Yale University Divinity School. His wife, Sylvia, also graduated from Phillips. Previously Dr. Gantz had been pastor of the First Christian Church of Tulsa.

When Dr. and Mrs. Gantz arrived on campus, they were met by more than 100 students, faculty members, and administrators. There was much cheering, singing, and speech-making. However, soon Dr. Gantz learned that unless the physical plant of the university was improved, the university would lose its accreditation.

Gantz and his staff developed a Growth With Quality plan that brought major changes in the physical appearance of the university campus in the first half of the 1960s. The Elliott-Goulter Apartments, Lankard Apartments, and the addition of a new wing on the Earl Butts Dormitory provided much needed space for students. The Journalism Building, the Government Building, and East Hall were torn down and a new Maintenance Building was constructed.

In 1963, the new four-story Zollars Memorial Library was completed. The basement and first floor contained classrooms and offices—the library was located on the upper two floors. December 18, 1963, was the date selected to move 60,000 bound books and thousands of unbound volumes of documents from the old to the new library. The outside temperature was 12 degrees. Nonetheless, volunteers and staff formed a continuous line between the two libraries and carried the books to their new home. Eventually the Zollars Memorial Library grew to 265,600 catalogued items—190,000 volumes, 60,000 microfilms, 15,000 audio-visuals, more than 1,000 current periodicals, and an archives and rare book collection. A network of computers connected the library to a nationwide Internet and interlibrary loan system.

The old library building was remodeled to house the School of Art, the Grace Phillips Johnson Art Gallery, and the Museum of the Cherokee Strip, which remained there

Autumn Leaves, sponsored by Tenth Muse, provided students with the opportunity to attend the first semi-formal dance of the year in 1962. Dancing had been prohibited on the Phillips campus in its early years but as times changed, administrators realized the importance of allowing such activities on campus, rather than forcing students to attend dances at other places off campus.

The Zollars Memorial Library opened in 1963. It quickly became the principal place of study for Phillips students. It was a modern facility that rivaled any college library in the region.

A New Generation: The Sixties and Seventies

ALMA MATER of PHILLIPS UNIVERSITY
ENID, OKLAHOMA

Eugene Rector, '34　　　　　　　　　　　　　　　　　　　Elizabeth Cleaver, '34

Verse: In rev-rance we stand and declare to the land, the glo-ry of our Phillips U. Her ban-ners un-furl and her challenge we hurl, Calling the loy-al and true Men who have con-quered stand read-y to do tri-bute to our Phillips U.

Chorus: Al-ma Ma-ter Al-ma Ma-ter Hail to thee for whose honor we'll be Ev-er faith-ful Al-ma Mat-er Al-ma Mat-er May we be wor-thy and hold ev-er high the standards of our Phillips U.

Band arrangement by Milburn Carey

Ira Morrison, professor of speech and oratory, joined the faculty at Phillips in 1945. In the 1960s he taught senior seminar and speech courses. Morrison held degrees from Kansas State University and the University of Missouri.

Far right: Dr. Robert Simpson, professor of religion and philosophy, and his daughter Megan Simpson, both graduates of Phillips University. Dr. Simpson served on the Phillips faculty for more than four decades. Megan Simpson became an attorney.

Dr. B. Kenneth Lewis came to Phillips in 1946 to teach chemistry and science. He was inaugurated as dean of the College of Arts in 1961. Dr. Lewis claimed his work was his hobby.

until 1973. During construction, new brickwork was placed over the first floor windows and the north entryway. To make the building blend with the new library and administration buildings, sand-color paint was applied to its exterior. Grace Phillips Johnson, the daughter of Thomas W. Phillips, funded the reconstruction. Phillips took a close look at itself in the 1960s, thanks to a Ford Foundation grant. Dr. Ton DeVos, a native of Holland who graduated from Phillips in 1950, directed the two-year task force that functioned as a fact-finding study group to make recommendations to policy-forming campus committees. The task force studied team teaching, presented a new core curriculum, and recommended methods of obtaining greater cooperation among university departments.

The changing times brought a new course for Phillips students in 1967. Professor Nancy Ogle taught the first course in human sexuality. One of her students, Dr. Patricia Huff, remembered, "We were apprehensive at first because that was a subject that had been limited to discussions with our parents. However, Professor Ogle presented the material scientifically, professionally, and with wit."

The 1970s brought more cultural changes to the Phillips campus. Students wore platform shoes, sandals, and paisley shirts. Students were suspicious of their national government and some began to believe conspiracy theories that Lee Harvey Oswald did not shoot President John F. Kennedy, that James Earl Ray did not kill civil rights leader Dr. Martin Luther King, Jr., and that Sirhan Sirhan did not shoot Senator Robert Kennedy in the previous decade. Phillips professors were cognizant that President Richard Nixon's role in the Watergate scandal caused students to question authority.

Problems associated with anti-war and anti-government feelings were dealt with in a variety of ways. The administration invited experts on topics in the news to the campus to openly discuss all sides of divisive issues.

In 1971, Phillips held its first Festival of the Arts. Concerned with low visibility of the arts on the campus, representatives of the Humanities Division and the School of Music planned a week-long celebration. The Oklahoma Arts and Humanities Council provided a 50 percent matching grant to fund the festival.

A New Generation: The Sixties and Seventies 101

The Everest Administration Building was occupied in December, 1963. It was named for trustee chair Harvey P. Everest, an Oklahoma City banker. The building contained the university offices and a boardroom for the board of trustees.

Operation Book Lift was a human conveyor belt to move 60,000 books and other documents from the old library to the new Zollars Library on December 18, 1963. In freezing temperatures, President Gantz joined 99 percent of the students and faculty in the operation. Students and faculty were dressed in sweatshirts, wool slacks and jeans, ear muffs, parkas, and gloves. After the book lift was completed, the accomplishment was celebrated that night at an all-school dance.

Edith "Mom" Mayberry was the first lady of Earl Butts Dormitory. The yearbook said she handled her responsibilities of running the men's dorm "with a graciousness that makes all her men proud of her."

Dr. Thayne Hedges administered hearing tests to all incoming freshmen each fall during a four-day introductory orientation program. Activities included taking personality and placement tests, meeting with academic advisors, and becoming acquainted with the university and each other.

102 In Reverence We Stand

The Sanford-Stunkle Drugstore in downtown Enid was a popular hangout for Phillips students in the 1950s and early 1960s. At one time there was a bowling alley, and later, a pool hall located on the second floor.

Below: A portrait of Dr. Stephen J. England was unveiled in 1965. Admiring the portrait of the legendary Phillips professor and dean are left to right, President Hallie Gantz, Bible College dean Dr. J. Daniel Joyce, Rev. James L. Christensen, and Dr. Wilfred Powell.

The 1964 Inter-Club Council was made up of representatives from various campus clubs to promote cooperation and harmony among the clubs. It also served as liaison between campus clubs and the administration. Front row, left to right, Clarence Warner, Bard McMullen, John Ruth, Paul Hopkins, Bill Wight, Nancy Staley, Jody Marshall, Virginia Angle, Dr. Beth Murphy. Back row, Jim Wiley, Jim Deming, Tal Black, Karen Wikoff, Janice Pettigrew, Pat Shiner, Nancy Christianson, Judy Abbey, Barbara Thornhill.

A New Generation: The Sixties and Seventies

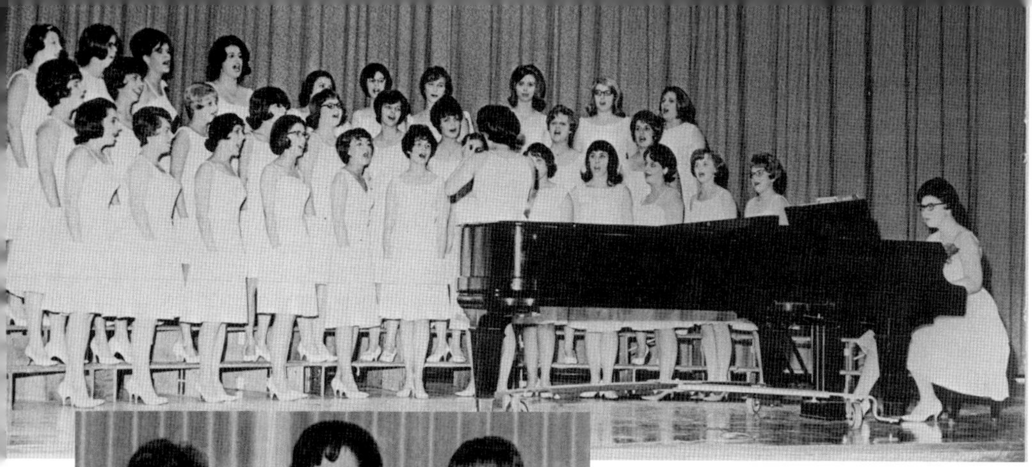

The Festival of the Arts ended with a performance of the Phillips Madrigal Singers. Associate professor of English Glenn Doyle wrote, "The long tables were laden with rib-eye beef, whipped yellow turnips, hot bread and lemon curd; and at the master's table, the great boar's head, ivy-twined, apple in mouth, reigned in fierce splendour. Candles gleamed, wassail cups were raised, and the plum pudding came riding aloft."

The festival was incredibly successful. The Department of English presented a program of student writing, featuring dramatic readings of stories and poems. Jesse Roy, a music composition major, performed several original guitar compositions.

The Music Department presented a choral concert, one of a series celebrating the 200th anniversary of Beethoven's birth. The concert was a joint production of the Phillips University Chorus and the Enid-Phillips Symphony Orchestra, conducted by Professor Max R. Tromblee.

Other programs of the first Festival of the Arts were silent films, sponsored by the Humanities Division, and dramatic performances by drama students. Paintings, metalwork, ceramics, photography, and other art forms were on display during the festival in the lobby of the Zollars Library.

One of the most significant events of President Gantz' administration was a reorganization of the College of the Bible. In 1971, the title "College of the Bible" was dropped and its deanship abolished. In its place, the Department of Religion and Philosophy was established. Its role was to prepare students for graduate professional training in a theological seminary, to offer courses on religion and philosophy to all students, and to aid students interested in church vocations. As part of the restructuring, Dr. Norman E. Jacobs became vice president for academic affairs and dean of the faculty.

Also in 1971 Alva, Oklahoma, senior Connie Bush became the first woman elected as president of the Phillips Student Senate. It was a year in

Mu Phi Epsilon was an international professional music sorority. This photograph shows the members of the Phillips chapter in 1965. At top, The Phi Mu Alphas sing in 1966.

Senior Class officers in 1966, left to right, Dale Herrick, president; Tom Genchur, senator; Nancy Yoder, secretary; Mike Miles, vice president; and Fred Randall, senator.

Sophomores Cerne Clark and Mike Duffy look on as Frosh Ben Goodman and Helen Harrian get ready to button for them. Frosh initiation was a major part of the Phillips spirit in the early weeks of the fall semester each year.

104 IN REVERENCE WE STAND

Members of the Student Education Association in 1970. Front row, left to right, Dorothea Rockwell, Lillian Reagan, Lerleen Williams, Carolyn Hostetler, Vonette Gettings, Cheryl Anderson, Linda Lively. Second row, Betty Peck, Irene Jefferies, Jim Baker, Jan Scott, Fran Sturgis, Donna Nickel. Third row, Professor Braley, Dr. John Ireland, Pam Parli, Janice Holcomb, Connie Lansdown, Craig McMahan, Galen Havner, Connie Johnson, Neil Wellman, Eileen Peil.

In 1969, a new president's house was built at 2602 East Maine. Dr. Gantz was the first president to occupy it. One of its most famous furnishings was Ralph Blakelock's *Indian Encampment Along the Snake River*, painted in 1871. Courtesy Jack N. Taylor.

which the Student Senate was transformed from a dormant creature of student government into a dynamic troupe of student leaders determined to correct what they saw were inequities of the past.

The unrest that existed on many American college campuses actually brought constructive reform to the Phillips campus. Dr. Gantz did not initiate all changes in student life, but he did create a mood that allowed for change.

A new constitution was written which contained a Bill of Rights and a Bill of Responsibilities. Among the rights listed was a section that allowed

In this 1970 photograph, a Phillips student uses a sign to convey his opinion that student demonstrations against American involvement in Vietnam might be helping the North Vietnamese cause.

Male students wore their hair longer in the 1970s than in the 1960s. Miniskirts were popular with both the female students who wore them and their male counterparts who observed them.

Jo Ann Hopkins was a well-liked accounting professor in the Business Administration Department.

Professor of Art Jim Bray showing his students an ink technique. Bray encouraged many Phillips students to develop artistic talents.

Susan Supernaw, a 20-year-old sophomore from Tulsa was named Miss Phillips University in 1971. She went on to become Miss Oklahoma and won a judges' scholarship at the Miss America pageant.

106 IN REVERENCE WE STAND

students to invite and hear any speaker, no matter how controversial he or she might be. The new constitution also gave students greater rights in dealing with living quarters issues. Searches were no longer allowed except in cases of extreme circumstances. A judicial system was set up—a Court of Appeals and a Student Government Court were created to have sole jurisdiction over violations of Student Government Association rules and regulations.

The Honor System, part of the old constitution written in the 1950s, required students to report violators of rules concerning cheating, stealing, and lying under oath. In supporting the new constitution, some students wore shirts that said the spirit of an honor system was good, but that everyone knew it did not work because many students would not turn in violators.

With a hearty endorsement from the Student Senate, Phillips students overwhelmingly approved the new constitution that gave students the huge responsibility of control over $63,000 of Class A funds that came from student dues. In the first year of the new responsibility, the Senate used some of its funds to finance a Black History Week and Indians' Concerns Conference.

In 1972, a scholarship fund in memory of Dr. Martin Luther King, Jr., was established with the help of Captain James Dixon, a flight instructor at nearby Vance Air Force Base, and Dorothy Jones, a prominent Enid citizen. Dixon, Jones, and other Enid leaders dedicated to helping the disadvantaged, approached Richard Anderson, director of graduate studies, and proposed the King scholarship, to be funded by contributions from the Enid Inter-Racial Club and Vance airmen.

The first Dr. Martin Luther King, Jr., scholarship was awarded to John Winters in 1974. Winters graduated from Phillips, took his master's degree from Kansas State University, and taught successfully in Oklahoma public schools. The scholarship program continued until the close of Phillips. Twenty-one students ultimately received scholarships making it possible for them to attend Phillips.

James Alan "Jim" Strain was editor of *The Haymaker* in 1971. Strain was a unique student who played intramural sports, served in the Student Senate, and was involved in a dozen other student activities. *The Phillipian* in 1971 wrote, "If you are around Jim for a little while, you realize that his charisma reaches mighty limits. In fact, he holds such an esteemed position that his friends respect his decrees. If Jim says someone 'is bein' all wrong,' they are definitely WRONG." After graduation, Strain was a member of the Phillips public relations staff before heading to Hollywood. He wrote the screenplay for a family film, *Bingo,* and co-wrote the screenplay for a big movie success, *Jumanji,* starring Robin Williams.

HOUSE RULE

1. All Players Must Sign In Prior To Beginning Play.
2. 20¢ Minimum Charge For All Play.
3. One Foot On The Floor At All Times.
4. All Phillips Students, Faculty, And Guests Are Welcome.
5. 5¢ Charge For Jumping A Ball Off The Table.

In January, 1972, the newly remodeled Coach House, the student center, was opened. The House rules for playing pool mandated a five-cent charge for jumping a ball off a table. When a fire gutted much of the building on September 12, 1972, students playing pool in the lounge managed to save one color television set and the money from the cash register. The residence hall was serving a picnic-style dinner at the Sunken Garden at the time the fire erupted. Students took their dinner plates across campus to the Coach House to watch the excitement.

Dr. Thomas Edward Broce became the fifth president of Phillips University in 1973. He resigned in October of 1975 following coronary-bypass surgery.

In just a decade, Phillips had gone from a spring May Fete, with May Poles galore, to Black Awareness Week. Attendance at class and chapel was no longer mandatory. Dances were allowed on campus with increasing frequency and tobacco use was no longer limited to the parking lots behind the Science Building and the Art Center. The 8:00 p.m. curfew for female students living in Clay Hall was moved to 11:00 p.m. Student enrollment was up because many students took advantage of the education exemption from the draft during the Vietnam War.

President Gantz always considered his service at Phillips as a ministry. Sylvia Gantz remembered, "He came to Phillips out of a sense of mission. He always knew God had placed him there for the important job of training Christian leaders to have an impact on the whole world."

When President Gantz died in July of 1972, he was replaced by Dr. Thomas E. Broce who held a Ph.D. from the University of Oklahoma, was director of development at Duke University from 1959 until 1967, and vice president of Southern Methodist University from 1967 to 1970.

Oklahoma City construction company owner Haskell Lemon, right, and his wife, Irene, were longtime financial supporters of Phillips University. To honor their contributions, a learning center bore their name.

Margaret Edwards held two degrees from Phillips and taught English and literature courses beginning in 1947.

John Randolph began teaching art at Phillips in 1948. He was known all over the Southwest for his unique paintings. He also taught art at the Phillips Summer Science Camp in Colorado.

108 IN REVERENCE WE STAND

Below: The Student Government Court was established in 1973 to hear all cases pertaining to violations of university policies. Standing around court chairman Chuck Shields, seated, are left to right, Teresa Grace, Ron Driskell, Arleta Edwards, Janet Gammel, and Dan Wiggs, members of the court.

Above: "We pledge allegiance to EBD" was the pronouncement of the officers in 1974 of the Earl Butts Dormitory. Seated, left to right, Mike Passmore, Mrs. Ruth Seamans, residence hall director, Bruce MacAllister, Gary Gee, Jamie Frazier. Standing, Kirk Board, Clark Bundren, Bryan Charlton, Alan Sayre, Jim Smith, Steve Torres, Greg McMahan.

The 1974 Homecoming Queen and her court. Queen Cindy Frazier, center, represented the sophomore class. Clockwise around Cindy are Arleta Edwards, Kathye Hill, Kris Karrenbrock, Susan Parham, and DuRee Bryant.

The changes of appearance of Phillips students in the 1970s is graphically displayed in this photograph of a freshman involved in Frosh Initiation.

A New Generation: The Sixties and Seventies 109

The Ladies of Clay Hall in 1975. Left to right, front row, Leanne Welch, Barbara Wonderly, and Ann Firkins. Second row, Anita Stroud, Laura Craddock, Debbie Hughes and Kim Fields. Back row, Nan Smith, Renee Johnson, Sydney Willey, and Arleta Edwards.

Enid native and American astronaut, Dr. Owen K. Garriott, Jr., was granted an honorary degree from Phillips in 1973. He presented the university two emblems which accompanied him on the Skylab II mission.

Coach Jim Stroup stands beside the lifeguard chair at the Phillips swimming pool covered by an air-inflated dome that made the pool accessible to students year round.

The comic strip "'Lil Abner" inspired the Phillips YMCA and YWCA to celebrate Sadie Hawkins Day, a fun annual event. In 1974, Janice and John Johnson had "done been hitched."

110 IN REVERENCE WE STAND

William Henning, left, art history curator of the Johnson Art Gallery, and Dr. James Beddow, professor of history, received a medal in 1973 for sponsoring the Copernicus Conference which featured the book *Sun Stand Thou Still*.

At the annual Fall Joust in 1975, Dennis Hughes, left, battles to become the Camelot Club Joust Champion. Jousting had been moved from the creek that fed University Lake.

The Hallie G. Gantz Student Center was opened in September, 1975, and was a modern facility for Phillips' students. Courtesy Jack N. Taylor.

Left to right, English professor Glenn Doyle; Adeline Shirley, wife of Dean Clifford Shirley; and Sylvia Gantz, wife of President Hallie Gantz, visit with Dr. Cecil Williams at a party to celebrate Williams' new book, *Memories of the Science Camp*.

The Mabee Center opened as a state-of-the-art indoor athletic facility in 1979. Courtesy Jack N. Taylor.

Just before being named president of Phillips, he served as the executive assistant to the president of the University of Oklahoma.

Broce immediately launched a campaign to secure adequate financing for Phillips' future. He remained the president of Phillips until October of 1975. During the three years of his service, gift support for Phillips increased 71 percent and a new academic master plan was developed.

Richard Anderson, director of graduate studies, headed a committee on international education in 1974 that decided an international campus program would be good for Phillips. Paul Denny, professor of art, suggested that Phillips establish a program in Sweden. After Anderson and Denny visited Mullsjo, Sweden, they recommended that city for the program that would provide Phillips students with classroom instruction, field trips, and travel. Mullsjo had a Folkhogskola, or "people's college," and a large number of citizens interested in exchange programs.

Phillips agreed to send a group of students and a faculty member to Mullsjo each semester and Swedish students would be sent to study on the Enid campus. In both cases, tuition and room and board were provided free for one semester. Two major field trips were required. One trip introduced students to the Soviet Union—the other excursion was to various points in Europe. Phillips was the first American university to form such a unique relationship with a Swedish university.

Professor Denny took the first group of 17 Phillips students to Sweden in the fall of 1974. In the spring of 1976, Professor Jerry Turpin took a group of students that presented a play, "The Lincoln Saga," in Mullsjo as well as several other cities in Europe.

The "Sweden experience" became so popular that students added their names to long waiting lists for acceptance to make the annual pilgrimage to Sweden. Richard Anderson reflected, "Students and faculty alike were able to draw on unique cultural and intellectual resources, to develop sensitivities to other cultures, and thus increase their appreciation of their own civilization."

Swedish students who came to Enid were enriched and a number of them completed degrees at Phillips. Another benefit of the program was the lasting friendships that were made when parents from each country visited each other. Anderson said, "The unique program represented the continuing emphasis of the Phillips concern for people everywhere."

Phillips' academic programs prepared students for success in the future. An example is Pete Earley who was *Haymaker* editor and graduated with a BS degree in business and mass communication in 1973. He worked as a reporter in Enid, Tulsa, Oklahoma, and Washington, D.C. before turning to writing non-fiction books. Earley has written books about the two most damaging spies in recent history, a sex-crazed religious cult, and a racially-charged unsolved murder in the Deep South. Earley said, "I want to take you places you normally wouldn't go and introduce you to people whom you normally wouldn't meet."

Circle K was a new campus club in 1976, founded on the commitment to lend a helping hand to those in need. The club sponsored a fund raising project to help send the Enid High School band to Washington, D.C. Front row, left to right, David Langston, Debbie Randolph, Linda Pounds, Beth Long, Pam Ousley, Karen Merrick. Back row, Ken Baker, Debbie Hughes, Susan Humphries, Jackie Foster, Dana Chisum.

A New Generation: The Sixties and Seventies

Attendance at the annual Homecoming weekend grew as the list of Phillips alumni grew. Typical events of Homecoming were a Homecoming dinner, club teas, a talent show for students and alumni, an awards luncheon, a presidential open house, and the crowning of a Homecoming queen. A Homecoming parade usually wound its way from campus to downtown Enid.

On September 30, 1975, the new Hallie G. Gantz Student Center was opened during Homecoming.

At a ribbon-cutting ceremony, Sylvia Gantz said the building named after her late husband was best described as "a place where hearts and minds touch."

The Gantz Center housed a dining room that seated 450, a lectorium that seated 200, a coffee shop, bookstore, drugstore, game room, faculty lounge, student lounge, and office space for the dean of students, student government, and student publications. To make room for the Gantz Center, the old Ladies' Gym was torn down. The White House, which housed offices of student publications, the Student Senate, and student government courts, was also torn down.

The Phillips campus family celebrated the Bicentennial of America in 1976 in grand style. Drama groups presented patriotic plays and music groups per-

The Millard Fillmore Society, formed by faculty members, honored President Millard Fillmore, who accomplished nothing, by accomplishing nothing in their meetings. After the Mabee Center was opened in 1977, the old Ladies Gym was torn down. Just before it was demolished in early 1979, the Phillips University chapter of the Millard Fillmore Society dedicated the old Ladies Gym as its new headquarters and renamed it the Millard Fillmore Memorial All Purpose Utility Building. Then Professor Dorothy Cozart, using a bottle of Ripple wine, christened the building just before the group marched back to classes as the Phillips University Kazoo Zoo Band played "When the Saints Go Marching In."

formed patriotic musicals. Star Spangled Entertainment, a variety show that replaced the Miss Phillips pageant, was a historical depiction of American entertainment of the previous two centuries. Dr. Ronald Cowan won the single/duet category with his performance as Mark Twain. Tenth Muse won the group competition with a barbershop quartet routine.

Dr. Samuel Everett Curl was named president of Phillips in 1976. Curl had received his Ph.D. from Texas A&M University in College Station, Texas, where he specialized in animal physiology and genetics. After graduation he joined the faculty at Texas Tech University in Lubbock, Texas. Curl served as a member of the regional board of directors for the Christian Church in Oklahoma and the Church Financial Council for America.

Phillips students reacted with shock and disbelief to President Curl's rejection of sweeping campus housing reforms in 1977. Living Options, an attempt to change dorm life, included recommendations for a quiet wing, extended visitation hours, and alternate floors of male and female students. Alternative floor living would have converted one wing of the Butts Dormitory into male-female quarters. Men would have lived on the ground floor and women on the second floor.

President Curl gave three reasons for rejecting the plan: (1) enrollment was up and dorms were full; (2) a majority of parents surveyed objected to the concept; and (3) he believed Phillips must maintain what he called a "distinctive" image. Student leaders criticized Curl's survey because only six percent of students' parents were contacted.

Angry students called for a sit-in demonstration to express student support for the Living Options. However, only a dozen students showed up for an 8:00 a.m. demonstration at the Administration Building.

Inaugurated as Phillips' sixth president in 1976, Dr. Samuel Everett Curl served until 1979 when he became dean of the College of Agricultural Sciences at Texas Tech University.

A new indoor athletic facility, the Mabee Center, was dedicated in 1979. The new gymnasium replaced older, outdated buildings in which the university's basketball teams had performed and which housed the indoor intramural sports such as volleyball. The 50,000 square-foot-facility was built at a cost of more than $2 million. Construction funds came from a Mabee Foundation $350,000 challenge grant and a $350,000 pledge from the Oklahoma Christian Church's Program of Progress.

Students, alumni, and faculty contributed to the building of the new athletic facility in the Buy-a-Brick Campaign. The Mabee Center was the last major building project completed by Phillips University.

The 1970s had been a challenging and an exciting time of stable growth for Phillips—but economic hard times lay ahead.

A New Generation: The Sixties and Seventies

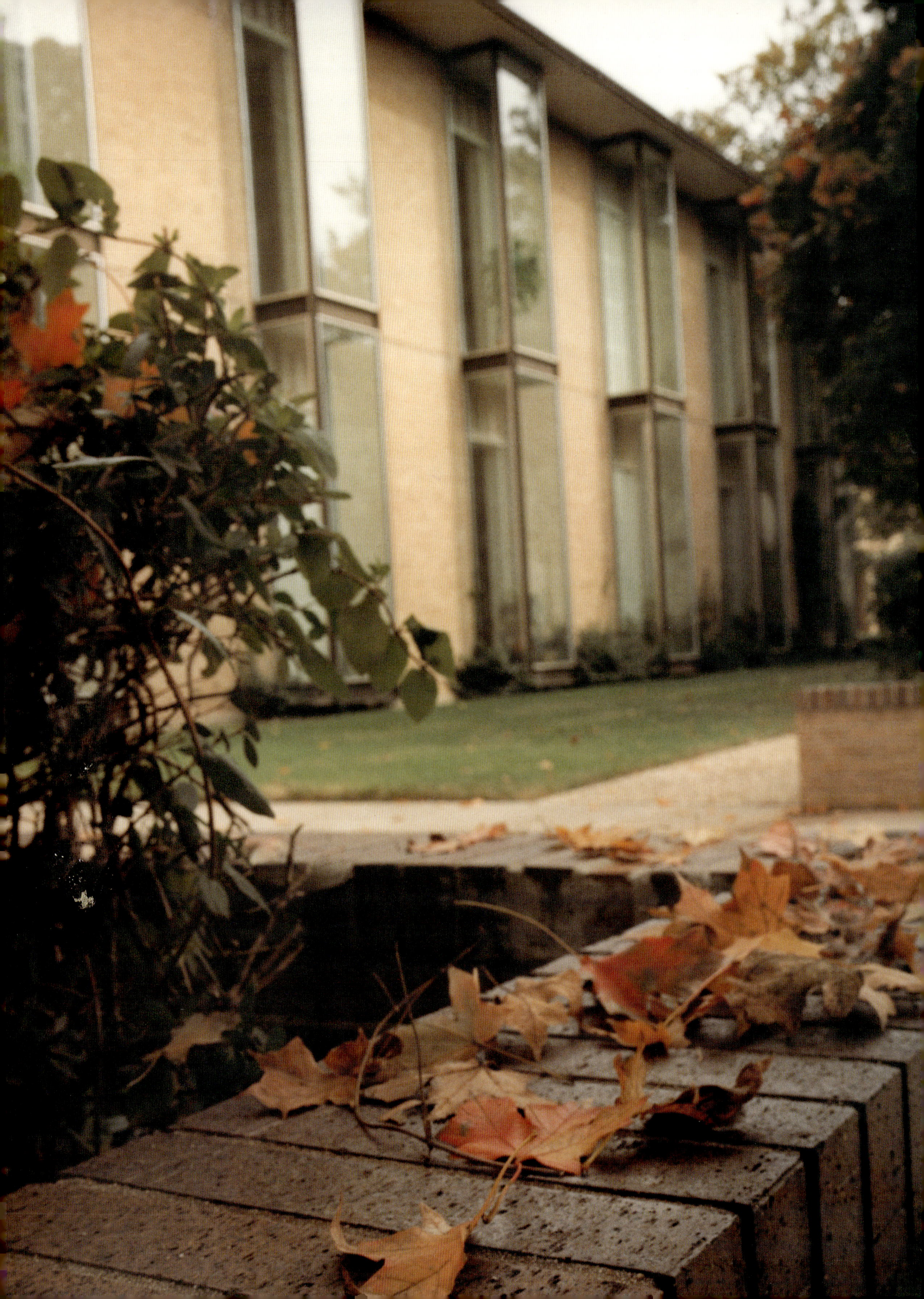

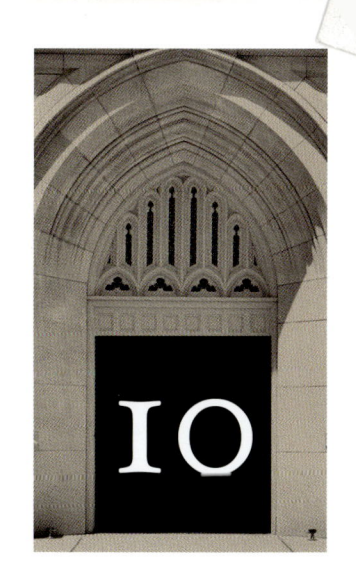

Economic Woes

The Eighties and Nineties

DR. JOE R. JONES was selected from a field of more than 70 candidates to become the seventh president of Phillips University on October 10, 1979. Oklahoma's Governor George Nigh joined a capacity crowd of faculty, students, community members, and church leaders to celebrate the occasion. After being officially installed, Jones reminded members of the Phillips family of the university's heritage and pledged that his personal theme would be "Decision for Excellence." Jones said the hallmark of his administration would be excellence in liberal arts education and a commitment to work closely with the Christian Church.

Jones received his Ph.D. from Yale University and spent a year as a research scholar at Oxford University in England. He was on the faculty of the Perkins School of Theology at Southern Methodist University before coming to Phillips as dean of the Graduate Seminary. He served on numerous boards and commissions of the Christian Church.

President Jones continued to expand Phillips' facilities. The university's Science Building was refurbished and renamed Harmon Hall in honor of the Pearl and Julia Harmon Foundation of Nowata, Oklahoma, which contributed $250,000 to its renovation. Another $40,000 came from the Arthur Vining Davis Foundation. A new ceiling, lighting, and windows were installed as well as air-conditioning, and most science labs were updated.

The 1980s saw an increase in student activities on the Phillips campus. A number of new ideas for student involvement were born, including a Brown Bag Opera. Ron Huggins directed vocal music students through operatic performances at high noon at the Gantz Center. One student observed, "Each member of the cast turned an otherwise prosaic noontime into one of life's most happy and hilarious 'Times to be Treasured' at Phillips."

The Madrigal Dinner was so popular that for many years it became a

From 1979 to 1988, Dr. Joe R. Jones was president of Phillips University. Dr. Jones was previously dean of the Phillips Graduate Seminary.

Professor C. Tibbie Shades was a popular professor of English at Phillips.

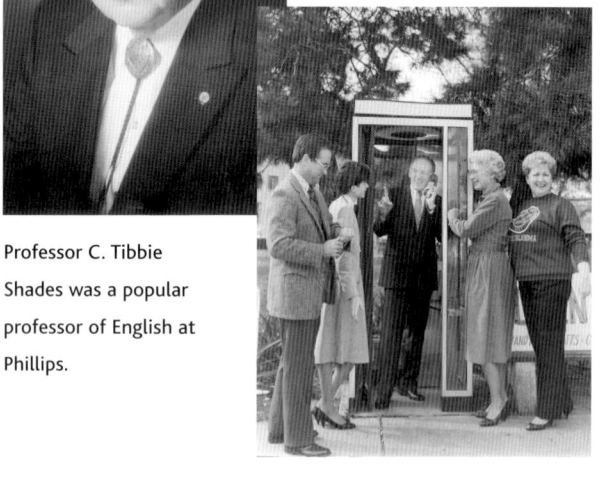

For most of its years, Phillips University enjoyed exemplary support from citizens of Enid. During a Phillips Day fund raising event, Enid leaders posed at a campus phone booth. On the phone is banker Bert Mackie. Outside the booth are, left to right, Stan Brownlee, Suellen Singer, Nancy Davies, and Mona Long.

John Sayre was the seminary librarian who guided a dedicated staff that made certain seminary students had full access to the latest printed material.

118 IN REVERENCE WE STAND

twice a year event for students and faculty to dress in medieval clothing and relive the days of the 15th century in medieval England. The Union Board brought a variety of musical acts to the campus for full-blown concerts in Briggs Auditorium and more intimate performances at several coffeehouses during the year.

In fall of 1980, a group of Phillips students formed the Philia Dona Clown Alley, better known as P. D. Clown Alley. The idea came from Bette Jayne Parrish. Ralph Glenn was the faculty sponsor for the project which was a part of the ministry to churches' youth. Lynette Alcorn was an early member of the group whose members spent many hours relating Bible stories, parables, theological ideas, and faith messages to youth.

Phillips students were introduced to a wide spectrum of American personalities and leaders. Special guests on campus included politicians, business leaders, magicians, hypnotists, and, in 1981, James Whitmore, whose creation of the spirits of Will Rogers, Theodore Roosevelt, and Harry Truman seemed to come alive before overflow audiences.

Phillips celebrated its Diamond Jubilee in 1982, celebrating 75 years of excellence. President Jones and university staff promoted a series of special alumni lectures that gave current students insight into the lives of former students. The University Women's Lecture Series provided enlightening talks on current topics of interest. Jones' idea of excellence went beyond academic areas into all phases of university life.

Eight major fields of study were available to Phillips students in the 1980s. The Division of Behavioral and Social Sciences included study in political science, psychology, and sociology. Biology, chemistry, geology, mathematics, computer science, medical technology, and physics were primary disciplines taught in the Division of Natural and Mathematical Science.

The areas of art and music were combined in the Division of Fine Arts. The Division of Language Communication included English, foreign language, speech, drama, literature, and mass communication classes. The goal of the Division of Education and Recreation was to train educators for service in elementary and secondary schools, special education, and library science. The Division of Education and the Division of Business Administration also provided accredited masters degrees to a large number of graduate students.

The Division of Business Administration prepared students for careers in accounting, economics, finance, business management, marketing, and business education. Giving students an overall view of human life and thought was the goal of the Division of Religion, History, and Philosophy. The school's close ties with the Disciples was a stated goal of President Jones' administration and courses in religion were emphasized in the Phillips curricula to enrich the values and attitudes of students while preparing them for a role within the church as lay leaders and as informed individuals.

The eighth area of study was the Division of Religion and Philosophy. Its purpose was to prepare students for

Professor J. Stam, kneeling, performs at a Madrigal Dinner, a return to the food and magical atmosphere of medieval times. From the 1960s until the close of Phillips, Tom Whittaker, associate professor of music and drama, played harpsichord music for the dinners.

Inset, above: Professor Jerry Turpin in his madrigal attire. Preparing for a Madrigal Dinner was often as enjoyable as the event itself.

Economic Woes: The Eighties and Nineties 119

Left: The "old" Phillips University science faculty at a 1980 reunion in Enid. Left to right, Dr. Beth Murphy, Dr. Cecil Williams, Dr. Lysle Mason, Dr. B. Kenneth Lewis, Dr. Philip Horton, Domer Dougherty, Dr. Vernon Baker, and Dean J. Clifford Shirley. Dr. Murphy, Dr. Mason, and Dr. Horton were still teaching at the time. Dr. Murphy called retired Dean Shirley "the greatest recruiter" Phillips ever had. Murphy said, "He attended summer church camps and the kids loved him. He remembered the names of every kid and usually knew where they were from."

Left to right, Steve Krebaum, Deborah Hackler, Bethany Bice, Eric Ramerez, and K.J. Reynolds pause during the 1982 Phillips University Choir Tour. The choir performed at many high school and community events.

Steve Maxwell, left, and Chris Evans make use of a lab during their Swedish Semester at Mullsjo Folkhogskola in the fall of 1981.

seminary and to make available religion courses for all students.

President Jones continued the Phillips tradition of a fine support staff. The academic vice president oversaw the academic life of the university. The Registrar's Office was responsible for everything from supplying official transcripts to registration for classes. Computers added in the mid-1980s helped provide fast and efficient help for students, faculty, and alumni.

The Phillips Development Office was charged with maintaining good relations with Disciples churches in the region and soliciting financial support from churches, individuals, and groups that were interested in the welfare of the university. The Business Office was often the center of activity on campus, whether involved in managing the financial affairs of the university or cashing a check for a student. The University Libraries continued to update collections to make certain students had the best selection of study materials.

The Admissions Department promoted the university to potential students and developed programs to encourage high school graduates to visit Phillips. The vice president for University Community Life headed a staff that handled housing and financial aid applications and managed activities in campus buildings. Behind the scenes, food service workers and the maintenance staff were important cogs in making a quality university life for students, faculty, and staff.

In 1983, Phillips began a close association with Northern Oklahoma

In 1983, members of the campus bluegrass band were, left to right, Paul Stewart, Lem Gordon, Justin Miller, Ray Person, and Mike Morgan.

College (NOC) at Tonkawa. Under the joint program, credits earned at NOC, a two-year college offering an associate degree, would be accepted toward a baccalaureate degree at Phillips.

Such programs allowed Phillips to maintain the highest academic quality of any college or university in Oklahoma. According to *Barron's Profile of American Colleges,* in 1984, Phillips was one of 168 colleges and universities of 1,500 nationwide that ranked "very competitive." In 1986, Phillips was among 315 colleges and universities listed in *Peterson's Competitive Colleges* with a high percentage of students with a composite score of 26 or more on the ACT admission test, above average scores on college board exams, and from the top half and top ten percent of their graduation class.

During these latter decades the admissions staff continued its earnest efforts to attract students to the campus. For most of its life, Phillips boasted the highest percentage of Disciples students on its campus of any Disciple-related college or university. Phillips hosted a variety of on-campus activities to attract high school students, including Applefest and Christian Youth Fellowship (CYF) Weekend. Visitors experienced dorm life as they integrated with the college students. Admissions experts knew that once a high school student actually came and spent time on the campus, there was usually a good chance that the student would enroll at Phillips.

Student ambassadors were deployed to church camps and conferences, regional and district assemblies, high school college fairs, and any other opportunity to expose the university to potential students. As Kirby Gould reflected, "These efforts were truly labors of love."

With student enrollment high and contributions from Disciples churches healthy, Phillips was doing well in the early 1980s. The oil boom in Oklahoma had increased the wealth of many Phillips supporters and the state's economy was good for members of churches who contributed regularly to the school. Oil and gas wells were drilled at a feverish pace all over the state. Car dealers prospered and jewelers sold Rolex watches in record numbers. Banks loaned money as fast as they could.

Then came the failure of Oklahoma City's Penn Square Bank in 1982, the first in a series of bank failures that reverberated throughout America's financial structure.

By 1984, the prosperity of the oil boom ended as quickly as it had begun. As world oil prices plummeted, the boom became a crash. Car dealers took back their fancy cars and jewelers bought back expensive jewelry.

There was an atmosphere of gloom as the state government budget shrunk, businesses failed, and men and women were out of work. It was a time of gloom that adversely affected all

Economic Woes: The Eighties and Nineties

Decades after it became an annual tradition, the Friendship Fire was a special time for students returning to class in the fall of 1985.

A dance concluded the 1986 Applefest, an annual attempt to attract high school students to the Phillips campus. The event was designed by the admissions department to give students an on-campus view of Phillips.

The 1985 Ambassadors were typical of Phillips' commitment to spreading the message about the university. The Ambassadors sang at churches and church dinners within a four-hour drive of Enid. They both entertained and informed audiences about the benefits of attending Phillips. Front row, left to right, Tracy Johnson, Gene Roberts, and Susan Kalka. Back row, Randy Johnson, Lucilla Nash, Lori Smith, Harriet Howell, and Elizabeth Hilligoss.

Tim Lovejoy, right, Jeff Evans smile as the tassels become reality at the 1985 Phillips graduation.

aspects of the Oklahoma economy, including Phillips University.

In spite of high academic rankings, expanded programs, and successful athletic teams, Phillips administrators faced hard economic times and the added burden of stiff competition from expanding public college education in Oklahoma. By design, public supported higher education in the state was inexpensive. The cost of tuition and fees for a full-time student at Phillips in 1985 was $4,064 per semester. The same student paid $858 at the University of Oklahoma and $828 at Oklahoma State University. The disparity in cost was beginning to affect Phillips' enrollment, and correspondingly, its income.

In 1983, a year before the oil bust, 543 Disciples congregations spread over six states were helping to support Phillips. Contributions from these churches and individuals accounted for 40 percent of Phillips University's budget. Tuition and fees brought in 46 percent and 14 percent was generated by the school's endowment fund. Nevertheless, by 1986, Phillips was forced to obtain a $1 million line of credit from the Board of Church Extension of the Christian Church (Disciples of Christ) to fulfill its financial obligations.

Despite all valiant and innovative efforts, Phillips' financial plight worsened, and in 1987, school administrators turned to Enid's city government for help. Many Enid citizens worked hard to save Phillips. A creative sale/leaseback plan was developed and Enid residents were asked to approve a three-quarter of a cent sales tax to fund a $24,000,000 city economic development plan. Fourteen million three hundred and fifty thousand dollars of the money would be used to purchase the 40 buildings and 130-acre campus of Phillips University. Phillips would then

122 IN REVERENCE WE STAND

lease the buildings and campus from the city for a period of twenty years, with Phillips having the opportunity to repurchase the school at any time.

The sale/leaseback plan would make the operation of Phillips a joint city-university project, with the school still affiliated with the Disciples and governed by the Phillips University board of trustees. The Marshall Building, which housed the graduate seminary and its library, was not part of the sale.

The innovative plan, according to observers such as Stephen Jones, extended the life of the university. Jones said, "Without the plan, Phillips would have closed its doors in 1987."

Enid voters approved the sales tax increase on June 2, 1987. However, it was by a margin of only 65 votes, 6,653 to 6,588. Collection of the tax began on August 1, 1987.

Almost immediately a group of Enid citizens organized the Political Action Group of Enid (PAGE) to block the sale of Phillips. Arguing that the arrangement would use public money to support a private institution, the group filed a lawsuit in Garfield County District Court in July of 1987, maintaining that the sale violated the separation of church and state principle because the university was affiliated with the Christian Church. The plaintiffs were Ted and Cathy Burkhardt and Richard Poindexter.

The trial was held in September of 1987 before district Judge Richard W. Pickens. In October, Pickens agreed that the public support of Phillips was unconstitutional and gave university and city officials 60 days to prepare a new agreement to sever the school's ties with the Christian Church (Disciples of Christ). One of his major concerns was that members of the board of directors of Phillips University and the separate seminary were the same people. Another concern was that the state constitution prohibited the loaning of public money to a private institution and because the university could repurchase

Participants in Phillips University's Semester in Sweden in 1985 were front row, left to right, Leigh Salzsieder, Julia Jordan, Greg Pratt, Nell Harfert, and Todd Salzsieder. Second row, Shawna McWaters, Michelle Schwinn, Tim Longman, Greg Hill, Todd Lucas. Back row, Becky Schovanec, Kris Keller, Mark Gillet, Butch Coffey, John Meyer, and Greg Murphy.

Stuart McLean was associate professor of Christian ethics at Phillips Theological Seminary.

Dr. Fred Craddock authored several books on religious life. *Time* Magazine listed him as one of America's top preachers. In 1978, he delivered the prestigious Beecher Lectures on preaching at Yale Divinity School. At Phillips, Dr. Craddock taught several religion classes.

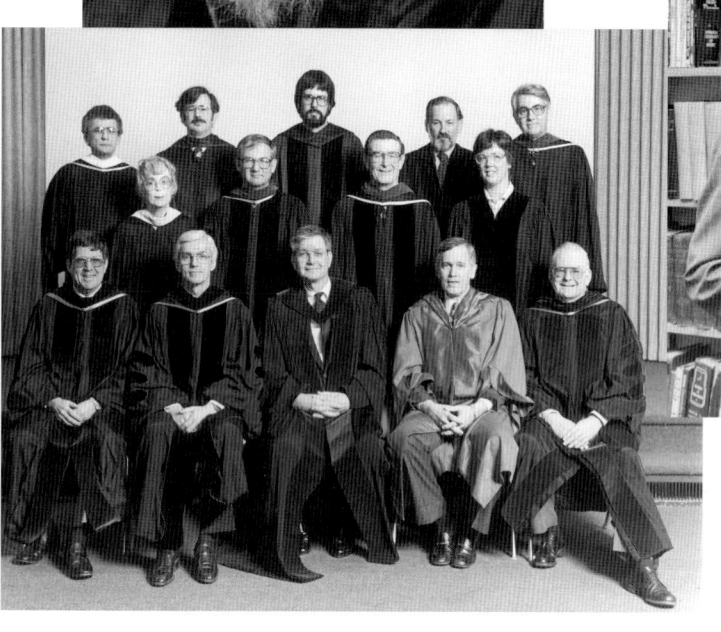

Members of the Phillips Seminary faculty and administration in 1986. Front row, left to right, Dr. Harold Hatt, Dr. Eugene Boring, Dr. Joe Jones, Dr. Roger Sizemore, Dr. John Sayre. Second row, Roberta Hamburger, Dr. David Richards, Dr. Rhodes Thompson, Mary Knutsen. Third row, Dr. Gary Johnson, Dr. Leo Perdue, Dr. Mark Toulouse, Dr. Stuart McLean, William Bryan.

the buildings and campus, the agreement between Phillips and the City of Enid appeared to be a loan.

An appeal from Judge Pickens' favorable ruling ultimately approving the sale/lease back plan was taken to the Oklahoma Supreme Court, which in a 7-2 landmark decision interpreting the freedom of religion clause of both the federal and state constitutions (*Burkhardt v. City of Enid*, 771 P.2d 608), upheld Judge Pickens in all respects. Phillips was represented by Enid attorney Stephen Jones and attorney Bryce Kennedy appeared for the City of Enid.

To comply with the judge's order, Phillips' trustees voted to separate the school from any operation of the seminary and prohibit any university trustee from serving as a trustee of the seminary.

In a major departure from past practices, the school's covenant with the Christian Church was modified.

Five Enid citizens, the mayor, and a member of the Enid City Council were made non-voting members of the Phillips board of trustees. Once this was done, on December 15, 1987, Judge Pickens approved the revised plan. Of the $14.3 million to be paid for Phillips' buildings and campus, $12 million would be placed in interest bearing accounts to provide scholarships and to increase student enrollment. An improved accounting system was implemented to watch over public money and university officials agreed to pay fair market value for the buildings and campus should they decide to repurchase. This removed the appearance of a loan by the city to the school that was prohibited by the Oklahoma constitution. In addition, the official relationship between the school and the Christian Church (Disciples of Christ) was reworded. On March 25, 1988, the ownership of the Phillips campus was officially transferred to the City of Enid. The university's board of trustees then leased the campus for $1,000 per month.

Even though Phillips did not own its own campus, there was no lessening of its commitment to training Christian leaders nor did it lose its close connection to the Disciples. "The school did not go secular," observed Janetta Cravens, "We still had chapel and religious studies." Phillips continued to offer a major in religion and administrators did not forget former President Briggs' admonition that "a Christian education was the hope of the world."

Phillips President Dr. Joe R. Jones, who, according to attorney Stephen Jones, was emotionally exhausted by his successful efforts to save the school, resigned effective May 31, 1988, to accept a position with the Christian Theological Seminary in Indianapolis, Indiana.

Dr. Robert Peck was appointed interim president and then president. During his March 31, 1990 inauguration, the university hosted a Renaissance Celebration to give outsiders a look at the school and to thank the citizens of Enid for helping the university keep its head above water. The celebration included a trolley ride, a country barbecue, displays, speeches and lectures, and an inaugural ball.

One of the programs that flourished during the Peck administration was Phillips University–Japan. In 1988, an agreement had been reached with the Kyoto Institute of Technology (KIT) in Japan for as many as 50 students to attend classes each year on the Phillips campus in Enid and at the Phillips Science Camp in Colorado. The agreement brought needed tuition revenues and the Kyoto Institute agreed to pay Phillips $100,000 a year for the right to use Phillips' name in recruiting activities.

Japanese education officials looking for an American partner found a willing prospect in President Peck. Dr. Robert Simpson, who headed the Phillips program in Japan in later years, remembered, "Dr. Peck believed that the American future rested with the Pacific Rim."

In 1989, Phillips established a 12-acre branch campus at the Kyoto Institute. All students were required to fulfill Phillips degree requirements including a one-year residency at the Enid campus. The same year, a branch campus of the Kyoto Institute was opened in Osaka, and in 1990, another branch campus was opened in Uji. Faculty members from Enid taught the classes in Japan and in August of 1989 the North Central Association of Colleges and Schools accredited Phillips' Japanese campus. By the beginning of 1990, there were approximately 2,200 students enrolled at Phillips' Japanese branches. In 1995, the branch campuses were reorganized as Phillips University International in Japan.

Stephen Jones remembered the value of the Phillips connection with Japan, "Relations with our Japanese partner were difficult, but the Japanese campus gave Phillips a presence in the Land of the Rising Sun and also made it possible for numerous Phillips students from Japan to come to Enid and for faculty members on the Enid campus to travel to Japan. It also represented a very important source of revenue for Phillips."

Dr. Simpson said, "Our presence afforded students who had fallen out of step with the lock-step educational system in Japan the opportunity to receive a high quality college education." The Japanese system also provided Phillips with outstanding instructors whom the government had forced to retire at the age of 65.

Japanese students studied English while engaged in their other studies in arts and sciences, taught mostly in Japanese. Phillips had rejected the idea that all classes would be taught in English, the norm for other American universities with branch campuses in Japan.

Three popular Phillips professors who served the university and its students for decades. Left to right, Dr. John Ireland, Dr. Edward Jorden, and Dr. Beth "Barracuda" Murphy.

The building on campus known as the "White House" was used for many purposes over the decades, as evidenced by a sign held by two students in 1987.

Economic Woes: The Eighties and Nineties 125

In 1987, Charlotte Kroeker was professor of piano and chair of the Phillips Fine Arts Department. From its inception, Phillips provided quality training for music and art students.

Dr. Roy Rakestraw was professor of mathematics. Phillips offered both basic and innovative math courses that rivaled those of state colleges and universities.

A group of students from Phillips University–Japan visiting the Enid campus in 1989. The Phillips program offered an alternative in higher education to the highly-structured colleges and universities in Japan.

Phillips became such a household word in Japan that a crossword puzzle in Japan's most widely read English language newspaper used "Enid" as the answer to "a four letter word that is the home of Phillips University." There was no doubt that Phillips was the best known American university in western Japan.

Jeanne Marie Kohr was a Phillips student who went to Japan for the two-semester exchange program. She said, "The skills I gained went far beyond just learning a little of the Japanese language. I learned self-confidence and had the opportunity to see what it feels like to be a minority. I was able to study the way in which culture and language affect world-view and philosophy."

The Phillips experiment in Japan was innovative, but was short-lived. Dr. Simpson explained, "Japanese universities are hard to get into, but easy to graduate from. All a student must do is to enroll for eight semesters and get an automatic degree. That did not fit well with the American expectation of four years of study that might not result in a degree. Once the difference was discovered, enrollment declined significantly."

Some of President Peck's decisions, including shutting down the school's baseball program, were not popular with some students and supporters of the university athletics.

Despite its national recognition as one of the country's finest private liberal arts universities, some Enid leaders wanted to sell the campus to the state. Enid business leaders represented a majority of the board's executive committee, but not nearly a majority of the entire board of trustees. Among the Enid board members were those such as Walter Scheffe, who was devoted to the university and gave of time and treasure to sustain it. Other Enid members, however, were less enthusiastic about the survival of Phillips as a private institution and did not want it to survive, preferring a state degree-granting institution.

ACADEMIC EXCELLENCE

American college experts recognized the excellence of academics at Phillips in the 1980s and 1990s. In 1986, the Fund for the Improvement of Postsecondary Education (FIPSE), a grant program of the U.S. Department of Education, funded a special project at Phillips to introduce classic texts into the university's core curricula. Two years later, FIPSE director Dr. Charles H. Karelis cited Phillips as one of the most promising projects his agency was funding. Phillips was one of only 45 colleges and universities nationwide to be awarded an unprecedented second grant to improve undergraduate curricula.

In 1989, *U.S. News and World Report* ranked Phillips the ninth best regional liberal arts college in the nation. That ranking was duplicated by the magazine in its annual "America's Best Colleges" report in 1992. Phillips was the only Oklahoma college included in the ranking that compared 400 regional liberal arts schools in the country. The magazine compared schools based upon quality of student body and faculty, reputation for academic excellence, the school's overall financial resources, and the level of student satisfaction as measured by the school's ability to graduate students it admits as freshmen.

In 1993, *U.S. News and World Report* moved Phillips to number five among the nation's private liberal arts colleges and universities. The national ranking was well deserved. Eighty-five percent of Phillips pre-law and pre-med majors were accepted to graduate schools of their choice. Phillipians scored highest among state schools on the Oklahoma Teacher Certification Test. Seventy percent of all accounting majors passed all parts of the Certified Public Accountant (CPA) exam on their first sitting. The 13:1 student/faculty ratio provided a highly regarded, personalized program of study. Phillips' Japanese campus was the largest American branch campus in Japan.

Clown Alley was a clown ministry group that helped people through the act of clowning. In 1989, members of the group were, front row, left to right, Angela Hermanzski, Rhonda Sommers. Back row, Brenda Dryburg, Gwen Poland, Elizabeth Johnson, Heather Fitzgerald. In the center is Laura Newman.

A benefit of Phillips' Sweden exchange program was that Swedish students came to the Enid campus. Marie Karlsson was a Swedish art student at Phillips in 1992.

The 1991-1992 staff of *The Haymaker*, the student newspaper voice of Phillips University since 1929. Left to right, Holly Hill, Jeanne Kohr, Scott Hemphill, Ali Gilmore, Cindy Lindsay, and editor Mindy Terry.

Longtime Phillips supporter Nancy Davies of Enid served as chair of the Phillips University Board.

Some on the Phillips administration team believed that the survival of the university could only be guaranteed if Phillips repurchased its campus. The possibility for that came sooner than expected. Within a year of the court's approval of the sale of Phillips to the City of Enid, university officials made plans to repurchase the campus.

In an agreement formalized on May 1, 1993, Phillips paid the City of Enid $2.5 million for the campus and $12 million for the bonds issued to support the school. At the same time Phillips officials agreed to sell the Enid Higher Education Program 21 acres of land for a 36,000-square foot building to house a university center offering classes from Northwestern Oklahoma State University, Oklahoma State University, and Northern Oklahoma College. The $162,525 cost of the land was deducted from the buy back price of Phillips.

News of the repurchase of the Phillips University campus was well received by students and faculty who hosted a party for citizens of Enid. A

128 IN REVERENCE WE STAND

Dr. Robert D. Peck spoke at commencement on May 1, 1994. Peck served as president of Phillips University from 1989 to 1993 and chancellor of the university from January to July of 1994.

The Phillips Ambassadors in 1992. Members of the group volunteered their time to perform in communities and churches far and near. Women, left to right, director Karen Lauer Ellis, Laine James, Cindy Lindsay, Jodie Barnett, Ali Gilmore, and Vicki Brazeal. Men, left to right, Rich Bruhn, Chuck Kemp, Eric Thomas, Ray Hilligoss, and Rod Benham.

parade down Broadway culminated in a celebration that night, including fireworks that illuminated the sky over University Lake.

There was an air of new optimism after the repurchase. Dr. John Ireland said, "You can't see it, but it's there. The feeling is evident. We're feeling like winners again . . . and that's half of what we need to win the race."

However, the repurchase of the university and its campus depleted much of the Phillips endowment fund. It also eliminated the approximately $1 million Phillips received annually from the City of Enid. To offset the losses, Phillips officials immediately launched a fund raising campaign.

Despite the constraints of smaller budgets, Phillips continued to offer students a wide variety of learning and social experiences. Dr. Tanya Whitmer Young remembered, "There were so many things to do . . . ice-skating with the Science Club and Dr. Beth Murphy, Quiz Bowl, Red Pepper pledge season, host families on band tours, volunteering at Leonardo's Discovery Warehouse, making pottery in the Art Building . . . and even a literature course solely about the legends of King Arthur."

Music therapy was a unique program that set Phillips apart from other schools in the early 1990s. Music therapy is the use of music by a professional music therapist to promote positive changes in behavior and overall rehabilitation and maintenance of mental and physical health. Sheri Wise, who after graduation established a music therapy program for terminal patients at the Kansas City, Missouri, Hospice, studied under music therapy professors Dr. Juanita McElwain and Dr. Cynthia Colwell. Sheri remembered, "I learned so much about the power of music . . . how music could be used to alleviate headaches."

A Somatron vibroacoustic chair sat in the Music Therapy lab. Many stressed-out Phillips students were given the opportunity to sit, listen, and feel the music throughout their bodies during multiple research projects conducted by music therapy students.

Financial problems shut down the Phillips Swedish exchange program in 1992. Professor Paul Denny took the last group of students to the Mullsjo campus in south-central Sweden. At a ceremony on the last day of the trip, eyes glistened and presents were exchanged in memory and thanks for the bond shared between the two countries in what was the nation's oldest European exchange program of any private university.

Trustees looked for ways to maximize income. Adopting a strategy proposed by President Peck designed to fill dorm rooms and help cover fixed costs on the campus, they offered free tuition for many students, a move that sparked an increase in enrollment. By the beginning of the fall semester of 1994, Phillips was forced to cut off freshmen enrollment because classrooms and dorm rooms were filled to

Economic Woes: The Eighties and Nineties

Dr. Jerry Turpin wrote, produced, and directed the play *Four Women West*, which was performed in the spring of 1993. Five cast members were left to right, Beth Chapman, Janetta Cravens, Jennifer Ahart, Faye Kiryakakis, and Audrey Spindle.

Sheldon Elliott, president of Phillips University from 1995 to 1996, right, introduces Richard T. Anderson as interim chancellor in 1994. Anderson was director of graduate studies before assuming the chancellor's post that he served in until 1995.

High school students from across the region attended the annual Tri-State Band Festival on the Phillips campus. The festival was one of the most attended festivals of its kind in the nation.

capacity. The first co-ed dorm was allowed on campus to make room for everyone.

But the prosperity was short-lived and soon the university was again facing financial difficulties. As the financial condition of the school worsened, some members of the board wanted to sell the campus back to the City of Enid. However, this move was opposed by its new chairman, Nancy Davies, and a majority of board members.

In 1994, Dr. Don Heath, a 1958 graduate of Phillips, replaced Dr. Peck as president. Heath was the first president of the university to be both an alumnus and a tenured faculty member. Heath, who had taught at Phillips for 27 years and had served as associate vice president for academic affairs and chairman of the Department of Religion and Philosophy, remained president until 1995. While Heath was president of Phillips, Richard T. Anderson served as chancellor of the university.

Heath's relationship with the North Central Accrediting Agency was key in keeping its confidence in Phillips for as long as it did. Anderson had been associated with Phillips for a long time and was also a source of stability during the difficult period.

When President Heath resigned, Sheldon Elliott, chairman of the university's board of directors, became interim Phillips president and an oversight committee was appointed by the board of trustees to assist him. Born in Paraguay of Disciples missionaries, Elliott moved to Enid in

130 IN REVERENCE WE STAND

For decades, members of the Enid community and students at Phillips University combined their talents to form the Enid-Phillips Symphony. In this photograph, symphony members rehearse for one of their annual performances.

1938 with his family when his father was named assistant to President Briggs as director of stewardship. Elliott was a graduate of Phillips, and after a successful career as a geophysicist with Phillips Petroleum Company, he retired and in 1988 was named to the board of trustees of the university. In 1992, he became chairman of the board of trustees, remaining in that office until he was named president. Elliott served without pay for the two years of his presidency. He stepped down in the early spring of 1996 shortly after he learned that Dr. G. Curtis Jones, Jr., had made a formal application to the search committee and plans had been made for an interview with the board. Elliott had been instrumental in recommending that Jones take the helm of the university.

Of Elliott's service, Stephen Jones said, "He brought a businessman's approach to management which was sorely needed. Assisted by Burrell Richardson, vice president for finance, Elliott developed an innovative plan for a revolving million dollar line of credit to keep the university open."

The Environmental Science Club cleaned the lake area on Earth Day in 1994. Front row, left to right, Vanetta Wallace, Shelly Burdick, James Hulse. Back row, Nathan Arnett, Sonny Ali, Ed Eargle, Joe Miller.

Economic Woes: The Eighties and Nineties

PHILLIPS UNIVERSITY

TRUTH

HOPE OF THE WORLD

COMBINING FUN WITH SERVICE

All through the history of Phillips University, social/service clubs were extremely important to campus life. Members sponsored events to raise money for local and national charities, helped keep the campus clean and blooming with flowers, and created innovative ways to serve both fellow students and the citizens of Enid. In the final decade of Phillips, many clubs supported feeding programs for the less fortunate and homeless and volunteered at retirement homes and at Leonardo's Discovery Warehouse, an innovative children's center in Enid.

Clubs successfully mixed countless hours of public service with having fun. They hosted formals, dances, and parties. There was both competition and cooperation among the seven clubs that remained at the university until its close. Intramural sports competition was spirited, with members' pride on the line in everything from softball to volleyball. However, when there was a need on campus or in the community, clubs came together to jointly sponsor fund-raising events. Often, two or more clubs jointly hosted parties or dances on special occasions.

Lifetime friendships were made in Phillips' clubs. Group retreats helped students get to know each other better. Quiet rooms became filled with laughter and smiles when club members gathered.

Each club had a special song or songs that were memorized by pledges and never forgotten by members. The Tenth Muse song said, "The years I spent at Phillips U. are sweeter because of you." The Zonta maidens sang, "Zonta maidens, grateful for our great forefathers. Carry on to serve our brothers and to prove ourselves trustworthy." Some wives jokingly questioned the last lines of the Gridiron club song, "Sweethearts and wives may fail you, but old G.C. never will."

Financial problems of the university in the 1990s resulted in a new role for the clubs—fundraising. Clubs were asked to contact former members to seek contributions to Phillips.

The sense of belonging to a Phillips organization took on new meaning with the very life of the university on the line.

Comets, left to right, Tara Gomez, Natalie Beebe, Susan Morford, Wendy Mack, and Gracie Aguilera prepare for March Madness in 1997.

Partygoers at the Boxer Rebellion had to wear their favorite pair of boxer shorts to be admitted.

In 1994, the president of the Zonta Club was Jennifer Redding, right, and the Zonta Brave was Scott Anderson.

The Comets, founded in 1940, was public service minded. Members coordinated Easter egg hunts at Booker T. Washington School in Enid, raised money for food drives, big brothers/big sisters, and Habitat for Humanity, and helped freshmen move into university dorms. For social activities, they hosted an all-school formal, a lil' bro and lil' sis party, and October Fest, complete with chicken dances, yodeling, and tug of war contest. Former Comet Club president Julie Bunton said, "With angels as our symbol, it gave us a sense of peace, safety, and purity." The Comets had a scriptural foundation, Luke 2:52—"And Jesus grew in wisdom and in stature, and in favor with God and man."

The Varsity Club began each fall semester with an event called the Boxer Rebellion. The men of Varsity comprised a close-knit group who worked together for the Four Pillars of the club: scholarship, service, fellowship, and unity. The "V-man" could be found in many leadership positions around the campus. Varsity was formed in 1939. In 1993, the club held a Varsity Olympics and sponsored a youth soccer team coached by Varsity alum Kevin Klamm.

The Zonta Club was organized at Phillips in 1926 and celebrated many Native American ideas. In 1993, the club co-sponsored a new service project for the Enid public school system—School and Family Enrichment (S.A.F.E.). Alisa West, the 1997 Zonta president, reflected, "Zonta taught me more about time management, organization, and leadership than any college course could do." One of the final Zonta projects was to participate in a community-wide effort to build a huge outdoor playground for children in Enid. The Zonta motto was "Forward forever, backward never."

The Red Pepper Club was re-activated in 1991 after ceasing existence in 1952. It was one of the oldest clubs on campus, established in 1923. The ten charter members of the new club included the traditions of pep and enthusiasm for the school plus the ideals of individuality, social awareness, and service to the community. Jeanne Marie Kohr helped breathe new life into the Red Peppers. She remembered, "Some of our first meetings were gut-wrenching—forming a mission statement, writing a constitution, baking pies for the homeless in the Gantz kitchen. Through it all, we remained open to the idea that a small group of dedicated women could, in fact, change the world."

134 In Reverence We Stand

In this 1994 photograph, Lady Dana Gerardy is surrounded by her knights.

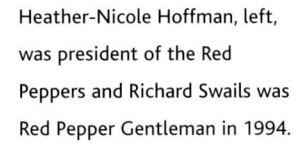

Heather-Nicole Hoffman, left, was president of the Red Peppers and Richard Swails was Red Pepper Gentleman in 1994.

The ladies of Tenth Muse in 1994 held a bowl-a-thon to support cancer research and auctioned a Homecoming Quilt to aid flood victims in Missouri and Kansas.

Geoff Beaty looks stressed after pressing the buzzer during competition as a member of the Gridiron Quiz Bowl Team.

The Camelot Club was founded in 1947 on the ideals of chivalry, honesty, and responsibility. In the latter years of Phillips, many campus leaders were members of Camelot. The Knights of Camelot participated in a variety of service projects, including coaching a grade school quiz bowl team, assisting at Leonardo's Discovery Warehouse, and babysitting for a mother's day out at Central Christian Church. For fun, they joined with the Zontas to sponsor the infamous CameZontalot Spooktaculur Halloween party.

Members of Tenth Muse, organized in 1927, were proud of their tradition to promote loyalty in service to school, friends, and God. Members found Romans 12:4-5 a guiding principle— "For as in one body we have many members, and not all the members have the same function, so we, who are many, are one body in Christ, and individually we are members of one another."

The Gridiron Social Service Club was founded in 1922 and was the oldest club on campus. In 1996, Gridiron members rebuilt the volleyball courts in front of the dorms and fielded strong intramural teams. 1996 Gridiron president Tim Drake said, "Gridiron gave me the opportunity to make some of the best friends I ever had and taught me to respect the traditions of Phillips."

Economic Woes: The Eighties and Nineties

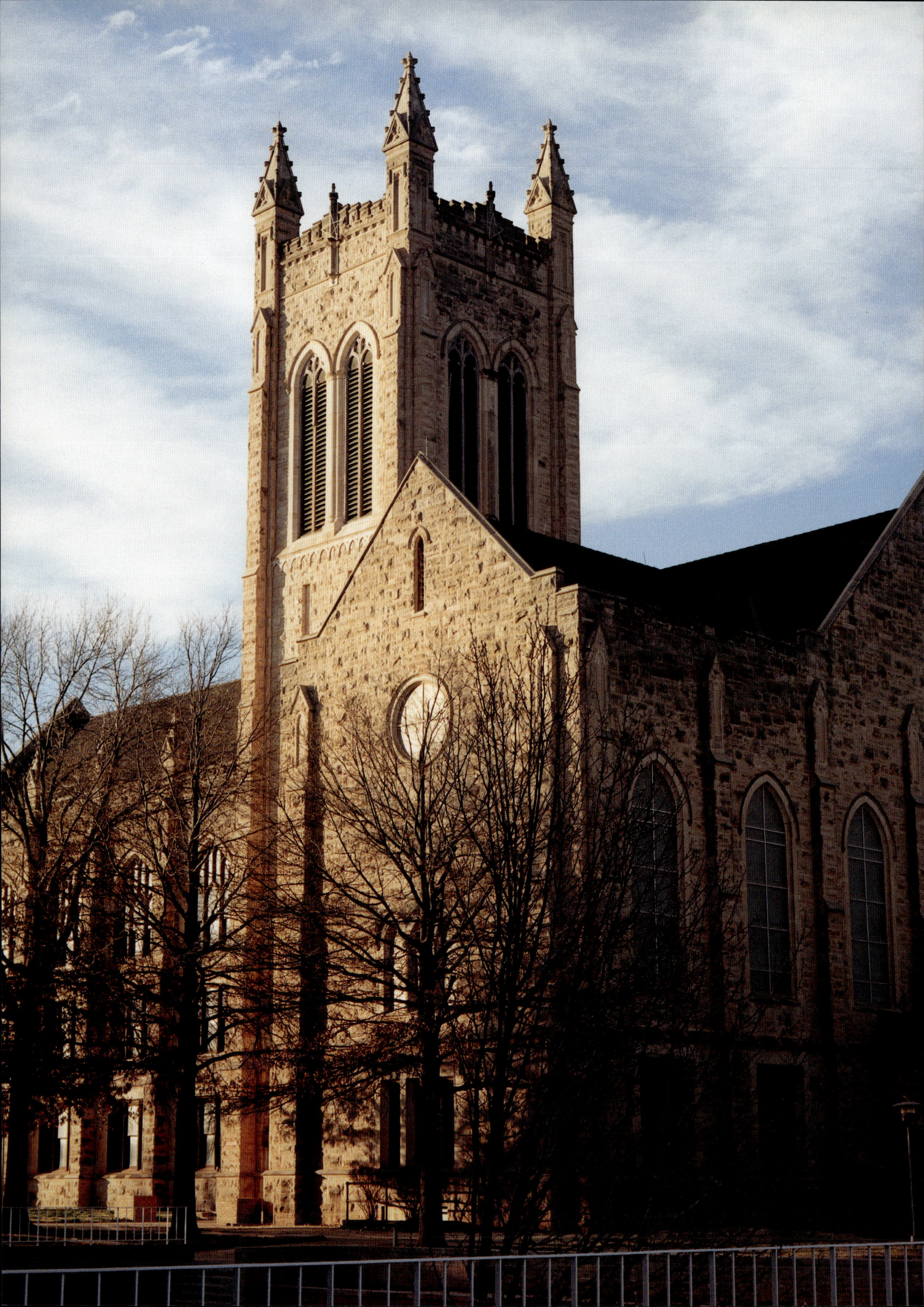

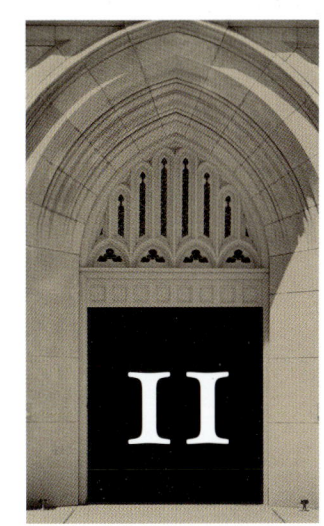

A Christian Learning Experience

THE IMPORTANCE of the Christian atmosphere on the Phillips University campus cannot be overstated. Students learned to respect the Christian heritage of the university and knew the high moral standard of conduct that was expected of them. As Reverend Don Alexander, longtime minister of Oklahoma City's First Christian Church, said, "The Christian atmosphere permeated every aspect of the university—it was a positive effect on both classroom and social activities." There is no doubt that the Christian influence made better citizens of the men and women who graduated from the university. Dr. Jerry Mash said Phillips was a school with a clear vision of what it was to the Church.

Above: Wherever they went, Phillips alumni tended to gather together. This is the Washington, D. C., Capital Area Phillipian Society on October 25, 1942. First row, left to right, Dorothea Harms, Henry Dugan, and Robert Geil. Second row, left to right, John Harms holding his daughter Mary Frances, Ivan Dugan, Hazel Carter, Virginia Davis, Mr. and Mrs. Maupin, and Mr. and Mrs. Glen Geil with their son, Earl. Third row, left to right, Lola Radcliffe; Pearl Harms, Gretchen Dugan, Clifford Carter, unidentified, and Ruth Gould.

Part of being a family is helping needy members of the family. Phillips was always available to help people in need. Like so many other Oklahomans who came to campus during a time of need, Jack and Lola Taylor moved their home and business to Enid from Vinita, Oklahoma, in 1984 to serve as both photographers and teachers. Jack operated the school's photographic studio until retirement in 1997.

"There was a passion for excellence and academic quality," Mash reflected, "but it was defined by the passion for the advancement of God's Kingdom."

The emphasis on creating a Christian learning atmosphere affected the way faculty were hired. Former chancellor Richard Anderson remembered, "The usual practice was for departments to recommend only Christians for vacant faculty positions . . . The great majority of faculty selected were able scholars . . . with high academic standards, and they practiced their Christian beliefs without proselytizing." However, adherents of other world religions also became members of the faculty.

138 In Reverence We Stand

"It was not an impersonal atmosphere," Don Angle said, "The professors impacted students' lives outside the classroom as well. They set examples of personal integrity. There was a real spirit of service to others that prevailed and influenced students for the rest of their lives. Attitudes learned at Phillips carried over to later lives."

The administration gave faculty great freedom to teach. The faculty always exercised primary control over academic standards because individuals they selected served on the curriculum and academic standards committee. Any measure passed by committee did not take effect until approved by the entire faculty. While the university president had an absolute veto power, it was rarely used. One president, Dr. Hallie Gantz, never used the veto. Chancellor Anderson remembered, "Although he would strongly argue for a different position at times, he would never say, 'I told you so,' even if future events proved him correct."

High admission standards set the tone for the type of student who attended Phillips. However, an unusually well-dedicated and caring faculty often looked beyond academic records and discovered students with less than desired past performance who could be rescued by faculty members who were willing to take the extra time to assist such students.

There were several fields of study at Phillips that required constant attention to very high academic standards. The Division of Science and Mathematics took great care to prepare students for medical school and science careers and never had a pre-med student who had been recommended by the faculty fail in medical school. Phillips became well known for sending highly qualified students to medical, osteopathic, nursing, pharmacy, medical technology, and dental schools. In addition, chemists, geologists, biologists, physicists, and mathematicians were graduated.

The Phillips administration made certain that Phillips laboratories were well equipped. Dr. Beth Murphy remembered, "All we had to do was to tell director of development Teri Holle what we wanted, how we would use it, and she did the rest." Graduates also helped the lab programs. When their companies were replacing equipment, Phillips often received the still-working instruments. Dr. Murphy said, "Many times, the older instruments were better for teaching because they did not have all the bells and whistles of newer models and were easier to keep in working order."

The Phillips board took a hands-on approach to helping the university excel. Once, when the chemistry lab needed new hoods, Sheldon Elliott heard about the need and appeared in the lab. He was horrified at the holes in the ducts and clanking motors and made the motion at the next board meeting to install new hoods.

Another special educational experience for the Phillips student was the small size of classes. Faculty understood that small classes meant more individualized instruction both in and out of the classroom. The result was an improved learning situation. A secondary effect was the development of long lasting friendships between faculty and students.

An example is Allison Tobola, who completed her undergraduate degree at the University of Science and Arts in Chickasha, Oklahoma, after the close of Phillips, and attended medical school at the University of Texas-Houston. Of her Phillips education, Tobola reflected, "I had professors who were extremely supportive. I could go to their offices anytime and their doors were always open."

Professors taught their own classes at Phillips, unlike large state universities at which graduate students often taught beginning classes. Faculty tried to coordinate the disciplines. The result was that papers presented in any class had to meet the same standards demanded by the English Department.

The Phillips faculty was always on the cutting edge of providing students with the latest information available in a field. One example was the Science Division that sponsored a Science Lecture Series at which professors or outside experts spoke to students. Professors hosted science fairs and lectured high school science classes when invited to do so.

From the early years of Phillips, science and mathematics were emphasized. One of the first college chemistry courses in the state was taught at Phillips. Faculty and students held that tradition closely. Photographs of early chemistry and physics laboratories hanging on the walls of the Science Building reminded them of their heritage of excellence.

One thing that remained unique to Phillips throughout its history was what many students called the "Phillips tradition." It was a bond between the university and its faculty and students that lasted far beyond one's college years. The Phillips community viewed itself as a family—a family that looked after one another, that made college fun, and promoted a Christian education. As Kirby Hughes Gould said, "Phillips was 'home,' not a mom and dad home, but a place which felt comfortable, friendly, nurturing, and fun." Dr. Jerry Mash remembered Phillips was like summer camp, "only you were given grades and a degree."

"Phillips had all the characteristics of a second family," said Bill Briggs, "by bonding students to each other through shared experiences of learning, persuasion, ritual, work, and social activities in small and large groups." Briggs equated the second family atmosphere at Phillips to that special feeling of members of a local church congregation.

A Christian Learning Experience

Professors at Phillips had a special availability to students and could be relied upon in times of need as a guide or confidant. They joined in sponsoring club activities and proved their humanness by poking fun at each other in humorous stunts at Stunt Night. Briggs remembered, "Their passion was the discipline they taught without a hidden agenda. Bible College professors challenged students to intellectually confront religious concepts that can't be proved but must be accepted on faith. No creeds of a church were taught." Jeanne Marie Kohr remembered, "The student body was encouraged to explore difficult questions of faith and religion in a safe and supportive environment."

Students were provided a wealth of viewpoints from outside the university. The first comprehensive academic conference was held in 1970 to commemorate the life and work of the great German philosopher George William Hegel, who is credited with reconstructing modern thought. Recognized Hegelian scholars were invited to address students and faculty. Many Phillips professors tied the conference to coursework in particular classes. In another conference, the achievements of Copernicus were studied.

In October and November of 1992, President Peck, assisted by a private contribution, invited the former Polish Ambassador to the United Nations, Stanislaw Pawlak, to give the annual Joe Jones and Sarah Jones Lectures. In addition, the veteran diplomat taught a class on the Cold War. Several hundred Enid residents and Phillips students attended Pawlak's historic address, giving an insider's view, "From the Other Side," of the Cold War conflict.

Not only experts, but also entertainers of the highest caliber were brought to the campus. Kirby Hughes Gould counts as the most significant event of her college career her participation in the Enid-Phillips University Symphony. She remembered, "Here in this little town I was performing on stage with Ethel Merman, Vincent Price, Ferrante and Teicher, and PDQ Bach. Those evenings in Briggs Auditorium were memorable and impressive."

Phillips professors were special and paid great attention to discussion and dialogue with students, unlike professors in other colleges that always had to be "right" and might become irritated when a student questioned his opinion. Connie Speer Cravens said, "Former students revere so many of the longtime professors at Phillips that this history would have to be doubled in size to mention them all."

There are hundreds of stories that reflect the "family" atmosphere at Phillips. Bill Nichols told the story of a 15-year-old who arrived on campus scared to death, but was taken in as a son, rather than just a number or a faceless student. Another student remembered Professor Lysle Mason spending countless hours outside the classroom tutoring her on complicated math concepts. And there is the story of Teresa Haney who worked in the Administration and Finance Office and went out of her way to resolve a big problem for one of the athletes. He was so relieved by Teresa's kindness, the six-foot, seven-inch young man cried unashamedly in her office.

When Jeanne Marie Kohr approached one of her professors about studying the function of pipe organs, he graciously offered to tutor her weekly, free of charge, during the summer months. Faculty members helped out in more than just academic situations. Jeanne remembered the occasion when she called a professor early one morning in a sheer panic—the toilet in her off-campus apartment was stopped up. The professor laughed at her predicament and graciously invited her to come to his home and borrow his plumbing tools.

M. Rick Hendricks was a shy freshman having a hard time making friends when Dr. Roger Carstensen showed up at his door and said in his booming voice, "Rick, I heard you got a box of cookies from your mother today. Are you going to invite me in or leave me standing out here?"

Within minutes, word of Dr. Carstensen's presence in the dorm spread. The room filled with students and the professor, whom students believed was surely consulted by God each day, regaled them with stories and kept his audience in stitches.

It was an example of the attention that professors gave students. Not only did the professor know that a student had received a box of cookies in the mail, he also knew that the student could use a little attention and guidance as well.

The cookie incident was certainly not unique. Hendricks reflected, "Professors at Phillips not only knew their students, they took time to become involved in their lives, and in that way, communicated some of their passion for their subject and instilled in their charges a passion for learning itself."

Janetta Cravens remembered, "Professors noticed when you were ill. They knew when you missed class. Professors taught you, one-on-one, how to outline your paper better so you might be a better writer. They cared about how you expressed yourself, how you thought through things, and what you eventually did with your knowledge. It was not sharing knowledge for knowledge's sake—it was sharing knowledge for people's sake."

University files are filled with letters from former students to faculty, thanking them for making their academic life brighter. After Susan Miller graduated in 1984, she wrote Dr. Russel Drumright, professor of education psychology, "I really learned a lot. You are very good at taking difficult informa-

Former students attended a 1993 symposium honoring Dr. Beth Murphy's 40 years of teaching at Phillips. Left to right, George Moore, M.D.; Michael Lambert, M.D.; Patrick Shaklee, Ph.D.; Ronda Voskuhl, M.D.; Dr. Murphy; Terry Lewis, Ph.D.; Susan Hauser, Ph.D.; Bard McMullen, M.D.; Charles Everly, Ph.D.; John Soper, Ph.D.; and Neil DeLapp, Ph.D.

tion and bringing it down to all levels .... As I continue my career as a teacher, I will try to remember to use so many of your positive qualities."

Dr. Drumright was at the forefront of the "teaching vs. research" controversy that plagued most college campuses in America. Some believed that professors should both teach and conduct research. Drumright favored the opposing viewpoint that most professors should concentrate on either research or teaching because both disciplines required different skills, different interests, and sometimes, different personalities.

Many former students believe that relationships developed while living on the Enid campus was the most important part of the Phillips experience. Jeanne Marie Kohr said, "It was a place which fostered constructive relationships, both inside and outside the classroom, that were integral to my growth and development in college years, and have continued to impact me even a decade later." Susan Morford, 1996 Homecoming Queen, and Representative Phillipian the following year, remembered, "Phillips' unique and intimate network provided a very special atmosphere for students whereby a multitude of one-on-one relationships were created, not just between students, but also with professors who connected on a personal level and were concerned with our lives even outside the classroom."

Barry Robinson, chairman of the Phillips board of trustees in 2003, agreed that personal relationships made his years at Phillips special, "The campus community was so small that everyone knew everyone else. An environment that stressed personal responsibility amidst intellectual inquiry—sprinkled with abundant fun and fellowship—led to personal connections that resulted in sustaining friendships and many, many marriages."

Robinson described what was happening at Phillips as a "nurturing environment." Forty years after his graduation, he remains grateful for the attitudes, approaches, and persistence of a number of faculty members. Journalism professor J. Louis Cozby, a war veteran and *Stars and Stripes* reporter, took Robinson under his wing and saw his potential in journalism. Margaret Edwards taught him an appreciation for correct use of the English language. Tibbie Shades helped him and other students develop writing skills so useful in careers and other applications. Don Seamans taught Old and New Testament courses that gave students a solid foundation in Bible study.

Attending Phillips was often a true family tradition. Among the many examples of multiple generations of the same family attending Phillips are Gene and Bonnie Frazier. The Fraziers, their children, and the spouses of their children all graduated from Phillips. Gene served two terms as Disciples Regional Minister for Oklahoma.

A Christian Learning Experience 141

Phillips alumnus Susan Pamerleau, left, rose to the rank of major general in the United States Air Force. Here she greets aviation author Charles Young, center, and Phillips librarian Rick Sayre.

Like many Phillips students during the Great Depression, Paul Sharp worked on campus to help pay his way through college. Sharp was editor of the 1938 *Phillipian* yearbook and the student newspaper. Sharp met his future wife Rose on the Phillips campus and later served as president of the University of Oklahoma.

Dr. Bill Snodgrass graduated from Phillips and became the first Oklahoman in history to win a Woodrow Wilson Scholarship. After receiving his Ph.D. from the University of Oklahoma, he returned to Phillips and taught until his untimely death in 1989. Of Snodgrass's teaching excellence, Richard Anderson said, "He was absolutely the best I have ever seen in terms of classroom presentations."

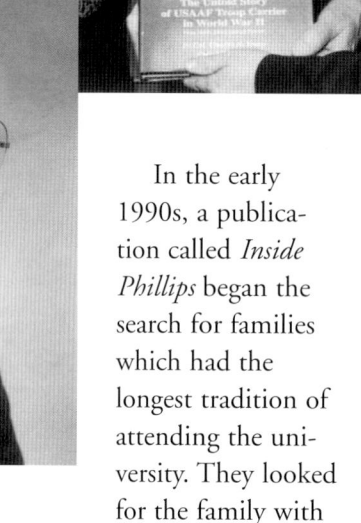

In the early 1990s, a publication called *Inside Phillips* began the search for families which had the longest tradition of attending the university. They looked for the family with the largest number of Phillipians and the family with the most generations of Phillipians.

After reviewing many entries detailing family histories, it was decided that the winner in the first category was the Lambert family, with 28 immediate family members graduating from Phillips. The Strain/Murphy family was second with 21 graduates. Placing third was the Smoot/Semones family with 17 graduates. In the "most generations" category, the family of Dr. Robert Young of Enid was the winner, with four generations of Phillipians. In second place, there was a 14-way tie with three generations of Phillips graduates.

Many students attended Phillips because their parents were graduates. Presidential scholar Jenni Gingerich came from Colorado Springs, Colorado, partly due to her mother being a Phillipian. She reflected, "At first, it was because my mom made me. Later, I could not imagine going to any other university."

Dr. Tanya Whitmer Young followed her parents and grandparents to Phillips. Her great grandfather, Thomas Holmes MacViers, was an early chief of maintenance at Phillips and helped build the Marshall Building in the late 1940s. When it came time for Tanya to pick a college in the early 1990s, she found Phillips to be her "home away from home." Her roommate's mother had been her mother's suite-mate a generation before. Many of her new friends' parents had been her parents' friends. Tanya met her husband, Jeremiah Young, in her first week on campus. It was a special time when Chaplain Kent Dorsey wed them in 1995 in the Bivins Chapel in the Marshall Building, built by Tanya's grandfather a half century before.

Many families assumed their children would attend college at Phillips—because they had, a generation before. Janetta Cravens grew up with stories of Phillips—from her parents, Ed Cravens, Jr. and Connie Speer Cravens, both Phillips graduates. She heard stories of the longevity of Phillips professors and wondered how wonderful the experience must have

142 In Reverence We Stand

been for faculty to stay so long at one institution. Janetta also heard about Phillips from her uncle, dean of students Pete Warren, and visiting ministers who had attended the university. Janetta was introduced to the Phillips Science Camp in Colorado because her parents had gone there as a young married couple and built a cabin for married students. She said, "There was a sense of ownership and awesomeness when I was at the Science Camp. My family helped make this place."

"Participating in Phillips because it was part of my family's story and heritage," Janetta remembered, "did not feel like playing out roles of identity or fulfillment, or even vicariousness. There was a greater sense of formation and involvement." Janetta said she attended Phillips, not because her parents went there, but because it was a place that would prepare her to be a person that represented the values she cherished in her family and because it would prepare her for her field. "Attending Phillips," she said, "was not just preparation to be a historian, musician, teacher, or whatever your vocation might be, it prepared you to be yourself." Janetta wrote, "I found my voice at Phillips."

The impact of the "Phillips experience" extended well beyond students and alumni. Each January, Phillips hosted Minister's Week, a definitive study and fellowship time for hundreds of ministers and their spouses from around the nation.

This three-day convocation, sponsored jointly by the university and the seminary, presented outstanding lectures and noted preaching personalities such as Dr. Fred Craddock, Dr. W.H. "Bill" Alexander, Barbara Brown Taylor, Tony Campolo, and G. Curtis Jones, Sr.

The flavor of the Phillips campus evoked fond memories of being back in seminary and provided a quality continuing education opportunity for ministers from many denominations. Reverend Don Alexander observed, "Bivins Chapel full of singing preachers was inspirational indeed!"

The proof of Phillips' excellence in academics lies with the astounding success of its graduates. "Phillips should be remembered," Barry Robinson wrote, "as a place that created leaders . . . leaders for the church and leaders in education, law, medicine, science, and in many other fields."

Kirby Hughes Gould said, "Future generations will know that Phillips' legacy rests in solid, committed people who know how to make a difference in their corner of the world."

The College of the Bible produced dozens of state secretaries and regional ministers and two general ministers and presidents of the national office of the Christian Church. In addition, numerous specialists in religious education who served in national and state offices of the denomination were graduates of Phillips, to say nothing of the hundreds of men and women who answered the call to serve in a local church.

Among alumni who served the church was George Oliver Taylor, who became the executive secretary of the Department of Religious Education of the United Christian Missionary Society and developed a total education program for the Christian Church. Spencer Austin was named national director of evangelism for the Disciples and later served as executive secretary of unified promotion in charge of raising missionary money for 70 agencies. Rolland Sheafor became executive director of the Board of Church Extension, Roland Huff was president of the Disciples of Christ Historical Society, and William Martin Smith was president of the Pension Fund. General minister and president Ken Teegarden directed the 1968 convention that revised the Christian Church (Disciples of Christ) constitution. Ronald Osborn served as president of the convention. Leon Whitney became vice president of financial management for the National Benevolent Association of the Disciples and Jim Reed was the first president of the Christian Church Foundation.

William T. Gibble was president and Cindy Ferguson Dougherty was the executive director of the National Benevolent Association. Duane Cummins was president of the Division of Higher Education and president of Bethany College, the institution of higher learning founded by Alexander Campbell in 1840. Jim Spainhower was state treasurer of Missouri, president of Lindenwood University, and president of the Division of Higher Education. These Phillips graduates and others had a major impact on the Disciples movement in the 20th century.

Even toward the end of Phillips' life as a university, Thursday morning chapel services emphasized the heritage of the university's Christian atmosphere. While some students did their homework or caught up on sleep, many other students attended University Worship in Bivins Chapel.

Rob Wonnell attended chapel to get "the extra push" he needed during the week. For Andrea Gould, chapel was personal. She said, "Being an active participant gives me the feeling that I am doing something for God instead of just watching other people." Chaplain Tammy Wooliver believed that chapel was a way to create unity among the student body, reflecting, "Chapel was the time to come together as a community to celebrate who we were…in the presence of God."

For all its years—during times of success and faltering—Phillips lived up to its motto that had been the creed of President Eugene S. Briggs: *Christian Education—the Hope of the World.*

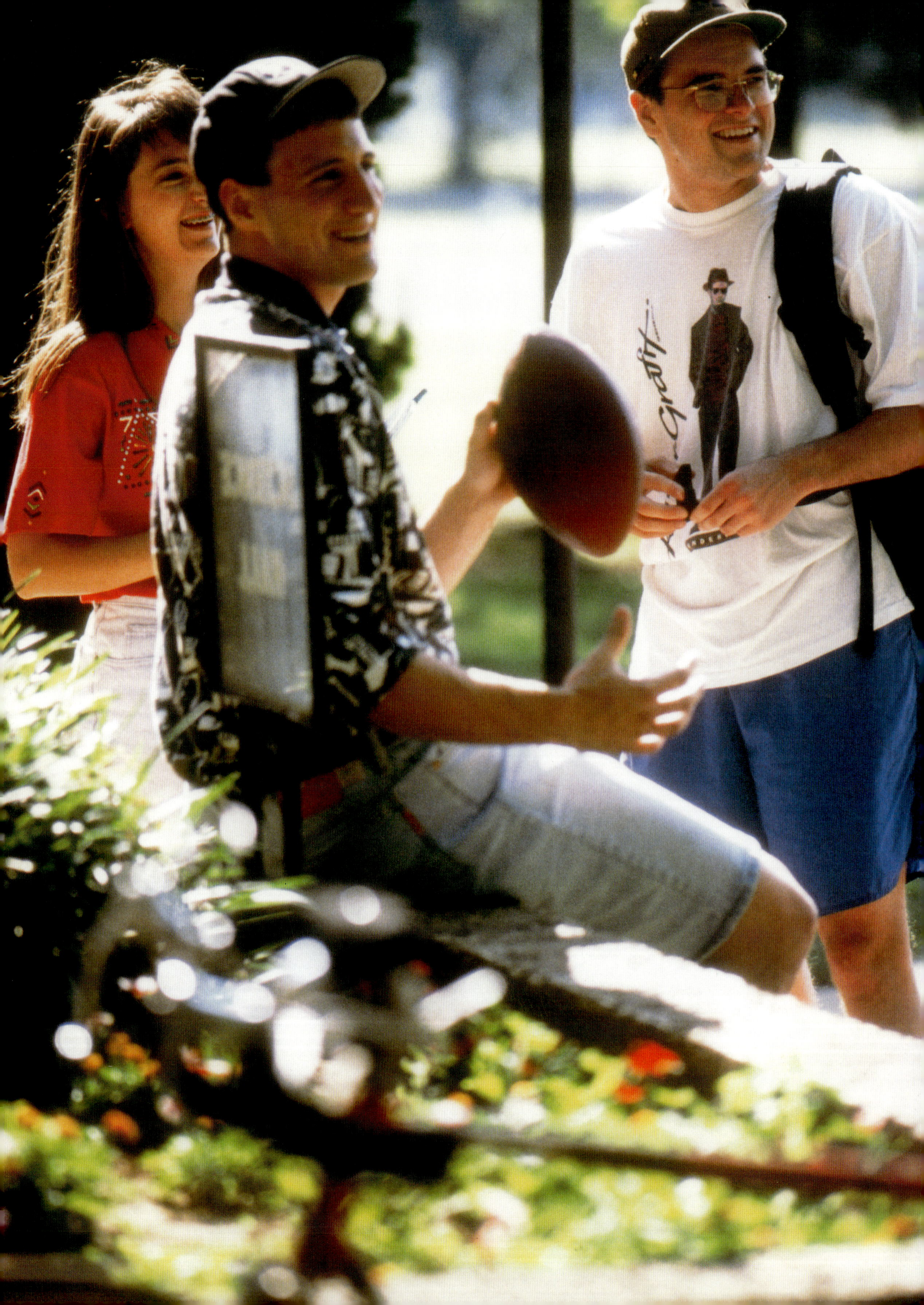

Excellence in Sports

FROM THE BEGINNING of Oklahoma Christian University, athletic competition was an important part of student life. The administration encouraged students to participate in both intercollegiate and intramural sports. A step toward an intercollegiate football program was taken in 1913 when Truman A. Copas was hired as physical education director and coach. The following year, on October 3, 1914, OCU officially launched its intercollegiate football program by losing to Oklahoma A&M, now Oklahoma State University, 134-0. The games were played on a large open area east of Old Main. Phillips also fielded intercollegiate basketball and baseball teams for the first time during the 1914-1915 school year. Until a gymnasium was completed, basketball games were played outdoors. The baseball schedule was limited to games with Methodist University, Oklahoma A&M, Conners Agricultural College, Henry Kendall College, Methodist College. The university's football team and other athletic teams were called the Lions until 1915.

Then came a major name change. The football field was used as a hay meadow in the off-season. Once when the football team was practicing, Professor Frank Wellman and Orville Chat were watching and yelled out "Are the boys making hay!" The name was picked up by Austin Cleveland, the athletic editor of the 1914 *Phillipian,* who called the field "Haymaker Meadow" as he reported on the football team. By November of 1915, *The Slate* was calling Phillips' football team the Haymakers.

Also in 1916, W. H. Cramblet was hired as the university's new coach. That same year Phillips fielded a track team, which, along with the baseball team, was second only in the state to the University of Oklahoma. Roy Curtis composed the Phillips song "Cheer, Cheer."

Cheer! Cheer! for victory,
Rip ram ba zoo
Phillips U
Maroon and White
Phillips might.
Our boys are beating,
Ring out the greeting,
Cheer! cheer! for victory,
Glorious triumph
We Proclaim
Deal the blow
'Gainst the foe
Hail the victory in Phillips name!

Although intercollegiate football was not officially organized at Oklahoma Christian University until 1913, students organized an informal football team in 1907.

The Haymakers hosted the major league Chicago White Sox in a 1916 exhibition game in one of the first baseball games played at Alton Field. The Haymakers lost 8-4 to the team that would soon become infamous because of the Black Sox scandal that blighted major league baseball immediately after World War I.

Cramblet compiled a disappointing record of three wins and four losses his first year and lost to OU 52-9 in 1917. As football fever swept the state, a group of local Enid businessmen offered to underwrite Phillips' athletic budget if the university would upgrade the competition and expand the athletic program. With such financial backing they hoped to bring the school into national prominence. To accomplish the task, John F. Maulbetsch, an all-American halfback at the University of Michigan in 1914-1916 was named coach and athletic director.

World War I shortened the 1918 football schedule and Maulbetsch was called to active duty with the Naval Aviation Corps after the second game, but continued to coach the team by mail. The Haymakers won four and lost one while outscoring their opponents 294 to 13 that year. Their only loss came to the University of Oklahoma 13-7 in a game played in Oklahoma City on November 23.

Maulbetsch returned for the 1919

The 1909 OCU tennis team. Front row, left to right, Charles Funk, John Harmon, unidentified, Frank Lash, Clyde Smith, and Ward S. Hutton. Second row, Paul Cook, E. A. Taylor, James Crain, Walter Friend, unidentified, William S. Rehorn, and Will Blackman. Top row, Claude C. Taylor and professor Rolla G. Sears. Note the freshman beanies worn by some of the players. The team was formed in 1908 by English Professor Roy J. Wolfinger who built a tennis court beside his home and organized a student tennis club.

Excellence in Sports 147

The 1909 Oklahoma Christian University men's baseball team included, front row, left to right, Artie Charlton, Roy Athey, Bill Frantz, Ed Shockley, unidentified, and unidentified. Second row, Jay Ratcliff, unidentified, Guy Pitts, Cliff White, Elmer Schenke, and Coach Bill Bates.

In 1916, Alton Field, named for local Enid merchant Harry Alton, became the new home of Phillips' football, baseball, and track teams. The field was the concept of T.T. Roberts, the school's financial secretary, and Dr. W. H. Cramblet, mathematics professor and football coach at Phillips. Alton Field was built east of University Lake, in a valley used to form a natural stadium. In cooperation with the City of Enid, 14,000 cubic yards of dirt was moved to extend and widen the valley to build a 400 feet by 400 feet athletic field. High embankments flanked three sides of the field. Two sections of concrete seats were built capable of holding 2,000 spectators.

season. Thirty players came out for practice. Fewer than 20 remained for the season opener and the 1919 Phillips' football team quickly acquired the nickname The Iron Men. Maulbetsch was such a disciplinarian he required his players to carry a rulebook at all times and gave frequent quizzes over game rules. Under his guidance, 1919 became the greatest season in Phillips University football history, capped by a 10-0 victory over the University of Texas on October 11. Four players, Doug Roby, Steve Owen, Dutch Strauss, and Ev Shelton, became national sports figures.

Roby was a halfback on the 1919 team. He then transferred to the University of Michigan. After his intercollegiate career, he became president of the United States Olympic Committee and a member of the International Olympic Committee.

Shelton, who had played halfback in the American Expeditionary Force football finals, went on to be head basketball coach at Phillips, the University of Wyoming, and Sacramento State University. He was inducted into the Naismith Basketball Hall of Fame in 1979.

The 1910 women's basketball team posing with their letter sweaters. Among the members were Pearl McClain, Bonnie Goode, Temple Palmer, Rhea Holland, Etta Charlton, Dahl Carrier, and Elizabeth Penn. Bill Bales was the coach and Ethel McCafferty was the team manager.

Steve Owen was All-State guard for Phillips in 1918 and 1919. From Aline, Oklahoma, he was described by the yearbook as having a "knack of hurling his elephantine proportions into an opposing line in such a way that it swept clear the whole side of the line."

Arthur "Dutch" Strauss was a 200-pound fullback who in 1917 scored a touchdown and drop-kicked a 55-yard field goal against Oklahoma A&M in spite of having two broken ribs. After college, Strauss played professional football with Kansas City.

Without a doubt the most famous football player from Phillips was Steve Owen. Born in Cleo Springs, Oklahoma, Owen went to high school in nearby Aline and then enrolled in Phillips. After playing at Phillips, Owen played professional football with the Kansas City Cowboys from 1924 until 1925, the Cleveland Bulldogs in 1925, and the New York Giants from 1926 until 1931. In 1931, he was named the Giants' head coach, a position he held until 1954. He won 153 NFL games, lost 108, and tied 17, for the ninth best record in NFL history. In 1933, Owen coached the New York Giants in the first official NFL championship game and lost to the Chicago Bears 23-21. Owen was credited with inventing the "umbrella pass defense," which became the zone defense, and a two-platoon playing system. In 1966, Owen was inducted into the Professional Football Hall of Fame.

The Iron Men began the 1919 season by defeating Kingfisher College 90-0, a game in which Strauss scored five touchdowns. Kingfisher made only one first down the entire game. In the second game, Phillips defeated Northwestern State Teachers College 27-0. The third game was against the University of Texas Longhorns. Roby had suffered a shoulder separation and would not be available for the Texas game. However, John Levi, a Cheyenne-Arapaho and the 1,001st student to enroll at Phillips, reported to practice five days before the game with Texas and became the team's punter. Phillips quickly jumped out to a 10-0 lead.

Excellence in Sports 149

Members of the 1922 Letter Club at Phillips. Members were men who lettered in any sport played at Phillips University.

The Philliboosters was the official pep organization of Phillips University in 1924. The yearbook commented, "The famous lock-step will long be remembered by all those who attended the games."

Douglas Roby was captain and fullback of the 1918 Phillips University football team.

However, the Longhorn depth—Texas played 35 men and Phillips 12—began to wear the Iron Men down. To preserve the victory, Maulbetsch had Levi punt on first down and then play defense. According to Owen, "John Levi could kick a ball a mile . . . and we played in Texas territory all day." After the game, the Texas athletic director proclaimed, "Phillips has the best team on the gridiron in this section of the country."

The season ended with a 57-0 defeat of Denver University. The only blemish on the Iron Men's 1919 record was a 7-7 tie with Oklahoma A&M.

The first season Phillips fielded a girl's basketball team that competed against other colleges was 1919.

Phillips, Northwestern State Teachers College, and Southwestern College at Winfield, Kansas, were the only other colleges in the region that allowed girl's intercollegiate sports so the three teams spent each season playing one another. Carol William, Lucille Babcock, Lena Dewell, Letha Snawder, Nina Smith, Elizabeth Sturman, Lenora Hinson, and Mary Schulter formed the initial team. They won only one of the four games they played. Under coach Ray Ballard, the Lady Haymakers lost only one game in the following two seasons, winning the Oklahoma Basketball Championship in 1920.

Phillips High School, the university's preparatory school, began a football program in 1919. Although only two students had played football before, the squad compiled a record of eight wins and one loss.

In 1920, Phillips joined the Southwest Athletic Conference along with Baylor University, Southwestern University, Texas A&M University, Oklahoma A&M, the University of Texas, and the University of Arkansas.

The 1920 football team managed four straight victories before beginning Southwest Conference play and losing to Texas A&M, Arkansas, and Texas.

Following the 1920 athletic season, Phillips left the Southwest Conference and participated as an independent in intercollegiate athletics. Eventually Phillips joined the Big Four Conference with the University of Tulsa, Oklahoma City University, and Oklahoma Baptist University.

On September 13, 1921, the Phillibooster Club was organized to support Haymaker athletics. Wearing white pants, maroon jackets, and a fez adorned with a tassel, the Philliboosters performed at every intercollegiate sports event at Phillips. Limited to 50 male members, the group was overseen by a yell leader and student marshals.

M. M. "Tubby" McIntyre became football coach at Phillips in 1921, having moved to Phillips from the University of West Virginia. McIntyre's second Phillips football team in 1922 was proclaimed the "Oklahoma Intercollegiate Football Champion." The Haymakers outscored their opponents 403 to 73 and lost only to the University of Texas in a game played in Austin by a score of 13-7.

The 1922 Phillips girl's basketball team won seven games and lost one to win the Oklahoma State Basketball Championship. The men's basketball team was 14-12. The Phillips High School girl's basketball team won all 17 of its games, scoring 548 points to its opponents' 162.

The girl's basketball team won another State Basketball Championship in the 1924-1925 school year. That same year, Phillips High School closed, ending its athletic history.

The 1926, 1927, and 1928 men's basketball teams won 84 games and lost only 23 for a .820 winning percentage. The 1928 Fighting Haymaker men's basketball team was used to promote Phillips University by playing a 16-game West Coast tour.

The team made a good enough impression on the nation's sportswriters that the school received much needed press coverage. When the players returned to Enid they were invited to play in the national tournament held in Kansas City, Missouri. Unfortunately, they lost in the opening round.

The Gridiron Club survived the football days of Phillips and became a service club. In 1937, members were, left to right, front row, Paul Cook, Vance Mills, Edgar Weeks, William Gibble, Wilfred Walker, Lawrence Bowlby, Martin Davis. Second row, Sterling Wees, Raymond Alber, Russell Palmer, Ardell Smiley, Ralph Williamson, Kenneth Weaber, Gene Moore. Third row, Roy Cody, Homer Harmon, James Behler, Harry Allen, Leslie Walker, Wicky Kingen.

Excellence in Sports 151

The infamous Phillips athletic bus. Equipment was hauled in the back of the bus or on top. Curtains on the windows allowed the student-athletes to sleep during their trips.

The Phillips University baseball team in 1961. Front row, left to right, Max Deffenbaugh, Larry Halbert, John Dahlem, Shep Surghnor, Tom Heydman, Durand Lugar. Back row, Coach Joe Record, Lynn Meech, Larry Geurkink, Stan Ogle, Jim Maples, Jerry Jeffrey, Mac Plummer, Gary Bloom, Charlie Buller.

The 1929 men's basketball team went 29-9 and was "Champion of Oklahoma," and runner-up in the national tournament. What became known as the Coast Trip became a tradition with the Phillips basketball team and was repeated in 1929 with the Haymakers playing both collegiate and National Amateur Athletic Union teams. Again the Haymakers were invited to the National Amateur Athletic Union basketball tournament. The Haymakers won the first three games but were knocked out of the tournament in a fourth game.

In 1930, Phillips again fielded a baseball team, beating Chilocco Indian School, Oklahoma City University, and Oklahoma Baptist University twice. The Haymakers lost to Oklahoma City University and twice to the University of Tulsa. The last game of the season was played against the touring Kansas City Monarchs, the most famous team of the Negro Leagues. Phillips lost 11-7. When the season ended the baseball team was disbanded for several years.

Also in 1930, Phillips won its first Big Four Basketball Conference men's championship, and won or shared the title for the next three years.

152 In Reverence We Stand

Richard "Dickie" Hood scored more than 2,000 points as a Phillips Haymaker from 1967 to 1971. For his distinguished career on the basketball court, Hood's number 43 was retired.

The Phillips University girls' field hockey team in 1974. Front row, left to right, Jean Moglle, Sandy King, Linda Wells, Sherrie Riebel, Sue Slavee, Gabriela Bochen. Back row, Marjorie Campbell, Annette Krocker, Mary Slane, Donita Gray, Rita Heenan, Debbie Stephenson, Nancy Van Boskirk, coach June Worley. Phillips offered women's competitive sports long before Title IX federal laws required increased emphasis on women's sports on college and university campuses.

Excellence in Sports

Dr. Joe Record celebrates after leading the Phillips baseball team to a victory in regional competition, heading to NAIA national competition for the first time in 1975. He was NAIA baseball coach of the year in 1973, was inducted into the NAIA Baseball Hall of Fame in 1975, and coached the U.S. baseball team in the World Games in Taiwan in 1976.

The Phillips Fillies won the NAIA womens' basketball championship in the 1974-1975 season. With a 21-7 record and a 99-point record game during the national tournament, the Fillies were led by volunteer coach, Spanish professor Lou Amaya. Pictured with the winning plaques are front row, left to right, Coach Amaya, Susan Gooden, Lisa Amaya, Peggy Hurley, Glenda Cameron, Janna Choitz. Back row, Karen Cannon, Judy Major, Pat Cook, Katy Martindale, Rachel Taylor.

154 IN REVERENCE WE STAND

The Phillips cheerleaders in 1983 were, left to right, Marsha McNelly, Debra Sveiven, Terri Schomber, Kerri Garrou, Shaunna Fields, Kathy Jones, and Carol McCoy.

Fillies basketball star Karen Cannon, number 30, drives on the goal during her brilliant career at Phillips. She was the highest scoring women's basketball player in school history. She was the Most Valuable Player of the 1977 national tournament. In 1978, Cannon's number was retired. After college she excelled in softball and was elected to the Oklahoma Softball Hall of Fame.

Excellence in Sports 155

Intramural sports were very popular with students throughout the life of Phillips. In this photograph, Glenn Davis was the pitcher for Varsity's entry into the intramural softball competition. Intramural basketball, flag football, and individual intramural competition were also successful.

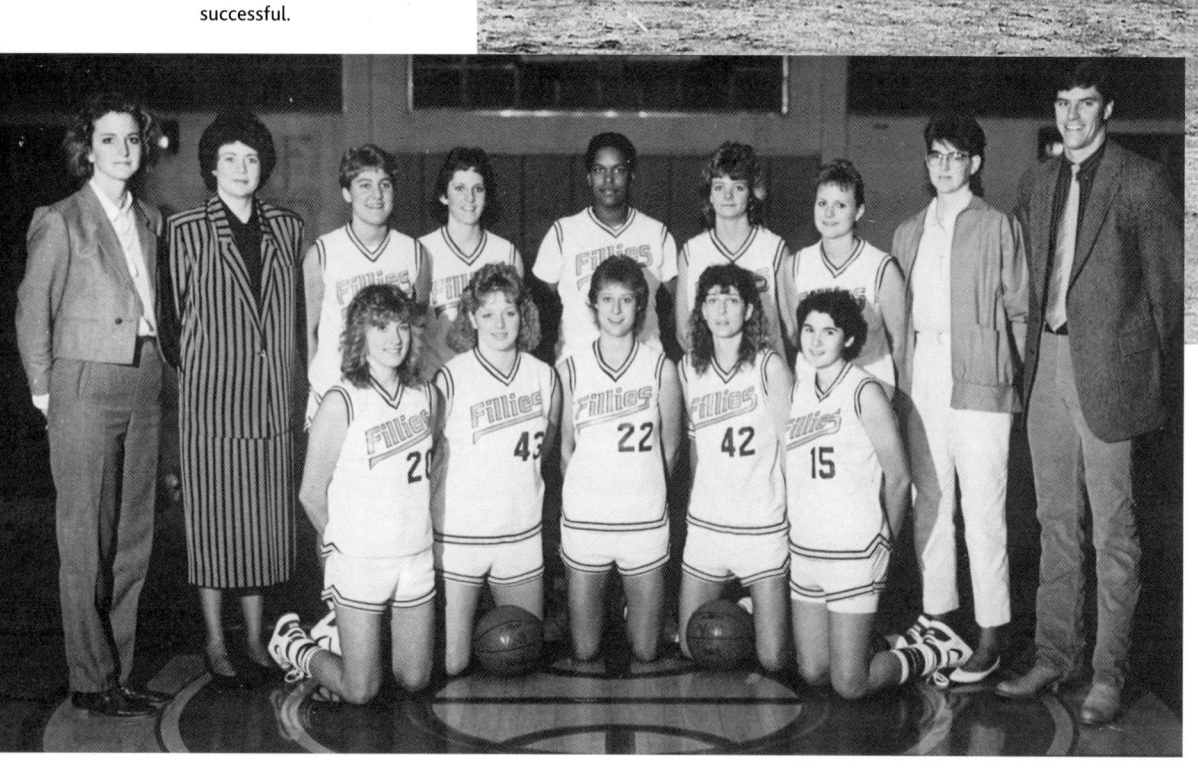

The Phillips University Fillies basketball team of 1986. Front row, left to right, Sandra Cermack, Laura Copenhaver, Kem Jones, Janet Van Winkle, Pam Kuehny. Second row, Melanie Freeman, Coach Jerrianne John, Sylvia Aughtry, Susan Canfield, Tammy Powers, Kristi Weldon, Kelly Gabeau, Jo Holland, Assistant Coach Rich Burkholder.

In an attempt to boost attendance, lights were installed at the beginning of the 1930 football season and games were played at night. The first night game was against the Oklahoma School of Mines and Metallurgy at Wilburton. Phillips won. Unfortunately attendance remained low.

The effects of the Great Depression on college athletics was especially hard on the minor sports of golf, track, and tennis. During the 1930-1931 school year, members of the track, golf, and tennis team volunteered to share the cost of travel and equipment to allow Phillips to field teams. To maintain membership in the Big Four Athletic Conference, Phillips was required to have at least three major sport teams in each two-semester school term. Following the disbanding of the Phillips baseball team, the university used track and field to round out its spring athletic teams.

The 1932 season proved to be the last for Haymaker football. As state supported schools became more active in offering financial inducements for football players, Phillips began to lose promising high school players to other schools. Phillips simply did not have the financial resources to compete, even though local Enid businessmen often contributed to student-athletes' finances. In an attempt to bolster falling football revenue, Phillips played five home games, each with a guarantee to the visiting teams.

Gate receipts for the entire five home games did not cover the money required for one guarantee. As a result, the Athletic Council recommended that the football program be dropped. Dean Stephen J. England explained the decision, "There was only enough

156 In Reverence We Stand

THE PHILLIPS MASCOT

For decades, Phillips athletics was officially represented as a Fighting Haymaker. However, in 1940, another mascot made its appearance. Several students saw a movie that featured a skunk in a cartoon. As the skunk appeared on the screen, so did the words, "Roses are red, violets are blue; If skunks had a color, they'd call it PU." The idea for Little Hay as Phillips' unofficial mascot was born.

Little Hay became the curse of school administrators who were horrified at the thought of a Christian university being represented by a skunk. Despite those fears, a student dressed as Little Hay made unofficial appearances at most school functions, especially athletic events. Faster than the authorities, he, or she, left before being apprehended while the crowd cheered. Students loved the prank. Once a student ran a toy skunk up the flag pole and then placed a lock on the chain so that it could not be taken down. In 1956, according to Leon Whitney, some unknown students painted a skunk on a full-size bed sheet and ran it up the campus flagpole. Again campus administrators were dismayed and the Enid Fire Department was called to remove the flag. However, the rope had been tied to the top of the pole and could not be lowered. To make matters worse, the pole had been greased and firemen discovered that their ladders were not tall enough to reach the top of the pole. Eventually a student agreed to climb the pole and remove the flag if he could have it. University administrators agreed, and after taking the flag down, the student placed it on the dormitory wall.

In an attempt to deflect the attention given to Little Hay, university officials adopted an apple as the new symbol, which according to Lynette Alcorn, represented the Biblical apple of wisdom and the academic pursuit of knowledge. However, students preferred Little Hay and it continued to appear at school functions. Alcorn, who studied advertising art at Phillips, once produced a cartoon version of Little Hay that was reproduced and stapled and taped all over campus for the Phillips University Diamond Jubilee in 1982.

When Dr. Curt Jones became president of Phillips in 1996, the air conditioning failed on the first night that he and his wife Becky spent in the president's home and they opened the windows. Unfortunately, there was a skunk that had taken refuge nearby. As Jones said, "I took this to be a sign that we should make our mascot a skunk." With the acceptance of Little Hay finally made official, two tame skunks were acquired from a breeding farm in Iowa. "Lil' Phil" and "Lil' Hay" were kept in the garage of the president's home and were escorted to all university athletic events.

"Lil' Phil," one of the two skunks that became official mascots of Phillips University in 1996. After the close of the university, Bennie Mullins and Dr. Joyce Yauk agreed to care for the skunks in their adoptive home on a farm in Carrier, Oklahoma. Both mascots died of natural causes in 2002.

Kristi Carano was the Phillips skunk mascot in 1995. She donned the skunk costume and appeared at most Phillips athletic events. The skunk mascot was a big hit with children.

money to pay either the football coaches' salaries or faculty salaries, but not both. Our choice was obvious!"

On March 7, 1933, the board of trustees concurred. Basketball, baseball, and track and field were retained and a comprehensive student physical education program was upgraded. All able-bodied freshmen and sophomore students at Phillips were required to enroll in gym classes. Also, an extensive intramural athletic program featuring touch football, volleyball, basketball, tennis, and archery was implemented. In the early 1950s, intramural softball, golf, track, horseshoes, and field hockey were added.

In 1934, P. J. Alyea was named as the new basketball coach and O. T. Autry became director of the university's intramural program. Autry rose to the rank of brigadier general in World War II and later was superintendent of schools in Enid.

During the 1935-1936 school year, the Fighting Haymaker basketball team won 19 of 21 games and was runner-up in the National Amateur Athletic Union Tournament in Denver, Colorado. In 1936, the Phillips basketball team had a .909 winning percentage. Unfortunately it dropped to .285 in 1937. But the Fighting Haymaker golf team won the 1937 Oklahoma Collegiate Conference Golf Championship.

The outbreak of World War II resulted in the cancellation of Phillips' baseball program in 1942 for the duration of the war. Phillips did field a basketball team during the war years despite losing most players to military duty. One of the big games of 1943 was against Oklahoma A&M and its center Bob Kurland, college basketball's first "big man." Phillips' strategy was to hold the ball to keep Kurland from scoring. Although A&M won, the Aggies were held to less than 30 points. Between 1938 and 1945, the men's basketball team posted a 54-120 record.

As the team's fortunes declined, so did revenue. James E. Strain enrolled at Phillips in September of 1941 and was a "walk on" for the men's basketball team before being granted a scholarship the next semester. Strain recalled traveling to the away games on a "broken down bus." Because there were more players than seats, freshmen were required to sit on the cracks between the seats.

The men's basketball team gained national prominence in 1945 when it went to the National Association of Intercollegiate Athletics (NAIA) national tournament. However, it was nearly four decades until the accomplishment was duplicated.

In 1953, Joe Record, an Enid native and Phillips alumnus, became Phillips' head baseball coach and athletic director, launched the university's modern baseball era, and built a comprehensive intramural program. Record had been a player-coach in his senior season at Phillips and returned as a full-time coach after spending one year in the Enid school system.

In 1961, the Haymakers baseball team won the Oklahoma Collegiate Conference championship with a 20-5 regular season record. Phillips' baseball team went to the NAIA national tournament in 1973 and 1975. Record's players not only excelled on the field but in the classroom. The coach was proud that he graduated his players who became corporate heads, bankers, dentists, doctors, and politicians. Record remained Phillips' athletic director until 1981. In his 29 years at Phillips, Record compiled a 649-249 mark.

158 In Reverence We Stand

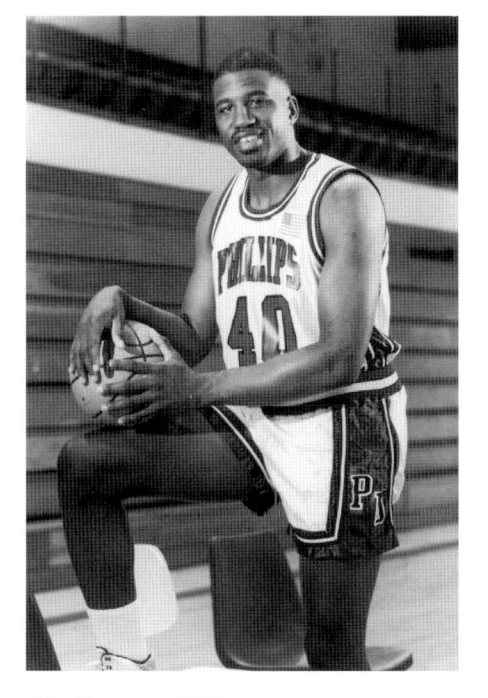

John Turner was NAIA first-team All American at Phillips in 1991. He was a first round National Basketball Association draft choice the following year.

Fillies Coach Carole Carter, center, with 1994 co-captains Kelly Curl, left, and Ann Smith.

Students passed many fall afternoons in intramural football competition. The university administration encouraged students to participate in organized and intramural competition.

Fans get excited during a 1988 Phillips soccer game. Soccer began as a varsity sport in 1974.

Excellence in Sports 159

Denny Price was a popular basketball coach and athletic director at Phillips University and in the City of Enid. His sons, Mark and Brent, were basketball stars in college and in the NBA. A third son, Matt, was a varsity basketball player at Phillips University. Price was only 62 when he died of a heart attack on July 7, 2000. To show its appreciation for Price, the Enid YMCA was named for him.

Former Phillips athletic star Nicky Emblem was named Northwest Oklahoma's Athlete of the 20th Century by the *Enid News & Eagle*. Emblem, a native of Edinburgh, Scotland, was playing on the Scottish national basketball team when Phillips Coach Carole Carter discovered her on a recruiting trip to Denmark in 1993. Nicknamed "Big Red," Emblem excelled in several sports at Phillips. She won the 1998 NAIA national championship in the javelin throw. In basketball, she was named all-conference and All-American three times. Emblem also played soccer at Phillips. After graduating in 1998, she became women's basketball coach at Enid High School. Another Scottish connection at Phillips was Craig Lidell, an excellent student and star player for the Phillips soccer team. Lidell is now the Enid High School men and women's soccer coach. Courtesy Jack N. Taylor.

The 1995 Phillips Haymakers men's basketball team. Front row, left to right, Matt Price, Mark Steltzer, Vernon Fitzpatrick, Theo Rambo, Billy Hawley. Second row, Phillip Christian, Steve Snyder, Terrance Turnage, Rich Burkholder, Brad Anderson. Third row, Coach Bob Cleeland, Sammy Jackson, Jay Woodruff, Mark Clanton, Kevin Chambers, Tim Carr, Assistant Coach Barry Gebhart.

Volleyball was one of the most popular intramural sports for students and faculty in the last years of Phillips.

Excellence in Sports 161

GOLF AT PHILLIPS

Golf was a premier sport at Phillips. The 1955 men's team won the Oklahoma Intercollegiate Tournament and finished third in the National Tournament. Although none of the players were on scholarship, the school still fielded a golf team in the 1990s. In 1996, new Phillips president Dr. Curt Jones, Jr., had been on campus only 10 days when he learned that the university's golf team had qualified for the national NAIA tournament in Tulsa. When the school's golf coach left because of a dispute over composition of the team, Jones and athletic director Denny Price took the team to the tournament.

One of the great success stories of athletic competition at Phillips is of the women's basketball team. It began in 1972 when Spanish professor Lou Amaya, who had been an All Big Eight guard at Oklahoma A & M under legendary coach Henry Iba, offered to coach a women's basketball team without remuneration. Amaya presented the idea to Graduate Studies Director Richard Anderson. The plan would cost the university nothing because Enid businessman Wesley Kroeker agreed to pay all costs, including transportation to and from games. Anderson remembered, "It was easy for me to agree that the idea was a good one and I recommended it to the president."

Amaya recruited players, began practice, and scheduled games with major colleges when he could. He played nine Big Eight teams and lost only once. Amaya, true to the tradition of his mentor, Iba, prepared his teams to play a tight defense, in an era when most women's college basketball teams emphasized offense. Within a season or two, Amaya had his women's basketball team playing at a championship level.

Sports programs at Phillips attracted many students to the school. Three sons of Bob and Jean McSpadden of Vinita came to Phillips because of its athletic emphasis. Robin McSpadden arrived on campus in 1972 and was named NAIA All American in baseball. His brother, Phil, remained in college sports after earning his degree and won several national titles as women's softball coach at Oklahoma Christian University. A third McSpadden son, Mark, played four years of baseball at Phillips while earning a business degree.

In 1983, Jeff Lawson was named to the NAIA All-American baseball team. That year Lawson set a NAIA record for the most home runs in a single season with 34 round-trippers.

In 1986, Denny Price was named men's basketball coach at Phillips. Price played basketball and baseball at the University of Oklahoma and coached with the National Basketball Association's Phoenix Suns and at Sam Houston State University in Huntsville, Texas. When Price resigned as coach in 1993, he was replaced by Bob Cleeland of Tulsa. Price remained the athletic director.

In 1988, the Phillips baseball team, under coach Allen Barker, won the Sooner Athletic Conference championship and placed third in the District Nine tournament. The team's season record was 29 wins and 9 losses. After the season, President Peck made the decision to drop intercollegiate baseball for financial considerations, a move that former coach Joe Record believed was a mistake. Record's reasoning was that Enid citizens were proud of the Phillips baseball tradition and that many outstanding students came to Phillips because of its excellent reputation in fielding superb baseball teams.

Phillips had been a top-level baseball contender for years. During the previous seven seasons under Barker, they were ranked at some point each season in the NAIA Top 20. They finished fourth at the national tournament in 1985, posting a school record 52 victories.

In February of 1989, Phillips dropped intercollegiate soccer. This left the university with two scholarship athletic programs—men's and women's basketball. It still fielded a tennis team, but none of the players were on scholarship.

"This is the day that alumni and friends of Phillips have waited for," President Sheldon Elliott said, in announcing the return of baseball to Phillips in 1996. The team competed in the Sooner Athletic Conference and Wayne Kennemer was named head coach. A former Phillips baseball player pledged $10,000 to help with the costs of returning baseball to the campus.

For the first time since 1977, the Phillips Fillies made it back to the national women's basketball tournament in 1994. Led by first-team All-American Birna Ballisager and Coach Carole Carter, the Fillies advanced to the Sweet 16 of the tournament and finished in ninth place in national rankings. The Fillies finished 26-8 for the season.

Both men's and women's basketball teams excelled in the final years of the university. Glory for the men's program had come in bits and pieces—a national tournament appearance in 1945, a NAIA District 9 title in 1984, and the selection of John Turner as a first-round NBA draft choice in 1991.

But under second-year coach Rand Chappell, the Haymakers moved into the elite of the NAIA in January of 1997 after upsetting top-ranked and defending national champion Oklahoma City University and snapping OCU's 52-game home court winning streak. The Haymakers won a trip to the national tournament but lost in the opening round to Georgetown College of Kentucky.

The final year of Phillips basketball, 1998, was an incredible year. By the middle of January, the men's team was 14-0, off to its best start in school history, and, immediately prior to the NAIA championship playoffs, was ranked No. 1 in NAIA Division I, the highest ranking the team had ever achieved. The team leader and high scorer was Joe Bunn, a 6'6" dynamo on the court.

Meanwhile, the women's team was 10-3, had won nine straight games, and was ranked No. 19 in the nation. Prior to the national championship playoffs, the Fillies were ranked No. 2 in NAIA Division I.

The success of the sports teams actually benefited the university. Michael Sohn was vice president for university advancement at the time and remembered, "We made a conscious decision to add baseball, soccer, women's soccer, and track and field. We needed students. We received criticism for emphasizing athletics but the athletes we were recruiting were truly student-athletes."

Allison Tobola was pitcher on the university's first competitive women's softball team in 1997. She remembered, "We had so much support from the school and the community. We developed into a competitive and successful team and formed a strong bond with each other."

Athletic competition was good for both Phillips University and its students. The university received much favorable publicity from the success of its teams. Caring coaches, who deliberately mixed teaching lessons of life with technical instruction of a particular sport, strengthened the character of student-athletes.

Excellence in Sports 163

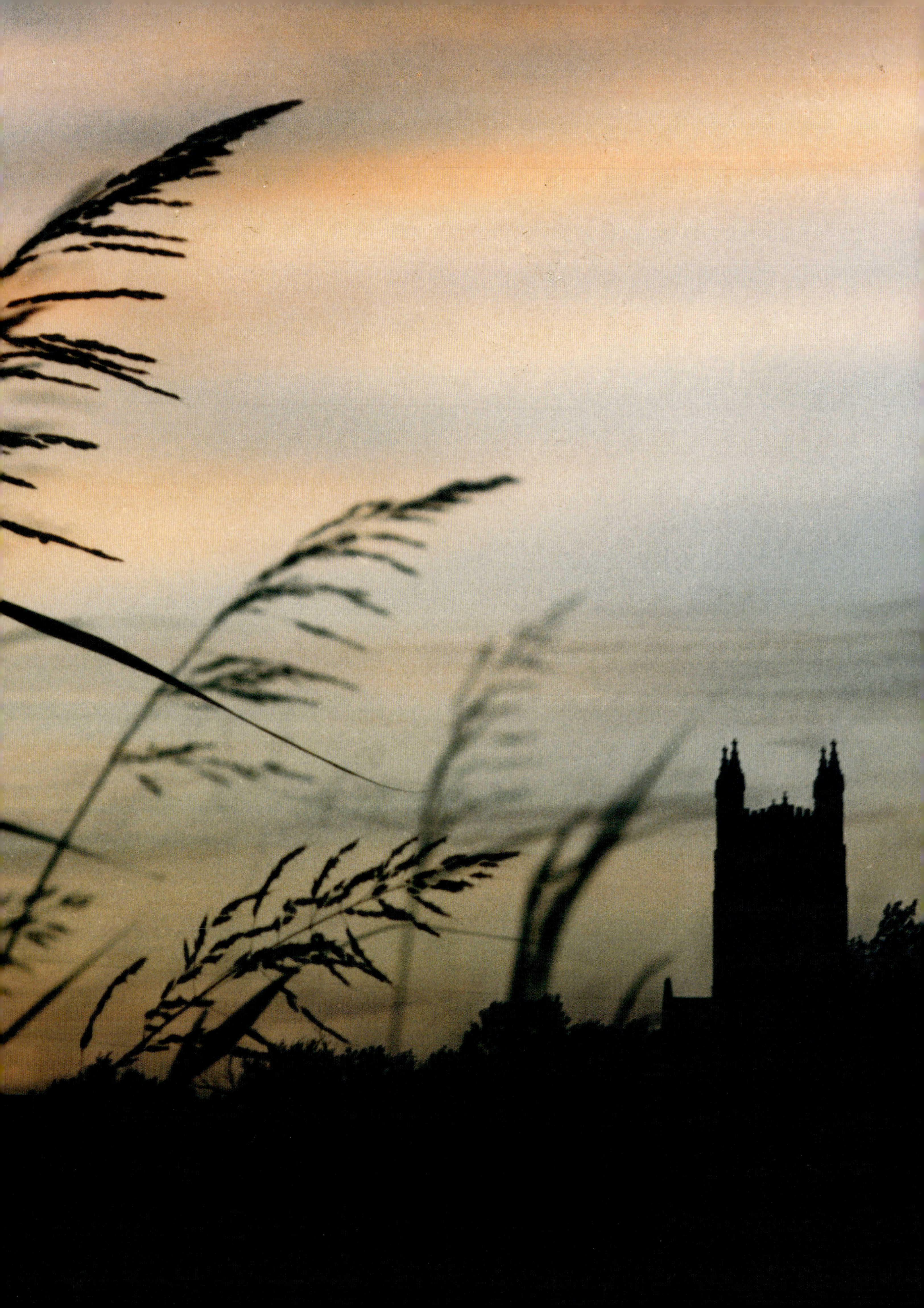

The End of an Era

DR. G. CURTIS "Curt" Jones, Jr., president of the Division of Higher Education for the Christian Church (Disciples of Christ), was selected as president of Phillips University on April 23, 1996, and was inaugurated on January 24, 1997. In the 11 days prior to Jones' arriving on campus, Virginia Groendyke, a member of the school's board of trustees, served as interim president. Jones received his B.A. and M.A. in political science and public administration from Texas Christian University, his law degree from George Mason University, and a doctor of humane letters from Eureka College. He came to Phillips with more than 30 years experience as a senior executive in government service, higher education, human resources, and job training. He worked for several federal government agencies before he became the Disciples principal representative to the 18 church-related colleges and universities, seven seminaries and foundation houses, and 80 campus ministry programs. Because of his work with Disciples colleges, Jones was no stranger to Phillips. When he arrived on campus, Jones discovered that Phillips' finances were worse than he expected. The university's endowment existed only on paper and there was little cash on hand. Jones turned to an old friend, James "Jim" Wright, a United Way official in Fort Worth, Texas, who had been a classmate of Jones at TCU. Wright, a proven fundraiser, became vice president for administration of Phillips. Jones described Wright as a "godsend."

President Jones hoped to remedy Phillips' critical financial situation by increasing student enrollment, which had dropped as word of the financial crisis spread. The incoming freshman class in the fall of 1995 numbered only 60 and the overall enrollment had fallen to 500 from a historical average of between 1,000 and 1,500 students. To encourage enrollment, Jones announced that Phillips would no longer rely on the ACT or SAT scores for admission, a move that hopefully would draw more students from the rural area surrounding Enid where test scores did not necessarily reflect students' academic potential.

Under the new requirements, enrollment increased without a significant decrease in the average grade point—3.2 in August of 1996. In addition, eight new athletic teams were added to help draw students.

Because it was a small school, Phillips was 85 to 90 percent tuition driven. The remainder of the budget had to be made up by outside funding, especially endowments. Prior to Jones' arrival, Phillips' endowment program had been largely depleted because of the repurchase of the school from the City of Enid.

To bring financial stability, Jones implemented an aggressive fund raising effort that succeeded in increasing the university's outside income. Jones enlisted the help of former students and alumni who knew their old school was in trouble and came to its aid.

One of the most noteworthy efforts was an alumni rally in the spring of 1996 at which hundreds of current students and alumni came together to protest the proposed merger of Phillips and Northwestern Oklahoma State University and raise more than $100,000 in an astonishingly short time. Emily Stuckey, a high school teacher in Covington, Oklahoma, and 1997 Phillips graduate in psychology, remembered, "Michael Sohn was running a fundraiser and we spent our evenings making phone calls. I always knew the student body was close, but I never saw people come together as we

Virginia Groendyke, a longtime Enid supporter of Phillips University, served as acting president of the university in 1996.

did.... There was not as much 'your club' and 'my club,' as there was 'we.'"

However, all efforts fell short. Because of financial problems, Phillips was placed on a two-year probation by the North Central Association of Colleges and Schools in August of 1996.

Much of the gloomy cloud hanging over Phillips was psychological. Looking back, Jones believes that, "alumni, the church, and the community had lost faith in the university and none of them were willing to assume any responsibility for the future of the institution." Jones believed that some previous administrations had either misread the depth of the university's plight, or had not been fully forthcoming with the university's supporters about the situation.

The Phillips board of directors at the time was controlled by Enid civic leaders and most supported the idea of selling the school to the city. Because of its uncertain future, efforts to raise outside money for Phillips were hindered. For example, when President Jones was seeking a loan for $12 million to $15 million, it took several board and executive committee meetings to obtain authorization to apply for the loan.

In May of 1997, the Phillips Theological Seminary moved to Tulsa where it continued to lease space from the University of Tulsa. A decade earlier, the Phillips seminary had joined forces to allow TU students to work toward a master's of divinity degree. On June 14, 2000, Quik Trip Corporation donated two single-story

Students posted a hand-painted "Not for Sale" sign under the Phillips University sign during the 1996 struggle over the future of the university.

The End of an Era 167

Members of the Phillips University band perform at the 1997 commencement exercises. A strong band program had been a hallmark of the university since the 1920s.

The Phillips University choir presents a concert in the chapel.

Acoustical guitarist and composer Michael Hedges, left, and his friend, Donnie Record, adjunct professor of music at Phillips University in 1997. A native of Enid, Hedges studied classical guitar at Phillips and won Grammy nominations for two albums in the 1980s. *Guitar Player* Magazine called him "the best steel string guitar player in the world." A short time after this photograph was taken, Hedges was killed in an automobile accident in northern California. Upon his death, Hedges was called "one of the most brilliant musicians in America" by David Crosby of Crosby, Stills & Nash. Hedges never forgot his Phillips roots, often wearing Phillips baseball caps during recording sessions and talking about his mentors at Phillips, Dr. Eugene Ulrich and Dr. Tibbie Shades.

office buildings located on 7.5 acres of land in Tulsa to be Phillips Theological Seminary's new permanent home.

In July of 1997, Phillips re-established its ministerial education program. The one-year program was designed to provide ministers for smaller churches and offered a bachelor of arts in ministry degree. It was not a substitute for a seminary degree, but would produce licensed, although not ordained, ministers and continue the university's service to the church.

The fall of 1997 brought increased enrollment at Phillips. Six hundred students from 24 states and 23 foreign countries attended classes. Phillips' faculty still boasted of a substantial number of Ph.D.s, a plus that helped maintain academic excellence. The average grade point of incoming students remained at 3.2. More flexibility was provided by reworking the core curriculum, reducing the number of majors, and streamlining the budget process.

By the end of 1997, membership on the university's board of directors had changed, giving Jones more support for his ideas. Barry Robinson, an alumnus and vice president of the Kansas City Federal Reserve Bank, became chairman. Other new board members were alumni such as Dr. Bill Briggs, a director of McDonnell Douglas Astronautics; Ray

168 IN REVERENCE WE STAND

Little, warden at the Fort Supply Correctional Institute; and Air Force Major General Susan Pamerleau. Also serving was Dr. Don Alexander, senior minister of the First Christian Church in Oklahoma City.

Little was a 1975 graduate of Phillips who was a shining example of the Christian education available at the school. Convicted of second-degree robbery in New York, Little enrolled at Phillips while still on parole. Granted a basketball scholarship by the university, Little called his time at Phillips the turning point in his life.

Supporters continued to contribute to Phillips. Dr. Richard Roberts, president of Oral Roberts University in Tulsa, sent a check for $10,000. His father, Oral Roberts, had attended Phillips as a young man. Other alumni and friends responded to the need with checks from $5 to $5,000.

Even with the positive steps being taken, the university was forced to file for Chapter 11 reorganization bankruptcy on April 1, 1998. The school was $3.8 million in debt, but had $21.5 million worth of real property. Phillips officials asked the court to remove the university's buildings from the restricted endowment fund so they could be used as collateral for a loan as part of a reorganization plan.

The school was dealt another blow in May of 1998 when a review team of the North Central Association of Colleges and Schools made a preliminary recommendation to revoke Phillips' accreditation. Unless the university's financial woes could be corrected, Phillips would lose its accreditation for the 1998-1999 school year.

Times were hard for students, faculty, and staff. Janetta Cravens had graduated and was hired as associate director of church relations. She remembered development director Michael Sohn calling staff into his office to say, "Okay folks. We have to raise $20,000 today or we don't make payroll." Sohn would then hand staff members a print out of donors and ask them to call them. Sohn remembered, "It was a terrible time, but one I'll remember forever. We were dedicated to the cause—to the belief that what we were doing had to be done, and our own personal sacrifice was secondary to the university and the people we served."

Every decision seemed critical. Sohn said, "We lived and died with each piece of news, everyday, all day

It was paint up-fix up day for members of the Christian Youth Fellowship in 1997. Social and service clubs at Phillips had a strong tradition of helping keep the campus attractive and helping the Enid community.

The End of an Era 169

Phillips president Dr. G. Curtis Jones, Jr., left, with Oklahoma United States senator Don Nickles in 1997. Jones came to Phillips with a background of exemplary federal government service and was acquainted with many federal and state officials.

Oklahoma congressman Frank Lucas spoke to Phillips students at the May 11, 1997 commencement ceremony.

long." The emotions were overwhelming. Offices began recycling paper—typing inner-office correspondence on the back of used sheets of paper.

There was a time when the university was not able to make payroll for its salaried employees. Professors and staff hung on, some until they drained their savings accounts. Janetta Cravens said, "We shared a vision. We were a team. We fought the good fight…raced the good race. We were loyal to the end."

Unable to secure funding to keep the school operating, the Phillips board of trustees voted on July 1, 1998, to suspend classes for the fall semester. Trustees still held open the option of reopening sometime in the future and refused to vote to close the school. They did vote to stay in Chapter 11 bankruptcy so that school officials could oversee the disposal of the university's assets. The board established three goals: (1) graduate the senior class; (2) assist students, faculty, and staff in relocating; and (3) repay creditors in full, plus interest.

The university's attorney, Stephen Jones, recommended the bankruptcy law firm of Kline & Kline in Oklahoma City. David Kline, Tim Kline, and Stephen Elliot handled the proceedings. Phillips is the only Chapter 11 case the firm ever recalled filing without requiring a retainer.

Tim Kline and Elliott had little to guide them. The Phillips University chapter 11 reorganization bankruptcy was one of only a handful of bankruptcy cases involving institutions of higher learning in America. The action was unique for a number of reasons, including public and private concerns; the exceptional review by the media, especially in the City of Enid; and the emotional concerns because of faculty and students and their loyalty to the school.

From the beginning, the objective was to keep Phillips University open. Dozens of alternatives were explored. President Jones led the trustees' search for new funds or any kind of arrangement, including sale or merger with another institution. Trustees worked overtime in many meetings to look at every possible option to keep the school open. But in the end, the decline in enrollment and tuition revenues and an inadequate endowment base caused the board to realize that there was only one option.

Efforts to refinance the debt in acceptable terms failed, accreditation pressures could not be satisfied, and the bankruptcy attorneys recommended, as a last alternative, that the school be permanently closed. As Tim Kline recalled, "When we arrived at the liquidation scenario and realized that the school could not reopen, the board was in total agreement because we all knew we had fully explored every alternative to keep the school open."

Nonetheless, when Barry Robinson, the chair of the board of trustees, called for a vote on the closing of the school, there was total silence. Bob Hall remembered, "No one would speak. They had tried so hard to keep the school open, but the answer was to close . . . and still no one could bear to say the words."

Economic problems that had existed since the early days of the university finally caught up with the school. As attorney Stephen Jones reflected, "Curt Jones could not have saved the university. But what he did do was arrange for an orderly transition."

Federal bankruptcy judge Richard Bohanon approved an innovative reorganization and liquidation plan. When the plan was completed, all approved creditors' claims were paid, plus interest. The sale of campus real estate was the major source of funds to repay creditors. At the time of the sale, the university's art collection was retained until more favorable market conditions existed. It was a good decision to wait because the increased market value

Mindy McCoy, left, and Janetta Cravens congratulate each other at the 1997 commencement.

The End of an Era 171

Phillips' final president, Dr. G. Curtis Jones, Jr., and his wife, Becky. At the closing of the university, Jones was named president emeritus. *Indian Encampment Along the Snake River,* by Ralph Albert Blakelock, is in the background. Courtesy Wess Gray Portraits.

allowed Phillips to accumulate significant funds for future purposes.

Almost immediately, Phillips' administrators made arrangements with Oklahoma Christian University of Science and Arts in Oklahoma City for Phillips' education majors to complete their class work. All current students were placed in other colleges or universities.

It was a torturous two weeks for the 700 students who remained at Phillips. Janetta Cravens and other staff members organized a college fair to assist students in finding a new school. Students helped each other—some chose to go together to new schools. There was both beauty and pain in the final experience for students, faculty, and administrators.

By that time, Janetta was one of the last church relations staff members on campus. It took her two days to write four paragraphs of a letter sent to Disciples churches in the region, announcing the close of the university and the severing of a 90-year relationship. She remembered, "It was the hardest thing I've ever had to do in my life."

Phillips held its final graduation ceremony on January 23, 1999. Dr. Don H. Alexander delivered the university's final commencement address in which he emphasized the key elements of the Phillips legacy:

A growing sense of self, an enlarging sense of self-identity in the larger context of the human family. This grew out of a very special flavor for living expressed in classroom and campus camaraderie, granting seriousness to life in the midst of enjoying life.

A keen sense of purpose, the giving of self to something larger than self, being able to define life not by saying, "This belongs to me, this belongs to me, this belongs to me," but by being able to say, "I belong to that!"

Phillips helped its students keep God at the center of their life equation. It helped them know the truth framed so articulately by Elizabeth Browning, "every common bush is aflame with God."

It was Alexander's belief that Phillips University would be "remembered by future generations for having stood at the crossroads of life for thousands of young people and helping them to choose the right roads." Alexander said, "Phillips provided a spirit in academics and in community that prepared students for making right choices. How could there be a better legacy than that?"

Dr. Paul Sharp lamented the closing of Phillips as "tragic." For more than 90 years, the school had filled a spot that public universities could not provide. Uniquely, Phillips helped students who needed embracing of the total person. Sharp said the school should be remembered for the host of incredible leaders it produced in a wide variety of disciplines for society.

172 IN REVERENCE WE STAND

As the liquidation of Phillips continued, the school's general and academic library was sold to Florida College in Tampa, Florida, on September 10, 1998. For months, it appeared that Northwestern Oklahoma State University (NWOSU) at Alva would purchase the Phillips campus. NWOSU had offered classes at a branch campus adjacent to Phillips and had nearly purchased Phillips in 1996. However, the sale stalled when NWOSU officials wanted guarantees that the Enid campus would never become larger than the main campus at Alva.

The other state college closely associated with Phillips was Northern Oklahoma College. In 1983, Phillips had agreed to allow NOC classes to count toward a bachelor's degree at Phillips. The close relationship paid off, and on May 21, 1999, the City of Enid and Northern Oklahoma College at Tonkawa paid $6.1 million for the 109-acre Phillips campus, 17 buildings, the university golf course, baseball field, swimming pool, and two indoor basketball courts. The City of Enid contributed $1.9 million of the purchase price, the Oklahoma State Regents of Higher Education another $800,000, and NOC the balance.

The leadership of the Joint Industrial Foundation and the City of Enid was unimpressed with the value of the Phillips art collection and indicated they were not interested in buying it, at any price. Ironically, the value of the art collection was nearly as much as the value of the other physical assets of the university.

NOC officials planned to spend an additional $6 million over the following three years upgrading the campus and buildings. On August 18, 1999, NOC began holding college classes on the former Phillips campus.

In August of 2000, Phillips was released from supervision of the bankruptcy court. By May of 2001, all debts of Phillips University had been paid and $3 million dollars remained. The university's trustees voted to give the money to the Phillips University Legacy Foundation. In a final symbolic act, President Jones carefully removed the school mascots from the garage of the president's house and found the two skunks a new home on a nearby farm.

As Kirby Hughes Gould explained, "Phillips was not an Ivy League school or a big college or research university. It was a simple school teaching basic classes to ordinary people. Those people went on to be ministers, teachers, doctors, lawyers, engineers, business administrators; to serve their communities, their churches, their society. The magic and mystery of Phillips University cannot be explained, it can only be experienced. The sadness of its closing is that no one else can have that experience."

A map of the Phillips University campus in the 1990s.

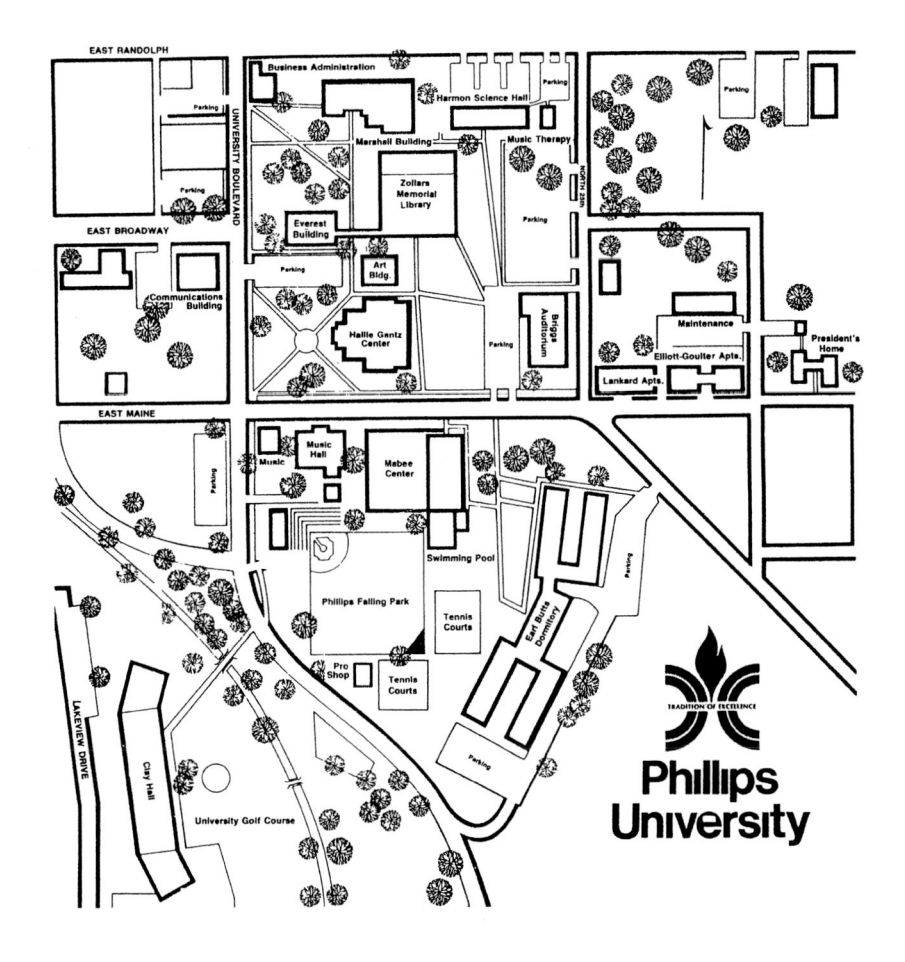

The End of an Era 173

THE GENEROSITY OF
GRACE PHILLIPS JOHNSON

A significant benefactor of Phillips University was Grace Phillips Johnson, the daughter of Thomas W. Phillips, for whom the university was named. In 1964, Mrs. Johnson contributed $75,000 to renovate the old library into a new Art Building, containing classrooms, the Cherokee Strip Museum, and an art gallery. More than 400 Enid citizens and friends of the university were present at a dinner on November 5, 1964, when President Hallie Gantz announced the gift.

Mrs. Johnson lived in New Castle, Pennsylvania, and owned one of the finest private collections of art in America. She had visited the Phillips campus just two months before announcing her cash gift and her donation of several pieces of art, including a Chinese sculpture, two Chinese screens, and two notable paintings—*By the Fire* (1921), by E. Irving Couse, and *Indian Encampment Along the Snake River* (1871), by Ralph Albert Blakelock.

Mrs. Johnson also gave the university a letter from President James A. Garfield to her father. It was an example of the large family collection of correspondence between the two old friends.

University officials used the cash gift from Mrs. Johnson to create an art gallery on the main floor of the Art Building. Paintings and art objects given by Mrs. Johnson, and previous artworks donated by Thomas W. Phillips and other members of the Phillips family, were displayed in the north room behind protective iron gates.

James "Jim" Bray, who taught art at Phillips for 28 years, oversaw the exhibition of student paintings and traveling shows in the south room of the first floor. He also cultivated the idea for a spring art sale, designed for students to display and sell works created during the school year.

At the same time the art gallery was being constructed, the Cherokee Strip Museum was created in the Art Building. Dr. Otho Whiteneck, president of the Sons and Daughters of the Cherokee Strip Pioneers, appointed a committee to work with Phillips to develop the museum portion of the building.

Phillips officials never knew how valuable the Blakelock painting was until two years after the university closed. The painting had in previous years been moved to the president's home on campus and was no longer available for viewing by the general public.

When the City of Enid and other suitors were bidding to buy the university, no one wanted the art collection because of the uncertainty of its worth. After bankruptcy, and the payment of all creditors, the university retained ownership of the collection until it was sold by auction and through the Internet in 2000. Sotheby's in New York estimated that the approximately 20 items would bring anywhere from $480,000 to $780,000. The Blakelock painting was valued at between $300,000 and $500,000.

In December of 1999, Phillips trustees approved the sale of the collection. They did so with a heavy heart because of the university's emotional attachment to the gifts from the Thomas W. Phillips family. However, they saw the sale as an opportunity to ultimately permit the legacy of Phillips to continue. Stephanie Johnson-Kiewlich, a former Phillips board member, was instrumental in explaining the necessity of the sale to the Phillips family.

In May of 2000, at a Sotheby's public auction, the Blakelock painting received a hammer price bid of $3.2 million, netting Phillips more than $3.1 million after the sales commission. The balance of the Phillips collection sold for more than $225,000.

After the auction, some suggested that Phillips should have sold the collection earlier, to keep the university alive. However, prices realized at auction surprised even the experts and the net benefit to Phillips would have constituted only one-third of the annual operating budget.

Indian Encampment Along the Snake River, by Ralph Albert Blakelock, was the most valuable painting Grace Phillips Johnson gave to Phillips University in 1964. When the university art collection was liquidated in 2000, Sotheby's sold the painting at auction for $3.2 million, nearly ten times its pre-auction estimated value. This was the largest painting created by Blakelock who is well known for oil paintings of landscapes and Indian scenes he portrayed during visits to the West just after the Civil War.

176 In Reverence We Stand

The Legacy Continues

The fierce loyalty that graduates of Phillips University feel for their alma mater may have reached a pinnacle during the meeting in 1996 when trustees faced a possible merger with Northwestern Oklahoma State University. Word of the trustee meeting quickly spread across campus, and about 60 students gathered outside the meeting room in the Gantz Center to sing the Phillips Alma Mater. Board members laid down their pencils and paper and sat and listened with an incredible feeling of pride and emotion. The singing lasted almost three hours. Although the efforts to save the school later failed, such a demonstration of loyalty to Phillips resulted in the creation of the Phillips University Alumni and Friends Association when the university closed on July 31, 1998.

Four key people helping maintain the archives and records of Phillips University are, left to right, Barbara Angle, Don Angle, Billie Hilbig, and James "Jim" Wright. Courtesy Jack N. Taylor.

Connie Cravens was secretary of the Phillips Alumni Association. Connie, her husband, Ed, and their daughter, Janetta, had all graduated from Phillips and Janetta worked in the university's office of church relations helping to recruit students and build financial support. The Cravenses' son, Matthew, attended Phillips but did not have the opportunity to graduate due to the closing of the school.

In 1998, Connie learned of the decision to close within minutes of it being made. She stepped into the office of Vice President Michael Sohn and asked if there was anything that she could do. Sohn simply said, "Take care of the alumni association." With a renewed vision, Connie was determined to keep the spirit of Phillips University alive.

It was a daunting task. There was no money, no tax-exempt status, no recognition as an organization by the state because the alumni group was part of the university, and it was just days before the scheduled Alumni Association meeting. Picking up a copy of *Robert's Rules of Order*, Connie outlined what steps had to be taken to officially close the Phillips Alumni Association and form a new organization.

A new group—the Phillips University Alumni and Friends Association—was organized on August 28, 1998. Michael Sohn served as its first president and Connie Cravens was its first secretary. Its mission statement was to serve as the collective voice of alumni and friends of Phillips University; to provide communication to and about its members and activities; and to perpetuate and preserve the history, traditions, and memory of Phillips University.

In May of 1999, the organization hosted the largest Phillips University reunion ever. Willo Lovell Clark chaired the "Celebrate the Life of Phillips" gathering which attracted more than 700 former students and faculty to reminisce, renew friendships, visit the campus, honor distinguished students and faculty, and participate in a closure service for the university. Ed Cravens salvaged the alumni database and created the first PUAFA Web page. Ed and Faye Kiryakakis, with the help of others, keep up with current addresses, news articles, and other information of interest to alumni. Don and Barbara Angle and other willing workers have identified, boxed, labeled, and provided secure storage for university artifacts.

The Phillips University Alumni and Friends Association also helped implement the Dr. Bill Snodgrass lecture series in May of 2001 and hosted a Phillips University luncheon at the General Assembly of the Christian Church (Disciples of Christ) meeting in Cincinnati, Ohio, in October of 1999, and in Kansas City, Missouri, in 2001.

One of the Association's most ambitious projects was the *The Glory of Our Phillips U,* a video produced in 2000. Produced by Spencer Briggs, it is filled with historic film clips of the university.

In 1999, Connie Cravens became president of the Phillips University

Alumni and Friends Association. On September 14, she proposed to the school's trustees the establishment of a living legacy, a foundation to provide scholarships in the name of Phillips University. Working with Bob Hall and Gene Challenner, Cravens completed details of the proposal by February 17, 2002, when Challenner, Cravens, Sheldon Elliott, Eric Hodson, and James Reed, as representatives of the Alumni and Friends Association, met with G. Curtis Jones, Jr., James P. Wright, Jr., Barry Robinson, Don Alexander, and Stephen Elliott, who represented the university, to form the Phillips University Legacy Foundation.

Dennis Landon, president of the Division of Higher Education of the Christian Church (Disciples of Christ), also was present at the historic meeting. Challenner was elected the first president of the Phillips University Legacy Foundation.

Three million dollars remaining from the liquidation of the assets of Phillips University was transferred to the Legacy Foundation. During the 2001-2002 school year, one-time grants were made to students who were enrolled at Phillips during its last two years of operation but did not graduate. A $20,000 donation was made to the Denny Price Memorial Foundation to benefit the Denny Price Family YMCA in Enid. The university retained sufficient assets to pursue its educational purpose in areas where the Legacy Foundation might not be able to function as effectively.

The first three Faculty/Professional Development Scholarships were awarded in December of 2001 to Stephanie Goh, a nursing faculty member at Midway College in Midway, Kentucky, for masters of science work at the University of Kentucky; Dr. Kathy J. Whitson, associate professor of English at Eureka College in Eureka, Illinois, for a sabbatical leave project at Eureka College; and Toni Wine Imbler, a former Phillips employee, for theological studies at Phillips Theological Seminary in Tulsa.

Eleven students were in the first group of Phillips Legacy Scholars for the 2002-2003 academic year. They included Lindsey B. Albert, Tulsa, Oklahoma, a senior at Drury University; Jacob E. Bullis, Waukomis, Oklahoma, a junior at Drury; Amanda R. Hall, Norman, Oklahoma, a freshman at Columbia College; Cara L. Haymaker, Hennessey, Oklahoma, a sophomore at Drury; Angela M. Inglish, Stillwater, Oklahoma, a freshman at TCU; Mary K. Krumrei, Springfield, Illinois, a freshman at TCU; Bethany A. Loader, Bardstown, Kentucky, a freshman at Transylvania University; Casey L. Peters, McKinney, Texas, a freshman at TCU; Cameron S. Wallace, Broken Arrow, Oklahoma, a junior at TCU; Mallory L. Watson, Little Rock, Arkansas, a freshman at TCU; and Kristin R. Wharry, Austin, Texas, a junior at TCU.

In October of 2002, Dr. Brad Lookingbill, assistant professor of history at Columbia College in Columbia, Missouri; Dr. Abdul J. Mia, professor of biology at Jarvis Christian College in Hawkins, Texas; and Dr. Richard H. Lowery, a former Phillips employee and currently professor of Old Testament at Phillips Theological Seminary, were awarded Faculty Development Scholarships.

In January of 2003, the Legacy Foundation awarded six Faculty Development Scholarships to seven individuals from four Disciples colleges. Recipients were Dr. Kerry Skora and Dr. Dennis J. Taylor, Hiram College; Sheila Putman, Culver-Stockton College; Dr. Thomas Shahady, Lynchburg College; Alison Critchfield, Midway College; Cindy Tucker, Midway College; and Roseanna Camacho, Midway College.

In the future, Legacy Foundation scholarships will be awarded to undergraduate students attending Disciples related colleges and universities, to faculty members of Disciples colleges for continuing education to enhance their teaching skills, and to former Phillips University employees. The scholarship programs are administered through the Division of Higher Education of the Christian Church (Disciples of Christ), but the Legacy Foundation board makes final selection of recipients.

The three Phillips University scholarship programs are a living legacy for the entire university family—students, professors, and administrators. They provide for continuing Christian education in the finest tradition of Phillips University. As Gene Challenner said, "Phillips University should be remembered as one shining moment in history."

The foundation's future is bright. The three scholarship programs are off to a good start. Also, if funds were available, the Legacy Foundation could establish an accredited higher educational institution; partner with an existing accredited higher educational institution; create a special focus institute with educational opportunities; and pursue other opportunities to educate and develop Christian leaders. As noted by Phillips University president Dr. Eugene Briggs, "Christian education is the hope of the world."

Barry Robinson hopes Phillips will be remembered for its outstanding success in blending a Christian environment with academic excellence in a setting that was never pious or forbidding, an environment that celebrated fun and developed deep personal relationships between and among students, faculty, and staff.

Even the physical campus of former Phillips University will always be special. Bryan Estabrooks remembers the piece of sacred soil on the university golf course that was known as the "V," where freshmen members of the Varsity Social Service Club stood at the bottom of the hill shouting "Yea, Yea, Varsity" every morning as upperclassmen gathered to test their mettle.

Of future trips to the Enid campus, Estabrooks said, "Every time the men of Varsity gather, rest assured we will journey to the 'V' once again, if for no other reason than to be reminded that Unity is still our most important product."

The contributions made by the thousands of Phillips graduates will never be overshadowed by the passage of time. For generations, the positive influence of a Phillips University education will be felt.

"Phillips should be remembered as a tightly knit community," reflected Jeanne Marie Kohr, "I find it awesome that three generations of families turned to Phillips for their college years, such as mothers and daughters relating and comparing tales of their dorm-life experience . . . or discussing how the face of Phillips changed over the years, and how it stayed the same."

Cheryl Carpenter, who preferred her unofficial title "Mom" to students over her administrative titles, said, "Phillips University will never die. Its legacy will continue through the good works and deeds of all who loved her."

Allison Tobola, a member of the Phillips student body during its last year, may have said it best, "Phillips was a small school, but there is nothing small about the imprint it has left upon my life."

The jewel-like living colors of the rose window on the south wall of the Bivins Chapel in the Marshall Building vary with every change in light. The twelve diagonal sections surrounding the inner circle depict symbols of prayer and praise, from praying hands to musical instruments. The open door at the center of the window represents the door of prayer, which is open continuously.

180 In Reverence We Stand

ACKNOWLEDGMENTS

We are extremely grateful to a number of people who made this history of Phillips University possible. Members of the board of trustees of the university and of the Phillips University Legacy Foundation were abundant in their contributions to the gathering of information.

Many people made Phillips University special. We have attempted to tell the story of administrators, faculty, staff, students, and alumni who contributed to the university's greatness. However, because of the sheer numbers of people involved and the 90-plus years of history, we have been unable to cover all significant events and personalities. For that, we apologize in advance.

Jim Wright, Billie Hilbig, Don and Barbara Angle, Cheryl Carpenter, and Dr. Curt Jones were invaluable in guiding the project to fruition. Jack N. Taylor, the resident photographer at Phillips for many years, and Wess Gray of Enid provided professional photographs for the book.

Many friends, former students, administrators, and alumni of Phillips sent letters, e-mails, and enthusiastically granted interviews. Stephanie Graves Ayala, Anna Hubbard, Shelley Dabney, and Debbie Neill helped with photographs and technical production.

Our editors, Gini Moore Campbell and Eric Dabney, worked with us to condense mountains of information into a readable and historically correct manuscript. Thanks to the Oklahoma Heritage Association and its chairman, Clayton I. Bennett, for a sterling commitment to preserve Oklahoma's incredible and unique heritage.

BOB BURKE
KENNY A. FRANKS

Retired Phillips University professors and alumni who assisted the authors in research. Front row, left to right, Dr. Beth Murphy, Dr. Robert Simpson, Dr. Kay Fortson, Dr. Russel Drumright, and Barbara Angle. Back row, Jack Taylor, Dr. Ed Jorden, Richard Anderson, Dr. John Ireland, Merle Phillips, Dr. Joe Record, and Don Angle. Courtesy Jack N. Taylor.

PRESERVING OUR LEGACY:
GIFTS TO THE PHILLIPS UNIVERSITY LEGACY FOUNDATION

Perpetuating the memory and history of Phillips University is important to many of us—alumni, faculty, staff and friends. You can help ensure our legacy with a gift to the Phillips University Legacy Foundation (PULF).

The Foundation was created through the generous support of the Phillips University Alumni and Friends Association (PUAFA) and the Phillips University Board of Trustees. Through an initial gift of over $3,000,000 from the Phillips University Board of Trustees, the Foundation is poised to fund scholarships and other programs in the University's memory. Because the Foundation is classified as a tax-exempt organization as provided under the Internal Revenue Code and its implementing regulations, all gifts are tax deductible.

Undergraduate Scholarships

The Foundation is pleased to award scholarships to undergraduates who wish to attend one of the 17 Christian Church (Disciples of Christ) colleges and universities. During 2002-2003, the Foundation awarded 11 scholarships to its first class of recipients, with 16 scholarships being awarded in 2003-2004. Some of these scholarships were awarded to children of Phillips' alumni.

Grants

In addition, the Foundation awards grants to faculty members employed by the Disciples of Christ colleges and universities and to former Phillips faculty and staff. During 2002 and 2003, 14 faculty members from eight institutions received grants to further their professional and leadership development, to benefit their peers and students, and to positively impact their church and community activities. The Division of Higher Education of the Disciples of Christ assists in administering Foundation scholarship programs.

Leadership Conferences and Seminars

In cooperation with the Christian Church (Disciples of Christ) Division of Higher Education, the Foundation will annually co-sponsor a Leadership Conference for Phillips University Legacy Scholars and the DHE Leadership Fellows. We are pleased to be able to further a very important educational thrust of Phillips University.

The Foundation will also endeavor to initiate and conduct leadership seminars and conferences tailored for Disciples of Christ lay members and clergy. PULF may also embark on other special programs, ministries, or interests that will enhance the memory of Phillips and benefit the church and communities which it historically served with dedication and vigor.

Preserving Phillips University Artifacts

The Alumni and Friends Association and the Legacy Foundation will work together to seek opportunities for the long-term preservation, storage, and display of its notable collection of memorabilia, artifacts, and records that have been carefully preserved since the University's closing. Your financial contributions will make this project a reality.

How You Can Help

Please consider a generous gift to the Phillips University Legacy Foundation. Your tax-deductible contribution may be payable in cash, a bequest in your will, real estate gifts, stocks, bonds or other securities, annuities, or life insurance. The Legacy Foundation's Board of Directors and staff will be happy to meet or visit with you confidentially at your convenience.

PULF genuinely welcomes your interest of support and can be contacted as follows:

Phillips University Legacy Foundation

MAIL
P.O. Box 2127, Enid, OK 73702-2127

OFFICE
808-810 W. Maine Street
Enid, OK 73701

PHONE
Voice 580.237.4433 or 580.237.1271
Fax 580.237.0124

E-mail: admin@phillips.edu
Web: www.phillips.edu

PRESIDENTS AND CHANCELLORS
OF PHILLIPS UNIVERSITY

Dr. Ely Vaughn Zollars, President, September 1907-1915
Oliver N. Roth, Chancellor, 1914-1916
Dr. Isaac Newton McCash, President, 1916-1938
Dr. Eugene Stephen Briggs, President, 1938-1961
Dr. Hallie George Gantz, President, 1961-1972
Dr. Thomas Edward Broce, President, 1973-1976
Dr. Samuel Everett Curl, President, 1976-1979
Dr. Joe Robert Jones, President, 1979-1988
Dr. Robert D. Peck, President, 1989-1993, Chancellor, January 1994-July 1994
Dr. Donald F. Heath, President, 1994-1995
Richard T. Anderson, Chancellor, 1994-1995
Dr. Sheldon E. Elliott, President, 1995-1996
Virginia Groendyke, Acting President, 1996
Dr. G. Curtis Jones, Jr., President, 1996-September 1998
*(Dr. Jones continued to serve as President Emeritus in 2003 and
headed efforts to establish and fund the Phillips University Legacy Foundation.)*

PHILLIPS UNIVERSITY BOARD OF TRUSTEES, 2003

Rev. Don Alexander, Oklahoma City, Oklahoma
Bill Briggs, St. Louis, Missouri
Rev. Donald E. Carter, Garden City, Kansas
Gene Challenner, New Braunfels, Texas
Connie Cravens, Newcastle, Oklahoma
Alanson Foreman, Wichita, Kansas
Dr. J. Harley Galusha, Tulsa, Oklahoma
Robert A. Hall, Norman, Oklahoma
Robert Harry, Oklahoma City, Oklahoma
Barry K. Robinson, Chair, Angel Fire, New Mexico
Walter P. Scheffe, Enid, Oklahoma
Dr. James E. Strain, Greenwood Village, Colorado

PHILLIPS UNIVERSITY LEGACY FOUNDATION BOARD OF DIRECTORS AND MEMBERS, 2003

Gene Challenner, Chair, New Braunfels, Texas
Connie Cravens, Secretary, Newcastle, Oklahoma
Sheldon Elliott, Director, Bartlesville, Oklahoma
Kirby H. Gould, Vice Chair, Olathe, Kansas
Eric W. Hodson, Treasurer, Broken Arrow, Oklahoma
James R. Reed, Director, Indianapolis, Indiana
Leon Whitney, Director, Manchester, Missouri
Todd Moore, Winfield, Kansas
Nancy Moats, Chickasha, Oklahoma
Don Angle, North Enid, Oklahoma
John Ireland, Enid, Oklahoma
Richard G. Castle, Enid, Oklahoma
Nancy Davies, Enid, Oklahoma
Bryan D. Estabrooks, Oklahoma City, Oklahoma
Pat Novak, Enid, Oklahoma

PHILLIPS UNIVERSITY
ALUMNI AND FRIENDS ASSOCIATION DIRECTORS IN 2003

*Barbara Angle, North Enid, Oklahoma
*Don Angle, Chair, History Committee, North Enid, Oklahoma
Jody Ann Woerz Britt, Norman, Oklahoma
*Robin Standley Bryslan, Enid, Oklahoma
*Lynne Adams Bussell, Chair, Reunions, Enid, Oklahoma
Beriece Creecy Castle, Enid, Oklahoma
Richard G. Castle, Enid, Oklahoma
*Sue Huckleberry Chael, Treasurer, Enid, Oklahoma
*Gene Challenner, Chair, Finance, New Braunfels, Texas
Marilyn Challenner, New Braunfels, Texas
*Willo Lou Lovell Clark, Enid, Oklahoma
*Connie Speer Cravens, President, Newcastle, Oklahoma
Richard A. Crum, Denver, Colorado
*Francis Ferne Davis DeVisser, Chair, Awards, Enid, Oklahoma

Kent Dorsey, Ponca City, Oklahoma
M. Rick Hendricks, Stillwater, Oklahoma
*Martha Bingham Hoad, Chair, Publications, Enid, Oklahoma
*John Ireland, Enid, Oklahoma
*Faye Kiryakakis, Secretary, Enid, Oklahoma
*Nancy McKeeman Moats, Vice President, Chickasha, Oklahoma
Todd Moore, Olathe, Kansas
Kathryn Penland, Fort Worth, Texas
Mary Randall Wallace, Broken Arrow, Oklahoma

* Members of Executive Committee

AWARD RECIPIENTS

DISTINGUISHED FRIENDS OF PHILLIPS UNIVERSITY

1999	Dr. Milburn E. Carey
	Dr. G. Curtis Jones, Jr.
	Dr. Walter P. Scheffe
	James P. Wright, Jr.
2001	Phillips University, Inc., Board of Trustees
	Rev. Don Alexander
	Dr. William B. Briggs
	Rev. Donald E. Carter
	Gene Challenner
	Connie Speer Cravens
	Alanson Foreman
	Dr. J. Harley Galusha
	Robert A. Hall
	Robert H. Harry
	Ray Little (posthumous)
	Major General Susan L. Pamerleau
	Barry K. Robinson
	Dr. Walter P. Scheffe
	Dr. James E. Strain
	Paul Wulfsberg

DISTINGUISHED ALUMNI

1963	Norman R. Stacey, Sr., '28
1968	Wing Sou (Dennis) Lou, Ph.D., '53
	Oscar T. Moline, '29
	Lawrence Vernon Scott, M.D., '40
1969	George G. Berry, '47
	Edna Poole, '25
	Paul Frederick Sharp, Ph.D., '39
1970	Lester D. Lacy, '14
	Nell Olney Lacy, '16
	Thomas O. McLaughlin, '16
	Thelma Diener Allen, '29
1971	Robert J. Murray, '54
	James E. Strain, M.D., '45
1972	George Howard Wilson, J.D., '26
1973	Harold S. Butler, Ph.D., '53
1974	Kenneth L. Teegarden, M.Div., '42
1976	Harley Galusha, D.O., '52
1977	Elaine Neill Davis, M.D., '58
1978	Thurman J. White, Ph.D., '36
1979	William C. Howland, D.Div., '50
1980	Ronald E. Osborn, D.Div., '39
1981	Cecil R. Williams, Ph.D., '34

DISTINGUISHED ALUMNI
(CONTINUED)

1982	O.T. Autry, '32
1983	Wayne Wray, Ph.D., '63
1984	Nathan Grantham, M.D., '66
1985	Keith Mielke, Ph.D., '56
1986	Jane Murphy, Ph.D.,'51
1987	Jim Gray. '61
	Carol Grever Gray, '62
1988	R.L. Rogers, '54
1989	Galen Havner, Ph.D., '71
1990	Sheldon E. Elliott, '48
1991	Robert Grey, Ph.D., '61
1992	Rev. A. Owen Guy, Jr., '67
1993	C.T. "Tibbie" Shades, Ed.D., '35
1994	Harold A. Pratt, '56
1995	Marion A. Christensen, Ph.D., '49
1996	Rev. Daniel Merrick, '48 A.B., '54 B.D.
1997	Phillip H. Porter, Ph.D., '59
1999	Fred B. Craddock, Ph.D., '53
	James H. Elliott, M.D., '48
	Rev. Larry W. Jones, '67
	Aigi Kamikawa, Ph.D., '48
	Kiyo Kamikawa, Ph.D., '45
	Robert L. Simpson, '55 B.A., '58 Ph.D.
	Beatrice Simpson, '56 B.S., '58 M.A.
	Druie L. "Pete Warren, Ph.D, '57
	Patricia Cravens Warren, M.Ed., '66
2001	Donald F. Clingan, Ph.D., '50
	Sarah Kathryn Alloway Couch, '31
	Judge Neil Phillip Mertz, M.A., '67
	Keith W. Purscell, M.Div., '70

OUTSTANDING YOUNG ALUMNI

1975	Tom Walker, J.D., B.A., '68
1976	Dr. Susan Jacobs, B.A., '67
1977	Dr. Charles Everly, B.A., '66
1979	Robert Arnold, B.A., '68
1980	David Collins, J.D., B.S., '75
1981	Pete Earley, B.S., '73
1982	Dr. John C. Bundren, B.S., '75
1983	Cynthia Dougherty, B.S., '77
1984	Terri Smyth Jones, '72
1985	Bradely E. Haddock, B.S., '77
1986	Dr. Tim C. Ireland, B.S., '74
1987	Dr. David Matousek, B.S., '75
	Richard K. Books, J.D., '74
1989	Dr. David Lambert, B.S., '76
1990	Connie Sloan Inglish, B.S., '76
1991	Carolyn B. Brafford, B.M., '80
1992	Bill Mayberry, B.S., '80
1993	D. Veston Rowe, B.S., '79
1994	Spencer G. Briggs, B.A., '80
1995	Dr. Rhonda Voskuhl, B.S., '82
1996	Heather Esslinger, '91
1997	Timothy P. Longman, '86
1999	Kirby Hughes Gould, B.M.E., '83
	Michael R. Sohn, B.S., '93

PUAFA is continuing to present awards to distinguished friends and alumni of Phillips.

For general contact or to recommend someone for recognition, please contact PUAFA:

Mail: Box 331, Enid, Oklahoma 73702
Voice mail: 580.237.4433
E-mail: puafa@fullnet.net
Web: www.puafa.org

PHILLIPS UNIVERSITY ENROLLMENT STATISTICS FOR UNDERGRADUATES AND GRADUATES ACADEMIC YEARS 1941-42 THROUGH 1997-98

ACADEMIC YEAR	FALL	SPRING	SUMMER
1941-42	704	827	187
1942-43	NA	NA	260
1943-44	502	463	267
1944-45	633	533	288
1945-46	707	803	340
1946-47	1,078	1,072	247
1947-48	1,135	1,053	382
1948-49	1,146	1,157	407
1949-50	1,241	1,186	412
1950-51	1,173	1,044	434
1951-52	1,110	1,016	356
1952-53	1,031	967	285
1953-54	990	952	285
1954-55	1,029	1,009	247
1955-56	1,109	1,137	255
1956-57	1,234	1,174	226
1957-58	1,118	1,062	186
1958-59	1,171	1,104	218
1959-60	1,190	1,121	242
1960-61	1,198	1,148	228
1961-62	1,193	1,149	252
1962-63	1,046	N/A	302
1963-64	1,038	N/A	332
1964-65	1,141	N/A	366
1965-66	1,099	1,074	388
1966-67	1,152	1,120	436
1967-68	1,120	N/A	478
1968-69	1,160	N/A	545
1969-70	1,007	903	376
1970-71	1,073	1,039	411
1971-72	1,058	N/A	393
1972-73	1,066	990	374
1973-74	1,030	875	N/A
1974-75	1,012	911	598
1975-76	936	886	547
1976-77	878	867	N/A
1977-78	972	876	594
1978-79	863	812	579
1979-80	824	811	530
1980-81	751	704	475
1981-82	703	682	403
1982-83	671	582	471
1983-84	675	621	433
1984-85	684	640	388
1985-86	660	587	411
1986-87	642	595	378
1987-88	539	502	333
1988-89	556	520	383
1989-90	599	581	453
1990-91	626	539	443
1991-92	588	542	401
1992-93	620	575	333
1993-94	622	539	314
1994-95	761	739	406
1995-96	567	501	314
1996-97	468	419	221
1997-98	473	439	156

Note 1: 1941–42 to 1961–62 fall and spring figures equal "total" enrollment.

Note 2: 1962–63 to 1997–98 fall and spring figures equal "full-time" enrollment.

Note 3: Summer figures equal "head count."

HONORARY DEGREES BESTOWED BY PHILLIPS UNIVERSITY

1926	Isaac N. McCash (DD)		Wilfred P. Harmon (DD)		Ned R. Graves (DD)
1930	Frank H. Marshall (DD)		William T. Pearch (DD)		Forrest D. Haggard (DD)
1934	Edwin F. Goldman (DMus)		John D. Raymond (DMus)		Frank C. Mabee (DD)
1935	Frank H. Rogers (DLaw)		Maxwell D. Taylor (DLaw)		James I. Spainhower (DD)
1936	Austin A. Hardin (DMus)		George C. Wilson (DMus)	1968	Howard C. Cole (DD)
1937	Claude J. Miller (DD)	1958	Leo K. Bishop (DMus)		Dan C. Kenner (DD)
	Orman L. Shelton (DD)		Carl M. Boyd (DLaw)		George L. Messenger, Jr. (DD)
	Tilford T. Swearingen (DD)		John M. Crawford (DSci)		William L. Miller, Jr. (DLtr)
1939	Herbert L. Clarke (DMus)		John Rogers (DHum)		William J. Moore (DLtr)
	Edwin R. Errett (DD)		Harry W. Seamans (DLaw)	1969	William L. Masters (DD)
	Daniel A. Poling (DD)		D. Bruce Selby (DLaw)		T. D. Nicklas (DHum)
1941	Frank Buttram (DLaw)		Charles F. Schwab (DD)		Ronald E. Osborn (DLtr)
1945	Ross J. Griffeth (DLaw)		Harold S. Stine (DD)		James Rainwater (DD)
	Thomas H. Johnson (DD)		Herman R. Thies (DSci)		G. Harold Roberts (DD)
1947	Paul Cook (DLaw)	1959	Lowell C. Bryant (DD)	1970	David M. Bryan (DD)
	Oswald J. Goulter (DD)		Ward A. Rice (DD)		Edward A. Flinn (DMus)
	Frank A. Wellman (DHum)		Ben Voth (DLaw)		Laurence V. Kirkpatrick (DD)
1948	Eugene S. Briggs (DLaw)	1960	Dyre Campbell (DD)		Edgar S. Sielert (DD)
	Judge J.H. Everest (DLaw)		Claude G. Large (DD)		Henry H. Tyler (DD)
	John D. Zimmerman (DD)		J. Clyde Wheeler (DD)		Ray Wallace (DD)
1950	George R. Davis (DD)	1961	Carlton D. Garrison (DD)	1971	Edward J. Aud (DHum)
	Gerald Sias (DD)		Oren E. Long (DHum)		Robert M. Elliott (DD)
1951	Harold G. Barr (DD)		W. S. Parish, Jr. (DD)		L.G. (Bud) Everitt, Jr. (DD)
	M.M. Hargrove (DLaw)	1962	Henry B. Bass (DHum)		Robert M. Greer (DHum)
	Walter H. Moore (DD)		Thomas O. Slaughter (DD)		Warren M. Hile (DD)
	Ray E. Snodgrass (DD)		James H. Tilsley (DD)		Ted D. Hurst (DD)
1952	Carl V. Covey (DD)	1963	Paul Ehly (DD)	1972	O.W. Coburn (DBus)
	John W. Harms (DLaw)		Mrs. Oswald J. Goulter (DD)		Robert M. Hall (DD)
	Loyal S. Northcott (DD)		Errett Newby (DHum)		Donald L. Helseth (DD)
	George O. Taylor (DD)		Kenneth Teegarden (DD)		Robert A. Langston, Jr. (DD)
1953	Cecil A. Denney (DD)	1964	John W. Boosinger (DD)		Jean Woolfolk (DLaw)
	J. Wayne Drash (DD)		Maurice F. Lyerla (DD)		Russell Wiley (DMus)
	Karl L. King (DMus)		Rolland H. Sheafor (DLaw)	1973	Margaret Buvinger (DLaw)
	Edwin L. Kirtley (DD)		Douglas F. Roby (DHum)		Eugene N. Frazier (DD)
1954	Spencer P. Austin (DD)	1965	Otwa T. Autry (DLaw)		John P. Jones (DHum)
	B. Roy Daniels (DLaw)		James L. Christensen (DD)		Paul Wallace (DD)
	Maxine S. Semones Miller (DLtr)		Dougald K. McColl (DD)		Thomas Wood (DD)
1955	S.R. Brentnall (DSci)		Norman R. Stacey (DD)		Owen K. Garriott, Jr. (DSci)
	Bayne E. Driskill (DLaw)	1966	Maude C. Butts (DHum)	1974	Yvonne Choteau (DHum)
	DeWitt Waller (DLaw)		James K. Hempstead (DHum)		Walter J. Lantz (DD)
1956	Harry F. Corbin (DHum)		Orval Holt (DD)		Timothy Woo Tag Lee (DD)
	Hallie G. Gantz (DHum)		Mary Louise Lankard (DHum)		Jack N. Tresner (DHum)
	Donald A. McGavran (DLit)		James C. Pippin (DD)		Larry E. Whitley (DD)
	Joseph J. Van Boskirk (DLit)		Frank E. See (DD)	1975	Joy Greer (DHum)
1957	Norval Luther Church (DMus)	1967	Barton A. Dowdy (DD)		Sam B. Howard (DHum)

HONORARY DEGREES BESTOWED BY PHILLIPS UNIVERSITY
CONTINUED

	C. William Nichols (DD)		Robert F. Glover (DD)		Jerry Thompson (DD)
	Judge George H. Wilson (DLaw)		H. Jackson Forstman (DD)	1989	Thomas J. Ligget (DD)
1976	Harvey P. Everest (DHum)	1983	Leslie L. Bowers (DD)	1990	Charles H. Karelis (DHum)
1977	Lloyd H. Lambert (DD)		Fred B. Craddock (DD)	1991	Barbara E. Walvoord (DHum)
	Forrest L. McAllister (DMus)		Paul Crow, Jr. (DD)	1992	Samir J. Habiby (DHum)
	Marvin G. Osborn, Jr. (DHum)		D. Duane Cummins (DHum)		C. J. Silas (DLaw)
	Beth Wells (DHum)		William M. Smith (DHum)	1993	William Tabbernee (DD)
	Darvin Wells (DHum)	1984	Dwaine Acker (DD)	1994	Nancy J. Davies (DHum)
	William B. Briggs (DSci)		Arthur Detamore (DHum)	1995	Paul G. Wulfsberg (DLaw)
1978	James A. Moak (DD)		Ben Duerfeldt (DD)		Jane Edwards Champlin (DHum)
	John K. Speck (DHum)		Charles R. Whitmer (DD)	1996	Sheldon E. Elliott (DHum)
1979	Dr. Angie Debo (DHum)		Donald P. Moyers (DHum)	1997	Richard L. Hamm (DD)
	M. Jasper Timbs (DD)	1985	Max E. Glenn (DD)		Walter P. Scheffe (DHum)
1980	Lloyd Cox (DD)		Harold R. Watkins (DD)	1998	Susan L. Pamerleau (DHum)
	Donald McEvoy (DHum)	1986	David L. Boren (DHum)	1999	None
	J. Wilfred Walker (DD)		Jerry D. Johnson (DD)		
1981	Henry Bellmon (DHum)		Kyle V. Maxwell (DD)		
	Don D. Brewer (DHum)	1987	William C. Howland, Jr. (DD)		
	Wilfred L. McEver (DD)		Joseph H. Williams (DHum)		
	Bishop Sul-Bong Park (DD)		James E. Womack (DHum)		
1982	J. Allan Clarke (DHum)	1988	Lynne V. Cheney (DHum)		
	William T. Gibble (DHum)		Ross O. Swimmer (DHum)		

DEGREE LEGEND

Degrees earned at Phillips are listed on the facing page.

Degrees in boldface are advanced degrees.

AA	Associate of Arts	BME	Bachelor of Music	BSM	Bachelor of Science in	MS	Master of Science
AB	Bachelor of Arts		Education		Music	MTh	Master of Theology
AM	**Master of Arts**	BMT	Bachelor of Music	BSMT	Bachelor of Science in		
AS	Associate of Science		Therapy		Music Therapy		
BA	Bachelor of Arts	BO	Bachelor of Oratory	**BTh**	**Bachelor of Theology**		
BBA	Bachelor of Business	BPSM	Bachelor of Public	**DMin**	**Doctor of Ministry**		
	Administration		School Music	MA	Master of Arts		
BD	**Bachelor of Divinity**	BS	Bachelor of Science	MBA	Master of Business		
BDA	Bachelor of Drama and	BSBA	Bachelor of Science in		Administration		
	Art		Business Administration	**MDiv**	**Master of Divinity**		
BDiv	**Bachelor of Divinity**	BSE	Bachelor of Science in	ME	Master of Education		
BE	Bachelor of Education		Education	MEd	Master of Education		
BFA	Bachelor of Fine Arts	BSEd	Bachelor of Science in	MRE	Master of Religious		
BM	Bachelor of Music		Education		Education		

UNDERGRADUATE AND GRADUATE DEGREES AWARDED BY DECADE

DEGREES	1908-19	1920-29	1930-39	1940-49	1950-59	1960-69	1970-79	1980-89	1990-99	TOTALS
AA	0	0	0	0	0	0	2	1	4	7
AB	142	501	422	390	136	0	0	0	0	1,591
AM	21	68	46	56	1	0	0	0	0	192
AS	0	0	0	0	0	0	0	0	15	15
BA	8	34	126	149	574	682	414	165	193	2,345
BBA	0	0	0	0	0	0	0	0	79	79
BD	0	22	52	108	202	191	3	0	0	578
BDA	0	0	9	12	3	0	0	0	0	24
BDiv	0	0	4	3	4	0	0	0	0	11
BE	0	0	0	0	0	0	0	1	0	1
BFA	0	0	6	22	21	33	63	43	26	214
BM	7	32	27	24	17	29	29	10	1	176
BME	0	0	2	40	48	34	57	50	21	252
BMT	0	0	0	0	0	0	0	0	8	8
BO	13	26	14	0	0	0	0	0	0	53
BPSM	0	0	21	0	0	0	0	0	0	21
BS	5	52	85	264	596	916	1,322	756	326	4,322
BSBA	0	0	0	0	0	0	0	31	323	354
BSE	0	0	0	0	0	0	0	0	75	75
BSEd	0	0	0	0	0	0	0	17	102	119
BSM	0	0	0	0	0	0	0	0	1	1
BSMT	0	0	0	0	0	0	0	0	3	3
BTh	3	0	4	2	0	0	0	0	0	9
DMin	0	0	0	0	0	0	71	79	0	150
MA	0	15	66	43	60	11	0	0	0	195
MBA	0	0	0	0	0	0	33	229	136	398
MDiv	0	0	0	0	3	51	235	170	0	459
ME	0	0	0	0	2	1	0	11	0	14
MEd	0	0	77	70	300	206	295	177	138	1,263
MRE	0	0	0	0	2	11	5	0	0	18
MS	0	1	3	0	3	11	62	34	0	114
MTh	0	7	0	0	0	2	3	0	0	12
TOTALS	199	758	964	1,183	1,972	2,178	2,594	1,774	1,451	13,073

BIBLIOGRAPHY

ORAL AND WRITTEN INTERVIEWS

Don H. Alexander. January 2, 2003, March 10, 2003.
Richard Anderson. December 26, 2002, March 10, 2003.
Don and Barbara Danforth Angle. January 8, 2003, March 14, 2003.
Annella L. Baker. Undated.
Eric W. Berg. July 10, 2002.
John E. Bloss. June 28, 2002.
LaVon Waldron Birdwell. June 30, 2002.
Robert Bonham. August 15, 2002.
Carl Books. July 9, 2002.
Joyce Bridgman. August 16, 2002.
William "Bill" Briggs. December 23, 2002, March 13, 2003.
Cheryl Carpenter. February 21, 2003.
Gene Challenner. January 6, 2003, March 13, 2003.
Sarah Kathryn Alloway Couch. July 8, 2002.
Glenn Cowperthwaite. Undated.
Fred Craddock. December 30, 2002.
Connie Cravens. January 3, 2003, March 13, 2003.
Ed Cravens. January 3, 2003.
Janetta Cravens. January 3, 2003, March 7, 2003.
Patricia Vandersall Crowl. July 19, 2002.
Shirley Cunningham. July 15, 2002.
Nancy Davies. December 12, 2002.
Russel Drumright. March 10, 2003.
Sheldon Elliott. December 30, 2002, March 7, 2003.
Bryan Estabrooks. March 5, 2003.
Joe Evans. February 21, 2003.
Kay Fortson. March 11, 2003.
Eugene N. Frazier. December 21, 2002 and December 28, 2002.
Sylvia Gantz. March 10, 2003.
Kirby Hughes Gould. January 16, 2003, March 13, 2003.
Tiny Murdock Grimes. Undated.
Virginia G. Groendyke. December 19, 2002.
M. Rick Hendricks, March 31, 2003.
Roland K. Huff. July 26, 2002.
Jeanette O'Connor Ice. September 3, 2002.
John Ireland. December 31, 2002, March 10, 2003.
Eldon Jandebeur. July 8, 2002.
Stephen Jones. January 3, 2003, March 7, 2003.
Ed Jorden. March 10, 2003.
Faye Kiryakakis. February 21, 2003.
Tim Kline and Stephen Elliott. December 12, 2002.

Jeanne Marie Kohr. March 7, 2003.
Earl N. Kragnes. July 5, 2002.
Robert A. Langston, Jr. October 1, 2002.
Robert E. Lee. January 11, 2003.
Nancy McKeeman Moats. February 21, 2003.
Louise Moddrell. July 11, 2002.
John P. Moore, Jr. July 11, 2002.
O. Eugene Moore. September 8, 2002, March 14, 2003.
Susan Morford. March 5, 2003.
Beth Murphy. March 11, 2003.
Sandra Nelson. July 3, 2002.
Jeannette Tonaki Okamura. July 26, 2002.
Merle Phillips. March 10, 2003.
Mary Agness Beck (Becky) Proudfoot. September 15, 2002.
Betty Suggs Quinn. Undated.
Geneva Randolph. July 15, 2002.
Randall Rasmussen. July 16, 2002.
Joe Record. December 26, 2002, March 10, 2003.
James Reed. December 26, 2002.
Sandra Anne Parish Remmert. July 23, 2002.
Verna Dean Smith Roberts. July 22, 2002.
Barry Robinson. March 14, 2003.
Art Scott. June 25, 2002.
Bob Seals. July 3, 2002.
Rose Miller Shaklee. July 2, 2002.
Paul Sharp. January 3, 2003.
Robert "Bob" Simpson. March 10, 2003.
Michael R. Sohn. March 17, 2003.
James I. Spainhower. December 28, 2002.
James Strain. July 16, 2002.
Emily Stuckey. March 6, 2003.
Jack Taylor. March 10, 2003.
Kay Taylor. March 10, 2003.
Allison Tobola. March 6, 2003.
Ewel and Mary Vaughan. July 28, 2002.
Elizabeth D. Votaw. July 19, 2002.
Druie L. Warren and Patricia C. Warren. July 2, 2002.
Robert Watkins. August 14, 2002.
Nancy L. Webster. July 14, 2002.
Thurman J. White. Undated.
Leon Whitney. Undated.
Cecil R. Williams. July 15, 2002, March 14, 2003.
Tanya L. Young. March 3, 2003.

MANUSCRIPTS

Lynette Alcorn. "Phillips University Reminiscences 1981-1983." Phillips University Archives. Enid, Oklahoma.

William B. Briggs. "My Story: Autobiography of Bill Briggs." Privately printed, n.d.

Connie Speer Cravens. "Phillips University Alumni and Friends Association." Phillips University Archives. Enid, Oklahoma.

Ernest E. Durham. "Thumb Nail History for Phillips University Alumni & Friends Association." Phillips University Archives. Enid, Oklahoma.

"It's A Woman's World, July 16, 1941." Transcript. Phillips University Archives. Enid, Oklahoma.

G. Curtis Jones, Jr. "Reflections on Phillips University." Phillips University Archives. Enid, Oklahoma.

Keith W. Mielke. "The 'Four Statesmen' A.K.A. 'Phillips Ambassadors.'" Phillips University Archives. Enid, Oklahoma.

O. Eugene Moore. "My Life Story." Phillips University Archives. Enid, Oklahoma.

James E. Strain. "My Recollections of Phillips University." Phillips University Archives. Enid, Oklahoma.

Dale E. Williams. "Memorable Associations with Phillips University in Enid, Oklahoma." Phillips University Archives. Enid, Oklahoma.

Ruth E. (Wolfinger) Williams. "Memorial Associations with Phillips University in Enid, Oklahoma." Phillips University Archives. Enid, Oklahoma.

Lois Moore Wimpey. "Memories of Phillips University, Enid, Oklahoma." Phillips University Archives. Enid, Oklahoma.

NEWSPAPERS

Daily Eagle. Enid, Oklahoma.

The Daily Oklahoman. Oklahoma City, Oklahoma.

The Phillipian. Enid, Oklahoma.

The Slate. Enid, Oklahoma.

PRINTED MATERIAL

Bivins Chapel, Phillips University. Enid: Phillips University, no date.

I. N. McCash. "History of Phillips University." *The Chronicles of Oklahoma*, Vol. XXV, No. 3 (Fall, 1947), pp. 181-197.

Stephen J. England. *Oklahoma Christians: A History of the Christian Churches and the start of the Christian Church (Disciples of Christ) in Oklahoma.* N.p.: Bethany Press, 1975.

_____. *In a Tall Shadow.* Midwest City, Oklahoma: Privately Printed, 1990.

Marquis James. *The Cherokee Strip: A Tale of an Oklahoma Boyhood.* New York: Viking Press, 1945.

Jerry Kirshenbaum. "Win One for the Nipper." *Sports Illustrated* (September 24, 1979), pp. 9-10.

Paul F. Lambert, Kenny A. Franks, and Bob Burke. *Historic Oklahoma: An Illustrated History.* San Antonio: Lambert Publications, Inc., 2000.

Gaston Litton. *History of Oklahoma at the Golden Anniversary of Statehood.* 4 vols., New York: Lewis Historical Publishing Company, 1957.

Frank H. Marshall. *Phillips University's First Fifty Years: Vol. I, The Early Days of Phillips University.* Enid: Phillips University, 1957.

Frank H. Marshall and Wilfred E. Powell. *Phillips University's First Fifty Years: Vol. II, The Turbulent Middle Decades.* Enid: Phillips University, 1960.

Frank H. Marshall and Robert G. Martin. *Phillips University's First Fifty Years: The Period of Greatest Advance.* Enid: Phillips University, 1967.

Ronald E. Osborn. *Ely Vaughn Zollars: Teacher of Preachers, Builders of Colleges.* St. Louis: Christian Board of Publication, 1947.

James Pippin. *A Miracle a Minute: The Unforgettable Story of a Life Lived with God!* Lake Mary, Florida: Creation House Press, 2001.

Stella Campbell Rockwell, ed. *Garfield County, Oklahoma 1893-1982.* Topeka, Kansas: Josten's Publications, 1982.

Jim Strain. "The Iron Men of Phillips Used Just 12 Players in Upsetting Mighty Texas." *Sports Illustrated* (October 19, 1981), unpaged.

Ruth E. Wolfinger Williams, Dale E. Williams, Birge M. Wolfinger, and Barbara Wolfinger Bellatti, compilers. *The Man Called "Wolfinger" As Seen Through the Eyes of His Students, Family & Friends.* Denison, Texas: National Press Printing, 1992.

INDEX

A. H. Ray's Grocery 72
Abbey, Judy 103
academic standards committee 139
Acappella Choir 57
accreditation 30, 169
ACT admission test 121, 166
Adams Elementary School 51, 72
Adams, DeWitt 54
Adams, Joan 57
AddRan Christian University 13
AddRan Male and Female Academy 13
Agra, Oklahoma 23
Aguilera, Gracie 134
Ahart, Jennifer 130
Aikins, Arthur 20
Alamosa River 87
Alber, Raymond 151
Albert, Lindsey B. 179
Alcorn, Lynette 119, 157
Alexander, Don 137, 143, 169, 172, 179
Alexander, W. H. 143
Alfalfa County 20
Ali, Sonny 131
Aline, Oklahoma 149
Allen, Harry 151
Allen, Louise 51
Alma Mater 5, 100, 177
Alpha Beta Kappa 74
Alton Field 147, 148
Alton, Harry 148
Alumni Association 76, 178, 179
Alva, Oklahoma 104, 173
Alyea, P. J. 158
Amaya, Lisa 154
Amaya, Lou 154, 162
Ambassadors 122 *(see Phillips Ambassadors)*
American Association of Colleges 28
American Association of Colleges for Teacher Education 28
American Association of Theological Schools 84
American Christian Missionary Society. 30
American Expeditionary Force 148
American Musical Art Foundation of New York 59
American University Women 62
Ames, Oklahoma 23
Anderson, Brad 161
Anderson, Cheryl 105
Anderson, Elinor 83
Anderson, Richard 107, 112, 113, 130, 138, 139, 142, 162
Anderson, Rose 54
Anderson, Scott 134
Angle, Barbara 84, 85, 178, 181
Angle, Don 84, 85 139, 178, 181
Angle, Virginia 103
anniversary, Phillips 25th 50
Applefest 121, 122
Ardmore, Oklahoma 14
Arizona Club 34
Arkansas 17
Arkansas Club 34
Armistice 31
Army Air Corps 67, 69
Army Air Corps base 69
Arnett, Nathan 131
Art collection 173, 175
Arthur Vining Davis Foundation 118
articles of incorporation 15
Ashcraft, Evelyn 57
Aten, Aaron P. 18
Athenian Hall 15, 19, 35, 36, 39, 52, 53, 67, 71
Athey, Roy 148
Aughtry, Sylvia 156
Austin, Spencer 143
Austin, Texas 179
Autry, O. T. 158
Ayala, Stephanie Graves 181
Aztec Theater 53

Babcock, Lucille 150
Babcock, Roscoe 74
Baker, Annella 55, 84
Baker, Jim 105
Baker, Ken 113
Baker, Vernon R. 55, 86, 87, 120
Balch, Ray 26
Baldwin, Barbara 57
Bales, Bill 149
Ballard, Ray 150
Ballisager, Birna 163
Band Day 53
Bank of Enid 15
Bank, Dorothy 60
Bankruptcy court 170, 171, 173
Baptist Association 13
Bardstown, Kentucky 179
Barker, Allen 163
Barnes, Enid E. 20
Barnett, Jodie 129
Barr, Mary Anna 83
Barron's Profile of American Colleges 121
Bates, Bill 148
Battle of Britain 67
Baxter Springs, Kansas 56
Baylor University 150
Beaty, Geoff 135
Beddow, James 111
Beebe, Natalie 134
Beecher Lectures 124
Behler, James 151
Belgian Congo 85
Bellmon, Ann 97
Bellmon, Shirley 97
Bellmon, Henry 97
Benham, Rod 129
Bennett, Clayton I. 181
Berg, Eric W. 69
Berkeley, California 31
Bethany College 13, 143
Bethany, West Virginia 13
Bible College Fellowship 84
Bible College scholarships 54
Bice, Bethany 120
Bickford, Elizabeth Cleaver 100
Big Eight Conference 162
Big Four Athletic Conference 156
Big Four Basketball Conference 152
Bilinski, Alex 90
Bingo 107
Bird, Alma 57
Bish, Robert A. 74
Bishop, Bessie Alyce 83
Bisophians 63
Bivins Chapel 80, 81, 142, 143
Bixler, Laura Frances 57
Black Awareness Week 108
Black History Week 107
Black Sox 147
Black, Tal 103
Blackman, T. W. 22
Blackman, Will 147
Blackwell, Oklahoma 14
Blake, W. R. 14
Blakelock, Ralph Albert 105, 172, 174, 175
Blakslee, Opal 37
Bloom, Gary 152
Bloss, John E. 67
Blue Key (honor society) 39
bluegrass band 121
Board of Church Extension of the Christian Church (Disciples of Christ) 122, 143
Board of Higher Education of the Christian Church 28
Board, Kirk 109
Bochen, Gabriela 153
Boggess, Mrs. 20
Boggy Creek 15, 19
Bohanon, Richard 171
Bonham, Robert 96
Booker T. Washington School 34, 134
Books, Carl 76
Boosters Club 84, 87
Boring, Eugene 124
Boston Fruit Store 79
Bourbon County, Kentucky 12
Bowlby, Lawrence 151
Boxer Rebellion 134
Bozo Lyles Barbecue Pit 79
Braley, Professor 105
Brawner, Gilbert 84
Brawner, Mrs. 20
Bray, James 106, 174
Brazeal, Vicki 129
Bridgman, Joyce 95, 96
Bridwell, Edward E. 91
Briggs, Eugene Stephen 56, 67, 69, 79, 89, 91, 94, 125, 131, 143, 145, 179
Briggs Auditorium 91, 96, 119, 140
Briggs, Charlie 56, 85
Briggs, Mary 56, 66
Briggs, Maude Butts 20
Briggs, Spencer 178
Briggs, William "Bill" 50, 52, 53, 67, 68, 69, 139, 140, 168
Broadway Dorm 72
Broce, Thomas Edward 108, 112
Broken Arrow, Oklahoma 179
Brown Bag Opera 118
Brown, B. F. 18
Browning, Elizabeth 172
Brownlee, Stan 118
Bruhn, Rich 129
Brush and Pencil Club 58
Brush Run Church 12, 13
Bryan, William 124
Bryant, DuRee 109
Buley, Mrs. 20
Buller, Charlie 152
Bullis, Jacob E. 179
Bundren, Clark 109
Bunn, Joe 163
Bunton, Julie 134
Burdick, Shelly 131
Bureau of Public Relations 50
Burkhardt v. City of Enid 124
Burkhardt, Ted and Cathy 123
Burkhart, Charles A. 20
Burkhart, Helen 57

Burkholder, Rich 156, 161
Busch, Carl 54
Bush, Connie 104
Butler, Missouri 85
Buttrey, F. W. 22
Butts, Mrs. Earl 88
Buy-a-Brick Campaign 62, 115
By the Fire 174

Camacho, Roseanna 179
Camelot Club 74, 111, 135
Cameron, Emory 45
Cameron, Glenda 154
CameZontalot Spookaculur Halloween party 135
camp meeting 12
Campbell, Alexander 13, 143
Campbell, Dorothy 57
Campbell, Gini Moore 181
Campbell, Marjorie 153
Campbell, Thomas 12, 13
Campbell, Tommy 67
Campolo, Tony 143
Campus Courts 72
campus protest 94
Campus Store 79, 95
Cane Ridge, Kentucky 12
Canfield, Susan 156
Cannamugh, Pennsylvania 12
Cannon, Karen 154, 155
Capital Area Phillipian Society 138
Carano, Kristi 158
Cardinal Key Club 39, 60, 79
Carey, Milburn 53, 54, 68
Carlson, Ray 63
Carnell, Hettie Ruth 63
Carney, Oklahoma 23
Carpenter, Cheryl 180, 181
Carr, Tim 161
Carrier, Dahl 149
Carstensen, Roger 74, 84, 140
Carter, Carole 159, 163
Carter, Clifford 138
Carter, Hazel 138
"Celebrate the Life of Phillips" 178
Central Christian Church 34, 54, 63, 135
Cermack, Sandra 156
Cerropian Literary Society 34
Challenner, Gene 179
Chamber of Commerce Building 15
Chambers, Kevin 161
Champlin Oil Company of Enid 48
Chancel Window 81
Chapman, Beth 130
Chapman, G. J. 23
Chappell, Rand 163
Chapter 11 bankruptcy 170
Chapter 11 reorganization 169

Charlton, Artie 148
Charlton, Bryan 109
Charlton, Etta 37, 149
Charlton, John 26
Chase, Herbert 94
Chat, Orville 146
Chenoweth and Green Music Company 69
Cherokee Outlet 33
Cherokee Strip Museum 174
Cherokee, Oklahoma 23
Chesnutt, Meta 13
Chicago Bears 149
Chicago White Sox 147
Chicago, Rock Island, and Pacific Railroad 23
Chickasha, Oklahoma 15, 139
Chilocco Indian School 152
Chisum, Dana 113
Choitz, Janna 154
Chou, A. C. Chi 88
Christensen, James L. 103
Christian Association of Washington, Pennsylvania 12
Christian Church 11, 12, 13, 14, 17, 19, 23, 28, 34, 39, 52, 56, 117, 118, 123, 124, 143
Christian Church Foundation 143
Christian College 56
Christian Missionary Society for Indian Territory 13
Christian Theological Seminary 125
Christian Youth Fellowship 169
Christian Youth Fellowship (CYF) Weekend 121
Christian, Phillip 161
Christianson, Nancy 103
Church Financial Council for America 115
Cincinnati, Ohio 178
Circle K 113
Civil Aeronautics Authority 67
civil rights 89
Civil War 175
Civilian Pilot Training Program (CPTP) 67
Clanton, Mark 161
Clark, Addison 13
Clark, Cerne 104
Clark, Randolph 13
Clark, Viola 58
Clark, Willo Lovell 178
Clay Hall 62, 64, 65, 67, 69, 74, 108, 110
Clay, Robert Henry 62
Clay, Sadie 62
Cleeland, Bob 161, 163
Clegg, Howard 85, 86
Cleo Springs, Oklahoma 23, 149
Cleveland Bulldogs 149

Cleveland, Austin 146
Cleveland, Lloyd 88
Cleveland, Maude 26
Cleveland, Mrs. Ora 20
Cline, Duane A. 96
Clown Alley 128
clubs 133
Coach House 79, 95, 108
Coast Trip 152
Cody, Roy 151
Coffey, Butch 123
Cohlmia, Casey 60
Cold War 140
College of the Bible 12, 14, 15, 20, 23, 28, 31, 34, 38, 42, 45, 50, 51, 52, 54, 84, 96, 104, 143
College Station, Texas 115
Colorado 17
Colorado Club 34
Colorado Springs, Colorado 142
Columbia College 179
Columbia, Missouri 56, 179
Colwell, Cynthia 129
Comets 62, 83, 134
Communication Building 20
Conley, Verna 58
Conners Agricultural College 146
Cook, Pat 154
Cook, Paul 54, 147, 151
Cook, Randolph 14, 15
Copas, Truman A. 145
Copenhaver, Laura 156
Copernicus Conference 111
corinthian columns 48
Cosmopolitan Club 56, 79, 90
Couch, Sarah Kathryn Alloway 54
Council Hill, Kansas 23
County Down, Ireland 12
County Poor Farm, 34
Couse, E. Irving 174
Covey, C. V. 50
Covington, Oklahoma 133, 166
Cowan, Ronald 115
Cowperthwaite, Glenn 72
Cozart, Dorothy 114
Cozby, J. Louis 141
Craddock, Fred 124, 143
Craddock, Laura 110
Crain, James 20, 147
Cramblet, W. H. 30, 146, 147, 148
Cravens, Connie Speer 140, 142, 178, 179
Cravens, Ed, Jr. 142, 178
Cravens, Janetta 124, 130, 140, 142, 143, 169, 170, 171, 172, 178
Cravens, Matthew 178
Critchfield, Alison 179
Crosby, David 168

Crosby, Marie 51, 54
Crosby, Stills & Nash 168
Crose, Jo Ann 83
Crowl, Patricia Vandersall 52
Crown Literary Society 34
Crum, Marilyn 83
Crum, Mike 96
Crusaders Club 84
Culver-Stockton College 179
Cumberland County, Illinois 30
Cummins, Duane 143
Cuppy, A. C. 74
Curl, Kelly 159
Curl, Samuel Everett 115
Curtis, Gene 88
Curtis, Roy 146

Dabney, Eric 181
Dabney, Shelley 181
Daerwiller, Kyla 123
Dahlem, John 152
Dallas, Texas 19
Dan and Bake's 79
dancing 53, 99, 108, 122
Danforth, Barbara 84
Danforth, Linda 75
Darst, Wilma Jean 57
Davenport, Wanda 88
Davies, Nancy 118, 128, 130
Davis Caldwell Academy 12
Davis, Glenn 156
Davis, Jerry 83
Davis, Martin 151
Davis, Virginia 138
Dean, T. R. 14
debate teams 38
Declaration and Address 12
Defense Bonds 69
Deffenbaugh, Max 152
DeLapp, Neil 141
Dellenback, Doris 57
Delmar Garden 33
Delphi Literary Society 34
Deming, Jim 103
Denny Price Family YMCA 179
Denny Price Memorial Foundation 179
Denny, Paul 67, 112, 113, 129
Denver University 150
Denver, Colorado 158
Department of Religious Education of the United Christian Missionary Society 143
depression 50, 51, 52, 53, 56, 59
(see Great Depression)
Des Moines, Iowa 30
desegregation 89
DeVos, Ton 101
Dewell, Lena 150
Diamond Jubilee 119, 157

Index 193

Dillinger, Alice, and John (see Library Endowment Fund) 56
"Dirty Thirties" 59
Disciples of Christ Historical Society 143
Division of Higher Education of the Christian Church (Disciples of Christ) 143, 165, 179, 182
Dixon, James 107
Dodson, Sarah A. 18
Dorsey, Kent 142
Dougherty, Cindy Ferguson 143
Dougherty, Domer 120
downtown Enid 18, 98
Doyle, Glenn 104, 112
Dr. Bill Snodgrass lecture series 178
Drake University 30
Drake, Tim 135
Driskell, Ron 109
Driskill, Bayne 50
drought 49
Drummond, Oklahoma 23
Drumright, Russel 140, 141
Drury University 179
Dryburg, Brenda 128
Duffy, Mike 104
Dugan, Gretchen 138
Dugan, Henry 138
Dugan, Ivan 138
Duke University 108
Dunnington, Norman 63
Durant, Oklahoma 56
Durham, Ernest E. 52, 91
dust bowl 49, 50
dust storms 50
Dyksterhus, Rein 18, 32

Eargle, Ed 131
Earl Butts Dormitory 88, 89, 94, 99, 109, 115
Earley, Pete 113
Earth Day 131
East Broadway 15, 35
East Hall 72, 73, 74, 96, 99
East Maine Street, Enid 18, 31
Eby, Noda 37
Edwards, Arleta 109, 110
Edwards, Margaret 108, 141
Edwards, Minnie Coleman 20
Ehly, A. M. 56
Ehly, Vic 96
El Meta Christian College 13
El Reno, Oklahoma 15
Elliott, Arthur 85, 94
Elliott, Dr. and Mrs. Arthur 96
Elliott, Sally 57
Elliott, Sheldon 94, 130, 131, 139, 163, 179
Elliott, Stephen 170, 179

Elliott-Goulter Apartments 96, 99
Ellis, Karen Lauer 129
Ellis, Marilyn 88
Embach, First Lt. H. E. 31
Emblem, Nicky 160
England, Stephen J. 15, 28, 42, 45, 50, 52, 67, 69, 72, 84, 96, 103, 156
Enid, Oklahoma 15, 18, 20, 22, 31, 34, 35, 39, 44, 50, 51, 52, 53, 56, 59, 62, 63, 68, 69, 74, 89, 91, 94, 97, 98, 103, 107, 113, 118, 120, 122, 125, 126, 128, 129, 130, 133, 134, 138, 140, 141, 142, 147, 151, 156, 158, 160, 163, 166, 167, 168, 169, 171, 173, 175, 180
Enid American Business Club 50
Enid Bank and Trust Building 48
Enid Building 61, 62
Enid Chamber of Commerce 15, 54, 61
Enid City Council 124
Enid City Library 90
Enid Eagle 34
Enid Events 61
Enid Commercial Club 28
Enid Fire Department 157
Enid Garden Club 50
Enid High School 33, 51, 160
Enid High School band 113
Enid Higher Education Program 128
Enid Inter-Racial Club 107
Enid Lions Club 79
Enid News & Eagle 160
Enid Pentecostal Holiness Church 74
Enid Police Department 53
Enid Symphony Orchestra 53
Enid University Investment and Development Company 15
Enid YWCA 54
Enid-Phillips Symphony Orchestra 104, 131, 140
Enid-Phillips University Concert Orchestra 94
Enos, Jack 63
entrance requirements 20
Environmental Science Club 131
Estabrooks, Bryan 179, 180
Eta chapter of Tau Beta Sigma 74
Eureka College 165, 179
Eureka Springs, Arkansas 55
Eureka, Illinois 179
Evans, Chris 120
Evans, Jeff 122
Everest Administration Building 73, 102
Everest, Harvey P. 66, 102
Everly, Charles 141

Everts, Rosecrans 19
Ewing, Edna 26
Ewington Academy 30

Faculty Development Scholarships 179
Faculty Participation Committee 50
Faculty/Professional Development Scholarships 179
Fall Joust 111
Farley, Eldon 63
Farris, Ruthella 83
Ferrante and Teicher 91, 140
Festival of the Arts 101, 104
Field Artillery Regiment (189th) 42
Field Placement Program 23
fields of study (at Phillips) 119, 139
Fields, Kim 110
Fields, Shaunna 155
Fighting Haymaker 151, 157, 158
Fillies basketball team 155, 156, 163
Fine Arts Building 15, 19, 38, 76, 174
Firkins, Ann 110
First Battalion Headquarters Detachment and Combat Training 42
First Christian Church in Oklahoma City 62, 137, 169
First Christian Church of Tulsa 99
First Headquarters Battalion 42
First Methodist Church 34
First National Bank, Enid 23
Fisher, "Bud" 47
Fitzgerald, Heather 128
Fitzpatrick, Vernon 161
Fleming, Robert 82
Florida College 173
Folkhogskola 112
Football Queen Contest 45
Ford 15
Forest Lake, Minnesota 69
Fort Supply Correctional Institute 169
Fort Worth, Texas 13, 82, 166
fortieth anniversary, Phillips University 78
Fortson, Homer 94
Foster, Jackie 113
Founder's Day 91
Four Statesmen 85, 86, 87
Four Women West 130
Fourth National Bank of Wichita, Kansas 25
Frank Hawkins Grocery 51
Frantz, Bill 148
Frantz, Edmund 15

fraternities and sororities 38
Frazier, Bonnie 72, 141
Frazier, Cindy 109
Frazier, Eugene 72, 79, 141
Frazier, Jamie 109
Freeman, Melanie 156
Friend, Walter 147
Friends University 13
friendship fire 75, 122
Froggie's 79
Frosh Initiation 35
Fund for the Improvement of Postsecondary Education (FIPSE) 127
Funk, Charles 20, 147
Future Teachers of America 28

Gabeau, Kelly 156
Gage, Oklahoma 91
Gamma Upsilon chapter, Phi Mu Alpha Sinfonia 74
Gammel, Janet 109
Gantz, Hallie G. 67, 97, 99, 102, 103, 104, 105, 106, 108, 112, 139, 174
Gantz Center 111, 118, 177
Gantz, Sylvia 99, 108, 112, 114
Garfield County 59
Garfield County Courthouse 15
Garfield County District Court 123
Garfield Exchange Bank 15
Garfield Memorial University 13
Garfield University 13
Garriott, Owen K., Jr. 110
Garrison, Sarah W. 22
Garrou, Kerri 155
Gebhart, Barry 161
Gee, Gary 109
Geil, Earl 138
Geil, Mr. and Mrs. Glen 138
Geil, Robert 138
Genchur, Tom 104
General Assembly of the Christian Church (Disciples of Christ) 178
George Mason University 165
Georgetown College 163
Gerardy, Dana 135
German Club 34
Gettel, Jean Claire 58
Gettings, Vonette 105
Geurkink, Larry 152
GI Bill 72, 74
Gibble, Mrs. William T. 20
Gibble, William T. 143, 151
Gibson, Arrell 85
Gibson, Mrs. Arrell 83
Gibson, Patty 83
Giffen, Ethel 88
Gillet, Mike 123

Gilmore, Ali 128, 129
Gingerich, Jenni 142
Girls' Drum Corps 47
glee club 54
Glenn, Ralph 119
Glory of Our Phillips U, The 178
Goh, Stephanie 179
Goldman, Edwin Franko 53, 54
golf 162
golf course 74, 179
Gomez, Tara 134
Goode, Bonnie 37, 149
Gooden, Susan 154
Goodman, Ben 104
Goodness, Betty 60
Gordon, Lem 121
Gorton, John E. 20
Gospel Team 84
Gould, Andrea 143
Gould, Bill 53
Gould, Kirby Hughes 121, 139, 140, 143, 173
Gould, Ruth 138
Goulter, Dr. and Mrs. Oswald 43, 96
Government Building 99
Government Military School 31
Grace Phillips Johnson Art Gallery 99
Grace, Teresa 109
Graves, Jones 45
Gray, Donita 153
Gray, Wess 172, 181
Great Depression 47, 49, 61, 91, 142, 156
Greek letter organizations 39
Green, Frederick 54
Gridiron Club 45, 59, 133, 135, 151
Gridiron Minstrels Club 59
Gridiron Quiz Bowl Team 135
Grimes, Louise 57
Grimes, Tiny Murdock 51
Groendyke, Virginia 165, 166
Growth With Quality plan 99
Guitar Player Magazine 168
Guthrie, Oklahoma 14, 15
Gwinn, Mary 57

Habitat for Humanity 134
Hackler, Deborah 120
Hages, Everett 26
Hahn, C. D. 51
Halbert, Larry 152
Hall, Amanda R. 179
Hall, Betty 88
Hall, Bob 171, 179
Hallie G. Gantz Student Center 111, 114
Hamburger, Roberta 124
Hamilton, F. L. 15

Hammer, Donna 63
Haney, Teresa 140
Harfert, Nell 123
Hargrove, Frank K. 20, 22
Harmon Hall 118
Harmon, Henry 54
Harmon, Homer 151
Harmon, John 147
Harms, Dorothea 138
Harms, John 138
Harms, Mary Frances 138
Harms, Pearl 138
Harris, Ethel Mae 29
Harrison, Vernal 58
Hart, J. S. 15
Hartshorne, Oklahoma 82
Harvesters Club 48, 59, 84, 86
Hatt, Harold 124
Hauser, Susan 141
Havner, Galen 105
Hawkins, S. R. 13
Hawkins, Texas 179
Hawley, Billy 161
Hayes, Frances 63
Haymaker, The 20, 47, 60, 96, 107, 113, 128
Haymaker Inn 44, 51
Haymaker Meadow 146
Haymaker, Cara L. 179
Haymaker, J. N. 25
Haymakers 146, 147, 151, 152, 156, 161, 163
Headquarters Battery 42
Healing Window 80
Heath, Don 130
Hedges, Michael 168
Hedges, Thayne 91, 102
Heenan, Rita 153
Hegel, George William 140
Helping Window 80
Hemphill, Scott 128
Hendricks, Rick 74, 140
Hennessey, Oklahoma 23, 179
Henning, William 111
Henry Kendall College 146
Henryetta First Christian Church 97
Henryetta, Oklahoma 97
Henson, Minnie 63
Hermanzski, Angela 128
Herrick, Dale 104
Heydman, Tom 152
Hibbs, Carl 20
Highland, Eugene 52
Hilbig, Billie 178, 181
Hill, Greg 123
Hill, Holly 128
Hill, Kathye 109
Hilligoss, Elizabeth 122
Hilligoss, Ray 129
Hilsabeck, Betty 60

Hinson, Leonora 150
Hiram College 13, 87, 179
Hiram, Ohio 13
Hitchcock, Oklahoma 23
Hobart, Henry 54, 55, 72, 74, 94
Hobart, Lois 83
Hodge, Orville 20, 22
Hodson, Eric 179
Hoffines, Ruth 57
Hoffman, Heather-Nicole 135
Holcomb, Janice 105
Holdenville 14
Holland, Jo 156
Holland, Rhea 149
Holle, Teri 139
Holm, Dallas 91
Holt, Bobbie Mae 58
Homecoming 109, 114
Homecoming Quilt 135
Honor System 107
Hood, Lorraine 60
Hood, Richard 153
Hope of the World, The 76
Hopkins, Jo Ann 106
Hopkins, Paul 103
Hopper, Kathryn 60
Horn, Samuel H. 18
Horne, George 84
Horton, Loren 60
Horton, Philip 120
Hostetler, Carolyn 105
Howard, T. J. 63
Howell, Harriet 122
Hubbard, Anna 181
Huff, Patricia 101
Huff, Roland K. 51, 143
Huggins, Ron 118
Hughes, Debbie 110, 113
Hughes, Dennis 111
Hulse, James 131
Humphrey, W. A. 14, 15, 22
Humphries, Susan 113
Hunter, Oklahoma 23
Huntsville, Texas 163
Hurley, Peggy 154
Hutchinson, George E. 42
Hutchinson, Kansas 85
Hutton, Ward S. 147

Iba, Henry 162
Ice, Jeanette O'Connor 54
Imbler, Toni Wine 179
Imhoff, Charlene Brannen 91
Indian Encampment Along the Snake River 105, 172, 174, 175
Indian Territory 17
Indianapolis, Indiana 125
Indians' Concerns Conference 107
Inglish, Angela M. 179
Inside Phillips 142

Inspiration Point 55
Inspiration Point Fine Arts Colony 74
Institute for Biblical Literacy 74
Inter-Club Council 39, 103
intercollegiate and intramural sports 145
International Olympic Committee 148
internment camps 69
intramural competition 159
intramural program 158
Intramural sports 156, 161
Ireland, John 67, 69, 71, 79, 82, 105, 125, 129
Iron Men 148, 149, 150

Jackman, C. M. 14, 25
Jackson, Dorothy 83
Jackson, Sammy 161
Jacobs, Norman E. 104
James, Laine 129
James, Marquis 33
Jandebeur, Eldon 67, 72
Japanese Christian Bazaar 56
Jarvis Christian College 179
Jefferies, Irene 105
Jeffrey, Jerry 152
Joe Jones and Sarah Jones Lectures 140
John, Jerrianne 156
Johnson Art Gallery 99, 111
Johnson Bible College 84
Johnson Club 84
Johnson, Connie 105
Johnson, E. B. 14, 15
Johnson, Elizabeth 128
Johnson, Gary 124
Johnson, Grace Phillips 101, 174, 175
Johnson, Janice and John 110
Johnson, Randy 122
Johnson, Renee 110
Johnson, Tracy 122
Johnson-Kiewlich, Stephanie 175
Joint Industrial Foundation 173
Jones, G. Curtis 143
Jones, G. Curtis, Jr. 119, 120, 125, 131, 157, 162, 165, 166, 167, 170, 171, 172, 173, 179, 181
Jones, Becky 172
Jones, Dorothy 107
Jones, Joe R. 117, 118, 119, 120, 124, 125
Jones, Kathy 155
Jones, Kem 156
Jones, Stephen 123, 124, 125, 131, 170, 171
Jordan, Julia 123
Jorden, Edward 125

Index 195

Journalism Building 99
Joyce, J. Daniel 95, 103
Jumanji 107

Kalka, Sue 122
Kansas City Cowboys 149
Kansas City Federal Reserve Bank 168
Kansas City Monarchs 152
Kansas City, Missouri 25, 151
Kansas City Symphony 54
Kansas Klub 34
Kansas Society of Friends 13
Karelis, Charles H. 127
Karlsson, Marie 128
Karrenbrock, Kris 109
Keen, Joy Lou 83
Keller, Fred 85
Keller, Kris 123
Kemp, Chuck 129
Kennedy, Bryce 124
Kennedy, John F. 101
Kennedy, Robert 101
Kennemer, Wayne 163
Kenney, Tom 86
Kentucky Classical and Business College 13
Kesnear, Mauritz 54
Kidd, Midge 83
Killian, Bob 86
Kim, Joe 90
King scholarship 107
King's Messengers Club 84
King, George 94
King, Karl 68
King, Martin Luther, Jr. 101, 107
King, Mildred 60
King, Sandy 153
Kingen, W. L. Wicky 54, 151
Kingfisher College 149
Kingfisher, Oklahoma 85
Kirtley, Edwin 79
Kiryakakis, Faye 130, 178
Klamm, Kevin 134
Kline & Kline 170
Kline, David 170
Kline, Tim 170, 171
Knights of Camelot 135
Knights of Knowledge 47
Knowles Physics Club 74
Knowles, Frank E. 42
Knoxville, Tennessee, 84
Knoy, Zane 88
Knutsen, Mary 124
Kohr, Jeanne Marie 126, 128, 134, 140, 141, 180
Krebaum, Steve 120
Kreie, Wanda 58
Krocker, Annette 153
Kroeker, Charlotte 126
Kroeker, Wesley 162

Krumrei, Mary K. 179
Kuehny, Pam 156
Kurland, Bob 158
Kyoto Institute of Technology (KIT) 125

Lacy, L. L. 51
ladies' gymnasium 29, 76, 114
Lady Haymakers 150
Lamb, Jefferson D. Hoy 45
Lambert family 142
Lambert, Lloyd 79
Lambert, Michael 141
Landon, Dennis 179
Langston University 89
Langston, David 113
Lankard Apartments 97, 99
Lansdown, Connie 105
Lappin, John C. 50
Larned, Kansas 54
Lash, Frank 20, 147
Last Will and Testament of the Springfield Presbytery 12
Latchaw, Ruth 58
Lawson, Jeff 162
Leadership Conference for Phillips University Legacy Scholars 182
Lear, C. E. 96
Lee, Robert E. 56
Lee, Timothy 90
LeMay, William N. 15, 18, 22, 23
Lemon, Haskell and Irene 108
Leonardo's Discovery Warehouse 129, 133, 135
"Let Every Student Buy a Bond" 69
Letter Club 150
Levi, John 149, 150
Lewis, B. Kenneth 101, 120
Lewis, Terry 141
Lexington, Kentucky 13
Libra Club 90
Library Building 18, 22, 24
Lidell, Craig 160
Lil' Hay (Little Hay) 157
Lil' Phil 157
Lincoln, Mrs. 20
Linden, Gladys 47
Lindenwood University 143
Lindsay, Cindy 128, 129
Lions International 79
literary societies 34
Little Rock, Arkansas 179
Little, Ray 169
Lively, Linda 105
Living Options 115
Livingston, Charles 54
Loader, Bethany A. 179
Logan County, Kentucky 12
Long, Beth 113
Long, Mona 118

Long, Phil 67
Long, R. A. 25, 27
Longfellow Junior High School 51
Longman, Tim 123
Lookingbill, Brad 179
Lounsbury, Lawrence L. 39, 56
Lovejoy, Betty Frances 60
Lovejoy, Tim 122
Lowen, Al 15
Lower Salem, Ohio 13
Lowery, Richard H. 179
Lucas, Frank 170
Lucas, Todd 123
Lugar, Durand 152
Lyberopoulou, Despina 90
Lynchburg College 179
Lyons, Kansas 30

Mabee Center 48, 62, 112, 114, 115
Mabee Foundation 115
MacAllister, Bruce 109
mace (of Phillips University) 67
Mack, Wendy 134
Mackie, Bert 118
MacViers, Thomas Holmes 142
Madison Debating Club 38
Madrigal Dinner 118, 119
Main Building 15
Maine Street 62
Maintenance Building 99
Major, Judy 154
Managbanag, Betty, Esther, Sarah, Ruth 79
Manahan, Ethel 58
Manley, Mrs. 20
Manley, O. Page 31
map (of the Phillips University campus) 173
Maples, Jim 152
March Madness 134
Marland, E. W. 49
Maroon Pencil Club 47
Marshall Building 20, 74, 78, 79, 80, 81, 123, 142
Marshall, Frank Hamilton 13, 18, 19, 28, 34, 52, 56
Marshall, Jody 103
Marshall, Mrs. Frank H. 18, 84
Martin, J. B. 14
Martin, Mrs. Robert 57
Martin, Robert G. 52
Martin, W. A. 15
Martindale, Katy 154
Martz, Matt 123
Mary E. Bivins Chapel 80, 81 (see Bivins Chapel)
Maryville College 96
Maryville, Tennessee 96
mascot (Phillips) 157
Mash, Jerry 137, 138, 139

Mason, J. R. 14
Mason, Lysle 86, 120, 140
Mason, Martha D. 37
Masquers Club 44, 45
Mathieson, T. H. 34
Maulbetsch, John F. 147, 148, 150
Maupin, Mr. and Mrs. 138
Mavon Club 69
Maxwell, Steve 120
May Fete 108
Mayberry, Edith 102
Mayberry, Everett 67
Mayberry, S. N. 20, 22
McCafferty, Ethel 149
McCash, Isaac Newton 30, 38, 45, 46, 54, 56
McCash, Marietta Tandy 45
McCash, Mrs. Isaac Newton 84
McClain, Pearl 149
McCoy, Carol 155
McCoy, Mindy 171
McDonnell Douglas Astronautics 168
McElroy, Ethel 23
McElwain, Juanita 129
McGready, James 12
McHugh, Barbara 83
McIntyre, M. M. 151
McKeever, H. G. 15
McKinney, Ed W. 15
McKinney, Texas 179
McLaughlin, Tom 56
McLean, Stuart 124
McMahan, Craig 105
McMahan, Deanie 83
McMahan, Greg 109
McMillan, Irma 37
McMullen, Bard 103, 141
McNaught, Roy 85, 86
McNelly, Marsha 155
McNutt, "Boob" 47
McSpadden, Bob 162
McSpadden, Jean 162
McSpadden, Mark 162
McSpadden, Phil 162
McSpadden, Robin 162
McWaters, Shawna 123
Medford, Oklahoma 23
Medicine Lodge, Kansas 62
Meech, Lynn 152
Meis, Armon 63
Memories of the Science Camp 88, 112
Men and Millions Movement 30
Merman, Ethel 140
Merrick, Karen 113
Messiah, The 95
Methodist College 146
Methodist University 146
Mexican mission 51
Meyer, John 123

Mia, Abdul J. 179
Miami, Texas 91
Midway College 179
Midway Dance Hall 34
Midway, Kentucky 179
Mielke, Keith 85, 86
Miles, Mike 104
Millard Fillmore Society, 114
Miller, Joe 131
Miller, Justin 121
Miller, Susan 140
Million Dollar Drive 50
Mills, Vance 151
Minco Christian Church 13
Minco, Oklahoma 13
Minister's Week 143
Ministerial Association 38, 58
Ministerial Institute of Oklahoma 14
Miss America 106
Miss Phillips pageant, 115
missionaries 43, 45, 85
Missionary Board of Indian Territory 14
Missionary Board of Oklahoma Territory 14
Missouri Club 34
Mitchell, David 86
Mitchell, Don 76, 86
Mittrata Club 79
Moats, Nancy McKeeman 72
Mogab's Grocery 51
Mogle, Jean 153
Money, Russell 88
Monroe, J. M. 13, 14, 15
Monsour, Naseef 30
Monte Vista, Colorado 87
Moore, Gene 12, 54, 91, 151
Moore, George 141
Moore, John P., Jr. 97
Moore, O. Eugene (see Moore, Gene)
More, Lorraine 57
More, Wilma 57
Morford, Susan 134, 141
Morgan, Dick T. 14, 15
Morgan, Mike 121
Morris, J. A. 52
Morrison, Oklahoma 23
Morrison, Ira 101
Morse, Mr. and Mrs. J. Russell 43
Moss, Esther Lillian 45
Mothers Association of Phillips 62
Mountain Home, Arkansas 85, 86
Mu Phi Epsilon 74, 104
Mullins, Bennie 157
Mullins, "Moon" 47
Mullsjo, Sweden 112, 120, 129
Murdock, Zeta 51
Murphy, Beth 103, 120, 125, 129, 139, 141

Murphy, Greg 123
Murray, R. J. 88
Museum of the Cherokee Strip 99
Music Building 63
Music Hall 40
music scholarships 39
Music therapy 129
Muskogee, Oklahoma 52
Mystic Harmony, The 81

NAACP 88, 89
NAACP Youth Conference in Houston, Texas 88, 89
Naftzger, S. M. 25
Nagasaki, Japan 69
NAIA 158, 159, 162, 163
NAIA Baseball Hall of Fame 154
Naismith Basketball Hall of Fame 148
Nash, Lucilla 122
National Amateur Athletic Union 152
National Amateur Athletic Union Tournament 158
National Association for the Advancement of Colored People (NAACP) 88, 89
National Association of Intercollegiate Athletics (NAIA) 158
National Association of Schools of Music Education 28
National Basketball Association (NBA) 159, 163
National Benevolent Association of the Disciples 143
National Football League (NFL) 149
National Guard 27, 44
National Youth Administration (NYA) 51
Neale, George A. 41
Negro Leagues 152
Neill, Debbie 181
Nelson, Jon 95
Nelson, Ralph W. 52
New Castle, Pennsylvania 26, 174
New Christy Minstrels 96
New Deal 51
New York Giants 149
Newby, Errett 56, 66
Newman, Laura 128
Nichols, Bill 140
Nichols, C. William 56
Nicholson, Jack 97
Nick H. Nicholas' grocery 51
Nickel, Donna 105
Nickles, Don 170
Nigh, George 117
Nixon, Richard 101
Noblitt, T. L. 18

Norman, Oklahoma 14, 15, 179
North Central Accrediting Agency 130
North Central Association of Colleges and Schools 27, 125, 167, 169
North Central Association of Colleges and Schools accreditation 30
North Enid, Oklahoma 72
North Middleton, Kentucky 13
North Platte, Nebraska 85
Northern Oklahoma College 91, 120, 121, 128, 173
Northwestern Oklahoma State University (NWOSU) 128, 166, 173, 177
Northwestern State Teachers College 149, 150

Oberg, Earl W. 44, 51, 79, 82, 84
Oberg, Mrs. Earl W. 82
October Fest 134
Ogle, Joseph 56
Ogle, Nancy 101
Ogle, Stan 152
Ohio State University 91
Okamura, Jeannette Tonaki 84
Oklahoma 17
Oklahoma A&M 145, 146, 149, 150, 158, 162
Oklahoma Arts and Humanities Council 101
Oklahoma Baptist University 151, 152
Oklahoma Basketball Championship 150
Oklahoma Christian Church's Program of Progress 115
Oklahoma Christian University 15, 18, 19, 20, 22, 23, 25, 26, 27, 32, 33, 35, 36, 37, 38, 145, 146, 148
Oklahoma Christian University Debate Team 37
Oklahoma Christian University Girls Glee Club 37
Oklahoma Christian University men's baseball team 148
Oklahoma Christian University of Science and Arts 172
Oklahoma City, Oklahoma 14, 15, 29, 121, 147, 170, 172
Oklahoma City University 151, 152, 163
Oklahoma Collegiate Conference Golf Championship 158
Oklahoma Heritage Association 181
Oklahoma National Guard 42, 67

Oklahoma National Guard Armory at Phillips University 42
Oklahoma School of Mines and Metallurgy 156
Oklahoma Softball Hall of Fame. 155
Oklahoma State Basketball Championship 151
Oklahoma State Board of Education 29
Oklahoma State Regents of Higher Education 173
Oklahoma State University 122, 128, 145
Oklahoma Supreme Court 124
Oklahoma Teacher Certification Test 127
Oklahoma Territory 33, 88
Oklahoma Territory Missionary Societies 17
Okmulgee, Oklahoma 56
Old Main 15, 16, 19, 38, 44, 52, 71, 76, 77, 79, 91, 145
Olympian Literary Society 34
opera club 54
Operation Book Lift 102
Oral Roberts University 76, 96, 169
Oregon Club 34
Orlando, Oklahoma 23
Osaka, Japan 125
Osborn, G. Edwin 52, 67
Osborn, Prudence 58
Osborn, Ronald 143
Oswald, Lee Harvey 101
Ousley, Pam 113
Owen, Steve 148, 149, 150
"owl" streetcars 34
Oxford University 118
Ozark Bible Conference 55
Ozarks 85

Page, Aletha 83
Page, Claudia Zollars 18, 26
Page, Harlan M. 22
Palmer, Mrs. W. I. 20
Palmer, Russell 151
Palmer, Temple 149
Pamerleau, Susan 142, 169
Panhandle of Texas 23
Parham, Susan 109
Park Avenue Christian Church in New York City 79
Parker, Helen 57
Parli, Pam 105
Parrish, Bette Jayne 119
Parsons, Jeanette 83
Passmore, Mike 109
Pawlak, Stanislaw 140
Payne, Clyde 37

Index 197

Payne, Effie 37
Payne, Ella 37
PDQ Bach 140
Peabody Seminary 30
Pearl and Julia Harmon Foundation 118
Pearl Harbor 67, 69
Peavey, Claud 26
Peck, Robert 67, 125, 126, 129, 130, 140, 163
Peck, Betty 105
Peil, Eileen 105
Pendleton, O. Edmund 78
Penn Square Bank 121
Penn, Elizabeth 149
pennant 35
Pension Fund of the Christian Church 143
Perdue, Leo 124
Perisho House 72
Perkins School of Theology 118
Perkins, Madison Love 53
Person, Ray 121
Peter, Wilma 57
Peters, Casey L. 179
Peterson's Competitive Colleges 121
Pettigrew, Janice 103
Phi Mu Alpha 104
Philia Dona Clown Alley 119 (see Clown Alley)
Phillibooster Club 151
Philliboosters 150
Phillipian 54, 75, 94, 107, 142, 146
Phillipian Choristers 57
"Phillipian Festival March" 68
Phillips alumni 138
Phillips Alumni Association 178
Phillips Ambassadors 85, 129 (see Ambassadors)
Phillips Campus Book Store 88
Phillips cheerleaders 155
Phillips Christian University 27
Phillips Fillies 154
Phillips High School 20, 26, 28, 30, 45, 150, 151
Phillips Legacy Scholars 179
Phillips Library 52
Phillips Lifetime Churches 56
Phillips Lunch (later the Haymaker Inn) 44
Phillips Madrigal Singers 104
Phillips Petroleum Company 131
Phillips Players 96
Phillips Science Camp 85, 86, 87, 88, 108, 125, 143
Phillips Service League 69
Phillips Speech and Hearing Center 91
Phillips Student Senate 104
Phillips Student Union 51

Phillips Theological Seminary 123, 124, 167, 168, 179
Phillips University Board of Trustees 182
Phillips University Choir 120
Phillips University Alumni and Friends Association 177, 178, 179, 182
Phillips University Band 42, 53, 79
Phillips University Chorus 88, 104
Phillips University Civilian Defense Committee 69
Phillips University Endowment Crusade 45
Phillips University International in Japan 125, 126
Phillips University Kazoo Zoo Band 114
Phillips University Legacy Foundation 173, 179, 182
Phillips University Press 79
Phillips University, origin of name 26, 27
Phillips, Thomas W. 13, 14, 26, 101, 174, 175
Phillips, Thomas W., Jr. 27,
Philolathuian Literary Society 34
Phoenix Suns 163
Physiological Laboratory 36
Pi Kappa Delta 74
Pickens, Richard W. 123
Pieratt, J. M. 15
Pippin, James 74
Pitts, Guy 148
PKs (preacher's kids) 51
Plank, Lorraine 57
Plummer, Mac 152
Poaster, Morris 85
Poindexter, Richard 123
Poland, Gwen 128
Political Action Group of Enid 123
Ponca City, Oklahoma 50, 67
Pond Creek, Oklahoma 23
Port Tobacco, Maryland 12
Pounds, Linda 113
Powell, Wilfred E. 52, 81, 103
Powers, Tammy 156
pranks 47
Pratt, Greg 123
Preaching Window 80, 81
Presbyterian doctrine 12
Presbyterian Synod 12
President's House 20, 46, 105
Presidential Singers 85
Prewitt, Aris 86
Price, Brent 160
Price, Denny 160, 162, 163
Price, Mark 160
Price, Matt 160, 161

Price, Vincent 140
Professional Football Hall of Fame 149
Proudfoot, Becky 18, 69
PUAFA (see Phillips University Alumni and Friends Association)
PULF (see Phillips University Legacy Foundation)
Pulitzer Prize 33
Pulpiteers 84
Purcell, Everett 15, 61
Putman, Sheila 179

Quik Trip Corporation 167
Quillin, Jean 60
Quintana, Dave 86
Quintana, Ray 86
Quiz Bowl 129

Race riots 93
Radcliffe, Lola 138
Rakestraw, Roy 126
Ramblers 34
Rambo, Theo 161
Ramerez, Eric 120
Randall, Fred 104
Randolph, Debbie 113
Randolph, John 87, 108
Rassmussen, Randy 85, 86
Ratcliff, Jay 148
Rather, Mildred 57
Ray's Grocery 51, 72
Ray, A. H. 51
Ray, James Earl 101
Reagan, Lillian 105
Record, Donnie 168
Record, Joe 152, 154, 158, 163
Rector, Joe Eugene 5, 100
red blizzards 50
Red Feather Cafe 89
Red Pepper Club 47, 65, 84, 129, 134, 135
Redding, Jennifer 134
Reed, Jim 143, 179
Reformers 12, 13
Regier, Anna 63
regimental band 42, 67
Rehorn, William S. 20, 147
Reiter, Arthur F. 18, 22, 28
Renaissance Celebration 125
Rennick, Verle 63
Reserve Officers' Training Corps (ROTC) 41, 42
Restoration Movement 12
Retail Merchants Association 54
Reynolds, Grace 18, 37
Reynolds, K. J. 120
Rhodes Scholars 56
Richards, David 124
Richardson, Burrell 131

Riebel, Sherrie 153
Rilford, Mrs. J. Lee 20
Roaring Twenties 47
Roberts, Gene 122
Roberts, Ison 18
Roberts, Katherine 18
Roberts, Oral 74, 169
Roberts, Richard 169
Roberts, T. T. 30, 148
Roberts, Verna Dean Smith 73
Roberts, Walter S. 20
Robinson, Barry 94, 96, 141, 143, 168, 171, 179
Roby, Douglas 148, 150
Rock Candy Mountain 55
Rockwell, Dorothea 105
Rogers, Will 119
Ronstadt, Linda 91
Roosevelt, Theodore 119
Rose Window 81, 180
Rossman, George 55
Roth, Oliver N. 23, 28, 29
Roy, Jesse 104
Royal Air Force (RAF) 67
Rustin, Bayard 89
Ruth, John 103

Sacramento State University 148
Sadie Hawkins Day 110
Salzsieder, John 123
Salzsieder, Leigh 123
Salzsieder, Susan 123
Salzsieder, Todd 123
Sam Houston State University 163
Sanford-Stunkle Drugstore 103
SAT 166
Saturday Bible School 34
Sawyer's Addition 15
Sawyer's Creek 15, 19
Sayre, Alan 109
Sayre, John 118, 124
Sayre, Rick 142
Scates, Walter G. 20
Scheen, Donna Jean 83
Scheffe, Walter 126
Schenke, Elmer 22, 37, 148
scholarship fund in memory of Dr. Martin Luther King 107
scholarship programs 179
Schomber, Terri 155
School and Family Enrichment (S.A.F.E.) 134
school mascots 173
Schovanec, Becky 123
Schulter, Mary 150
Schwinn, Michelle 123
Science Building 50, 79, 118, 139
Science Camp (see Phillips Science Camp)
Science Club 129
science fairs 139

science laboratory 22
Science Lecture Series 139
Scott, Art 89
Scott, Jan 105
Scott, Vernon 63
Scoville, Charles 55
Scoville, Mrs. Arlene Dux 55
Scrivner, Mary 63
seal (of Phillips University) 66
Seals, Bob 84
Seamans, Don 141
Seamans, Ruth 109
Sears, Rolla G. 38, 147
Seibel, Glenn 63
Selman Hall 79
Semester in Sweden 123 (see Swedish Semester)
Semones, Barbara 83
Severinsen, Doc 91
Shades, C. T. "Tibbie" 118, 141, 168
Shafer, Ronnie 86
Shahady, Thomas 179
Shaklee, Patrick 141
Shaklee, Rose Miller 52, 55
Shane, William L. E. 15, 20, 22
Shannon, Kathleen 57
Shapp, Lloyd 20
Sharp, Paul 54, 142, 172
Sharp, Rose 54, 142
Shawnee, Oklahoma 15
Sheafor, Rolland 143
Sheeks, Virginia 63
Shelton, Elaine 63
Shelton, Ev 148
Shields, Chuck 109
Shiner, Pat 103
Shirley, James Clifford 50, 52, 63, 67, 87, 95, 112, 120
Shirley, Mrs. James Clifford 63, 95, 112
Shockley, Ed 148
Siegal, Henrietta 18
Silvee, Ruth 60
Silver City, Indian Territory 13
Silver Moon Cafe 79
Silver Scroll 39
Simmons Grocery 53
Simpson, Lois 60
Simpson, Megan 101
Simpson, Robert 101, 125, 126
Singer, Suellen 118
Sizemore, Roger 124
Skora, Kerry 179
skunk mascot 157, 158
Skylab II 110
Slane, Mary 153
Slate, The 23, 31, 47, 146
Slavee, Sue 153
Smiley, Ardell 151
Smith, Andrew G. 20, 26, 37

Smith, Ann 159
Smith, Bill 54
Smith, Clyde 147
Smith, Jim 109
Smith, Lori 122
Smith, Margaret 51
Smith, Mart Gary 15, 20
Smith, Nan 110
Smith, Nina 150
Smith, O. L. 14, 15, 22
Smith, Sam 60
Smith, Walter A. 23
Smith, William Martin 143
Smith. S. M. 52
smoking 76
Smoot/Semones family 142
Snack Shack 53, 79
Snawder, Letha 150
Snodgrass, Bill 142, 178
Snyder, Oklahoma 91
Snyder, Steve 161
social clubs 39 *(see clubs by name)*
Sohn, Michael 133, 163, 166, 169, 178
Solomon, Peter 79
Sommers, Rhonda 128
Sons and Daughters of the Cherokee Strip Pioneers 174
Sooner Athletic Conference 163
Soper, John 141
Sotheby's 175
South McAlester, Oklahoma 14
South University Avenue 20
Southern Methodist University 108, 118
Southwest Athletic Conference 150, 151
Southwest Young People's Summer Conference 44
Southwestern College 150
Southwestern University 150
Spainhower, Jim 143
Spiller, Jim 88
Spindle, Audry 130
Spokane University 30
sports 148
Springfield Presbytery 12
Springfield, Illinois 179
Staley, Nancy 103
Stam, J. 119
Star Spangled Entertainment 115
Stars and Stripes 141
State Basketball Championship 151
State Board of Education 29, 30
State Teachers College in Lebanon, Ohio 30
Steltzer, Mark 161
Stephenson, Debbie 153
Stephenson. Helen 60
Stewart, Harold 86

Stewart, Paul 121
Stillwater, Oklahoma 179
Stober, Buena 43
stock market 22
Stone, Barton W. 12
Stone, Keith 86
Strain, James Alan 107
Strain, James E. 158
Strain/Murphy family 142
Strauss, Arthur "Dutch" 148, 149
Strecker, Betty 83
streetcar line 15, 23
Stroud, Anita 110
Stroup, Jim 67, 110
Stuart, Wayne 86
Stuckey, Emily 133, 166
Student Army Training Corps (SATC) 31
Student Center 20, 95
Student Council 35
Student Education Association 28, 105
Student Foreign Aid 56
Student Friendship (War) Fund 31
Student Government Association 107
Student Government Court 107, 109
student loans 50
Student Ministerial Alliance 34
Student Senate 106, 107
Student Union 62, 63
Student Volunteers 34
Students' Foreign Aid Fund 56
Stunt Night 52, 140
Sturgis, Fran 105
Sturman, Elizabeth 150
Suley, Mrs. Fred 20
summer music camp 55
Sunken Garden 35, 48, 58, 59, 108
Supernaw, Susan 106
Surf Riders 96
Surghnor, Shep 152
Sveiven, Debra 155
Swails, Richard 135
Sweden exchange program 112, 113, 128, 129
Swedish semester 120
Sweet Sixteen Opera Company 55
Sweet, May 82

T. W. Phillips Foundation 91
Tacoma, Washington 52
Taft, Harold 82
Tampa, Florida 173
Tapps Grocery 51
Taylor, Barbara Brown 143
Taylor, Claude C. 20, 22, 37, 52, 147
Taylor, Dennis J. 179

Taylor, Elbert A. 20, 147
Taylor, George Oliver 143
Taylor, Gerard 85
Taylor, Lola 138
Taylor, Jack N. 64, 89, 91, 96, 105, 111, 112, 138, 181
Taylor, Kay 47
Taylor, Rachel 154
Teaching Window 80
Tecumseh, Oklahoma 23
Teegarden, Ken 60, 143
tennis club 147
Tenth Muse 47, 57, 99, 115, 133, 135
Tenth Muse Club Sweetheart 95
Terre-Blanche, Henry 90
Terry, Mindy 128
Texas A&M University 115, 150, 151
Texas Christian University 13, 18, 165, 179
Texas Club 34
Texas Houses 72
Texas Panhandle 50
Texas Tech University 115, 165
Theis, Mrs. 20
Thomas, Eric 129
Thomas, Leroy 86
Thompson, Rhodes 124
Thornhill, Barbara 103
Thorp Spring, Texas 13
Thurman, Dorothy Ann 60
Time Magazine 124
Timothy Club 34
Title IX 153
Tobola, Allison 139, 163, 180
Tomlin, Lillie 91
Tonkawa, Oklahoma 121, 173
Toronto, Canada 87
Torres, Steve 109
Toulouse, Mark 124
Training Board of American Speech and Hearing Association 28
Training School for Nurses 20
Transforming Window 80
Transylvania Presbytery 12
Transylvania University 179
Traveling Players 97
Tri-State Band Festival 53, 54, 68
Tri-State Missionary Movement 30
Tri-State Music Festival 53, 54
Tri-State Piano Scholarship 54
Triple R 47
Tromblee, Max R. 104
Truman, Harry 119
Tucker, Cindy 179
tug-of-war 57
Tulsa 15, 76, 163, 167, 169, 179
Turnage, Terrance 161
Turner, John 159, 163

Index 199

Turpin, Jerry 113, 119, 130
Twin Territories 50
Tye, Wilma Moore 51
typhoid fever 19

U.S. Department of Education 127
U.S. News and World Report 9, 127
Uji, Japan 125
Ulrich, Eugene 168
Umphries, John W. 30
Underwood, A. Elmer 20, 22
Union Board 119
United Christian Missionary Society 45
United States Department of State 54
United States Marines 67
United States Olympic Committee 148
United War Work Campaign 31
United Way 166
University Band 53
University Dames 20
University Endowment Crusade 45
University Hospital 20
University Investment and Development Company 15, 22, 23, 26
University Lake 15, 30, 31, 35, 39, 44, 50, 56, 57, 62, 64, 69, 111, 148
University of Arkansas 150, 151
University of Kentucky 179
University of Michigan 147, 148
University of Minnesota 54
University of Oklahoma 54, 108, 122, 142, 146, 147, 163
University of Science and Arts 139
University of Texas 89, 148, 149, 150, 151
University of Texas-Houston 139
University of Tulsa 151, 152, 167
University of West Virginia 151
University of Wichita 91
University of Wyoming 148
University Place Christian Church 30, 34, 70
University Post Office Station 44
University Service League of Women 69
University Women's Lecture Series 119

Van Boskirk, Nancy 153
Van Winkle, Janet 156
Vance Air Force Base 107
Vance, Patty 63
Varsity Club 59, 134, 179
Varsity Courts 72
Varsity Shop 76, 79
Vaughan, Ewel 80, 84
Vaughan, Mary 84
Veteran's Village 72, 74
Veterans Administration 28
Veterans Affairs 72
veterans, Phillips University 69
Vietnam 106
Vietnam War 93, 108
Vinita, Oklahoma 138, 162
Voskuhl, Ronda 141
Votaw, Elizabeth D. 69, 72

Waco, Texas 13
Waldron, Richard Allen 91
Walker, Leslie 151
Walker, Paul 86
Walker, Wilfred 151
Wallace, Cameron S. 179
Wallace, Vanetta 131
Wallingsford, Betty 57
Warner, Clarence 103
Warren, Druie L. "Pete" 50, 143
Warren, Ohio 29
Warren, Patricia Cravens 50
Washington, D. C. 138
Watergate 101
Watkins, Muriel 60
Watson, Mallory L. 179
Watts, Anna Louise 83
Waukomis, Oklahoma 179
WAVES 69
Weaber, Kenneth 151
Webster and Lincoln Debating Society 38
Webster, Nancy 69, 72
Weeks, Edgar 151
Wees, Sterling 151
Wehner, Walter 95
Weibels 79
Welch, Leanne 110
Welch, Rosa Page 89
Weldon, Kristi 156
Weleetka, Oklahoma 14
Wellman, Frank A. 30, 52, 54, 146
Wellman, Mrs. Frank 20
Wellman, Neil 105
Wellman, Victor 84
Wells, Linda 153
Welty, Mrs. Reuben 20
West, Alisa 134
West, Loretta 57
Wharry, Kristin R. 179
White Castle 79
"White House" 73, 125
White Way 34
White, Cliff 148
White, Thurman J. 50
Whiteneck, Otho 174

Whitmer, Tanya 129
Whitmore, James 119
Whitney, Leon 143, 157
Whitson, Kathy J. 179
Whittaker, Tom 119
Who's Who in American Colleges and Universities 39
Wichita, Kansas 13, 14
Wiens, Joel 86
Wiggs, Dan 109
Wight, Bill 103
Wikoff, Karen 103
Wilburton, Oklahoma 156
Wiley, Jim 103
Wiley, Russell L. 53, 54
Willet Stained Glass Company 80
Willet, Henry Lee 80
Willey, Sydney 110
William, Carol 150
Williams, Bill 85, 86
Williams, Bob 84
Williams, Cecil 52, 86, 87, 88, 112, 120
Williams, Dale E. 76
Williams, Dixie 37
Williams, Flo 37
Williams, Lerleen 105
Williams, Lucile 86
Williamson, Ralph 151
Wilson, Aline 54
Wimpey, Lois Moore 72
Winfield, Kansas 150
Winters, John 107
Wise, Sheri 129
Wolfinger, Birge 51
Wolfinger, Roy J. 23, 28, 51, 147
Wolfinger, Ruth 23
Women's Auxiliary Corps 69
women's basketball 149, 163
Women's Self-Governing Association (WSGA) 58
women's sports at Phillips 153
Wonderly, Barbara 110
Wonnell, Rob 143
Wood, Mary E. 18
Woodford, Burton 18
Woodring Air Field 67
Woodrow Wilson Scholarship 142
Woodruff, Jay 161
Woodward, Oklahoma 14
Wooliver, Tammy 143
World Games 154
World Student Service Fund of the Intercollegiate Christian Council 79
World War I 27, 30, 41, 44, 147
World War II 55, 56, 62, 67, 68, 69, 71, 72, 73, 79, 86, 88, 94, 158
Worley, June 153

Wright, James P. "Jim" 166, 178, 179
Wright, Nona 50, 51
Wright, Rose 47
Wright, W. J. 26
Wyoming 17

Yale University 118
Yale University Divinity School 99, 124
Yauk, Joyce 157
Yewell, Monette 63
YMCA of Enid 160
Yoder, Nancy 104
Young family 142
Young Men's Christian Association (YMCA) 31, 110
Young People's Conferences 44, 80
Young Women's Christian Association (YWCA) 31, 34, 54, 79, 110
Young, Charles 142
Young, Jeremiah 142
Young, Lois 83
Young, Maida 26
Young, Robert 142
Young, Tanya Whitmer 142
Yukon, Oklahoma 23

Zelotai Club 45, 62, 84
Zollars, Ely Vaughn 13, 14, 15, 18, 20, 22, 23, 25, 26, 27, 29, 30, 34, 36
Zollars Hall 39
Zollars Memorial Library 99, 102, 104, 172, 173
Zollars Literary Society 39, 44
Zonta Brave 134
Zonta Club 44, 47, 65, 133, 134, 135